# The Trinity

## and

# The Unicity of The Intellect

*By*

St. Thomas Aquinas

*Translated by*
Sister Rose Emmanuella Brennan, S.H.N.

WIPF & STOCK · Eugene, Oregon

Wipf and Stock Publishers
199 W 8th Ave, Suite 3
Eugene, OR 97401

The Trinity and The Unicity of The Intellect
By Aquinas, Thomas
ISBN 13: 978-1-60608-509-7
Publication date 4/14/2009
Previously published by B. Herder Book Co., 1946

# FOREWORD

St. Thomas Aquinas wrote no more masterful treatises than the commentary on Boethius' *De Trinitate* and *De Unitate Intellectus*. They are essential for an understanding of the thought and the character of the Angelic Doctor. The almost inexplicable surge of interest in Thomistic thought by students not familiar with Latin has found these basic writings inaccessible. Sister Rose Emmanuella Brennan has done a great service to these students and to the ever-widening influence of Thomism in turning these scientific treatises into English. Sister is eminently fitted for this task as the reader of these translations will discover.

Needless to say, all scholars will welcome any contribution which enables them to acquire familiarity with St. Thomas' teaching through the text itself rather than through synopses and interpretations.

It is consolatory to find members of the gentler sex adding their support to movements that arm to make truth sovereign. Their services are needed both for the dissemination of sound philosophy and for the public manifestation of their increasing philosophical efficiency. Of this efficiency many are not yet aware and from this angle, too, these translations will be enlightening.

IGNATIUS SMITH, O.P.

# CONTENTS

## COMMENTARY ON *DE TRINITATE*

|  | PAGE |
|---|---|
| Translator's Preface | 1 |
| St. Thomas' Introduction | 8 |
| Boethius' Preface | 12 |
| St. Thomas' Commentary | 14 |
| Question I: Concerning the Knowledge of Divine Things | 20 |
| Question II: Concerning the Manifestation of Knowledge of Divine Truth | 45 |
| Lectio I | 67 |
| Question III: Concerning Those Things That Pertain to the Knowledge Possessed by Faith | 74 |
| Question IV: Concerning Those Things That Pertain to the Cause of Plurality | 99 |
| Lectio II | 125 |
| Question V: Concerning the Division of Speculative Science | 131 |
| Question VI: Concerning the Modes Attributed to Speculative Science | 169 |

## UNICITY OF THE INTELLECT

| CHAPTER |  | |
|---|---|---|
|  | Translator's Preface | 201 |
| I. | The Purpose of the Author | 209 |
| II. | That the Intellectual Soul Is the Act and Form of the Body | 211 |
| III. | The Intellect as a Faculty of the Soul | 227 |
| IV. | The Opinions of Other Peripatetics | 237 |
| V. | What Ought to Be Held | 242 |
| VI. | The Possible Intellect Not One for All Men | 256 |
| VII. | Reasons for Proposing the Unicity of the Intellect | 264 |
|  | Appendix | 278 |
|  | Index | 283 |

TWO OPUSCULA

BY

ST. THOMAS AQUINAS

COMMENTARY OF ST. THOMAS ON

BOETHIUS' *DE TRINITATE*

TRANSLATED BY

SISTER ROSE EMMANUELLA BRENNAN, S.H.N.

## TRANSLATOR'S PREFACE

When in 1258 St. Thomas wrote his Commentary on the *De Trinitate* of Boethius,[1] he not only established for all time the fame of a sixth-century opusculum, but, together with his own explanation of certain doctrines concerned with the Trinity, he set forth a philosophy of human knowledge.

For the logician, the mathematician, the scientist, the philosopher, and the theologian, this Commentary remains a source book, rich in explicit principles and implicit doctrine. The explanation of merely a few of its teachings in the light of present-day attitudes of thought has, to cite one example, inspired many of the chapters of Jacques Maritain's *Degrees of Knowledge*.

In itself, the Commentary is brief, consisting of 47 pages in the Parma edition. These embody an explanation of the Prooemium of Boethius' own work, six main *Quaestiones*, and two *Lectiones* (short excerpts from Boethius' treatise) inserted after the second and the fourth Questions. Short as the Commentary is, it runs to fully ten times the length of the early medieval original. St. Thomas' work, on the other hand, is much more concise than that of St. Augustine, to whom Boethius refers as the source for certain teachings of his *De Trinitate*.[2]

It was in 524, shortly before his imprisonment and execution, that Boethius wrote his treatise. It is addressed, with

[1] Date assigned by Father Mandonnet, O.P., in Vol. I of the *Opuscula omnia*.
[2] In concludng his Prooemium to Symmachus, Boethius says: "You must, however, examine whether the seeds sown in my mind by St. Augustine's writings have borne fruit."—Loeb Classical Library edition of the *Theological Tractates* of Boethius, Trans. by H. F. Stewart and E. K. Rand, Harvard University Press, 1936, p. 2. (Treatise on the Trinity, Latin and English, pp. 2-31.)

a request for criticism, to his father-in-law, Quintus Aurelius Memmius Symmachus, who, like himself, held the rank of patrician and ex-consul. Not long afterward, Symmachus met the same fate of imprisonment and death by order of Theodoric, the Ostrogoth ruler of the Western Empire, in whose service both men had attained honors, until the time when charges of treason were brought against them.

The *De Trinitate* may have hastened Boethius' death. Certainly it could well have caused loss of favor with Theodoric, who was an Arian, since Emperor Justin had shortly before proscribed Arianism throughout the West. At any rate, the *De Trinitate,* like the other theological treatises, indicates an ardent apologetic activity which made Boethius a marked man in those times of doctrinal disputes. But it was on charges of treason that Boethius was imprisoned, forged letters supposedly sent to Emperor Justin being used as evidence to show that Boethius was stirring up revolt in favor of a recovery of the former independent position of the Roman Senate. These charges he denied, but no mitigation of sentence was allowed.

During the time left to him, he wrote at Pavia the book which is almost exclusively associated with his name, *De consolatione philosophiae.* It later became not only the most influential and popular serious book of the Middle Ages, but one of the great "prison books" of history. Yet many who are familiar with that work know little or nothing of the *De Trinitate,* which also ranks as a work of great importance, particularly in medieval tradition up to the time of St. Thomas. Equally with the *De consolatione philosophiae,* it marks Boethius as worthy to be called "the last of the Roman philosophers and the first of the Scholastics." It is remarkable that a Roman consul, in the midst of a public career that was splendid and honorable, wrote, in addition to works on logic and ancient philosophy, five theological treatises.

The importance of the *De Trinitate* is threefold: First,

it removes any doubt about Boethius' having been a Christian, a point which in the past was questioned because of the strictly philosophical character of the *De consolatione philosophiae*.

Secondly, it indicates the great ambitions which prompted Boethius in his literary career, as well as the breadth of his learning.

Thirdly, the *De Trinitate* and his other treatises manifest certain ways in which he anticipated and inspired later medieval endeavors, especially those of St. Thomas. Particularly is this to be noted in his attitude toward faith and reason; his attempt to establish the harmony of pagan and Christian truth; his desire to harmonize Plato and Aristotle; his use of original sources when possible; his classification of the sciences; and his concept of a hierarchy of faculties or powers of knowing in the individual.

St. Thomas in his Commentary on the *De Trinitate* of Boethius maintains, as has been pointed out, the same division of the discussion into six parts. But the order in which various doctrines are considered differs, as will be apparent from the accompanying diagram. All the problems that Boethius touched upon find expansion and clarification in the Commentary. In addition to this, St. Thomas also deals with certain doctrines of St. Augustine's earlier treatise that had inspired Boethius, and likewise develops others which thirteenth-century interests made especially important.

St. Thomas, for example, undoubtedly had St. Augustine's work in mind when treating of the possibility of knowledge of the Trinity by reason alone. Much of St. Augustine's treatise, particularly chapters 8–13 and the concluding summary of chapter 15, dealt with analogies of the Trinity in creatures. The resemblances of the Holy Trinity, traceable especially in human nature, St. Augustine regarded, not as logical proofs of the revealed doctrine, but as striking indications of its truth. Thus he points to what he terms an "inner trinity" in man: his memory, understanding, and will; and to another, concerned with bodily sight: the eye, vision itself, and the memory of objects seen.[3] St. Augustine emphasizes, however, that the Trinity, as regards our knowledge, is a matter of faith, not of reason; he dwells upon the incapacity of human thought in fathoming the depths of the nature of God.

St. Thomas brings into his remarkable discussion of the relationship between philosophy and revelation, as found in the Commentary, certain points of Augustinian doctrine left unmentioned or only implied by Boethius.[4]

In this summary we can merely point out the more important divisions of the Commentary. The first three Questions are a compendium of major epistemological doctrines. They are not exclusively so, of course; for the psychologist will be equally concerned with them, especially with Questions I and II; and the theologian will regard the discussion of faith in Question III as belonging essentially to his domain. Question IV and Article 3 of Question V deal with fundamental problems of mathematics: unity and plurality, concrete and abstract number, quantity and number, bilocation, and the relationship of mathematics to the physical sciences and to metaphysics in the hierarchy of the sciences. Questions IV and V are devoted especially to a discussion of the degrees of abstraction, and to corresponding degrees of science and of the faculties of knowledge.

Apart from their theological importance, therefore, the three treatises on the Trinity by St. Augustine, Boethius, and St. Thomas are of major value and significance in revealing the evolution of philosophical thought regarding the following problems in the fields of logic, mathematics, and epistemology:

[3] St. Augustine, *De Trinitate*, chaps. 10 and 11; Vol. VIII of *Works of Aurelius Augustine, Bishop of Hippo* (T. and T. Clark, Edinburgh, 1873).
[4] The first three Questions of St. Thomas' *Commentary* as well as the concluding Question are of particular importance in this respect.

1. *Reason and language:* the validity and the limitations involved in employing human thought and language with regard to God, spiritual beings, and revealed truth.

2. *Mathematics:* the nature of unity and plurality. Plurality differentiated as generic, specific, and numerical. The kinds of number; quantity; intelligible matter.

3. *Degrees of science:* the divisions and methods of the speculative sciences. The place of experiment, imagination, reason, and abstract speculation.

4. *The categories* and their relation to finite and to infinite being.

5. Special consideration of the category of relation and the predicates of relativity.

## COMPARISON OF CONTENTS OF TREATISES ON THE TRINITY

| ST. AUGUSTINE | BOETHIUS | ST. THOMAS' COMMENTARY |
|---|---|---|
| 1. Unity and Trinity of God. Testimony of Scripture. | *Dedication to Symmachus* Difficulty of task. No desire for applause. Use of brevity and obscure language. Human mind is limited. Source: St. Augustine | Explanation of Boethius' Prooemium. I. Relation of human mind to knowledge of God: —No need of new light. |
| 2. The equality of Persons in the Trinity. | | |
| 3. Appearances of God as told in the Old Testament. | | —Possible concept of God. —God, not first known. |
| 4. The sending of the Son of God. | I. Trinity: An essential doctrine of Catholic faith. | —Natural reason would not give idea of the Trinity. |
| 5. The Son is one substance with God. | —Essence of plurality: "otherness." | II. Faith and reason: —Permissible to speculate about divine things. —Philosophical science of truths of faith, possible. —Permissible to employ philosophical reasoning. |
| 6. Unity and quality of the Three Persons. | | |
| 7. Unity of power and wisdom. | —Sameness may be: generic, specific, numerical (by reason of accidents, as in different men). | |

| ST. AUGUSTINE | BOETHIUS | ST. THOMAS' COMMENTARY |
|---|---|---|
| 8. Knowledge of God from our concepts of truth, supreme good, righteousness, love. | | —Use of new and obscure language justified. (Lectio I: from Boethius) |
| | II. Divisions of speculative sciences. | III. Knowledge of truths of faith: —Necessary for mankind (five reasons given). —Relation to religion. |
| 9. Human trinity in man. Man as image of God. | Physics: Matter in motion. Mathematics: Forms of bodies considered apart from matter; not altogether separate. | —True faith is Catholic. —The Trinity, an essential doctrine of faith. |
| 10. Memory, understanding, will, knowledge and love of self. | | IV. Plurality —"Otherness" (*alteritas*). —Variety of accidents. —Bilocation. —Variety of location and influence in determining numerical difference. (Lectio II: from Boethius) |
| 11. Trinity in outer man: the eye, sight, recollection of object seen. | Theology: Forms abstract or abstracted from matter and motion. Method of sciences 1. Scientific 2. Systematic 3. Intellectual | |
| 12. Difference between wisdom and knowledge. | III. Differentiation of Persons of the Trinity. | V. Divisions of the sciences. —Natural philosophy —Mathematics —Divine science (theology) Natural philosophy —Matter and motion Mathematics —Intelligible matter Divine science: —No matter or motion. |
| 13. Trinity of knowledge. Commendation of Christian faith. | IV. The categories and finite and infinite being. | |
| 14. True wisdom of man: memory, understanding, and love of God. | V. Category of relation. | |
| 15. Summary: human bliss consists in the | VI. Manifoldness and relation. | VI. Methods of the sciences. |

| ST. AUGUSTINE | BOETHIUS | ST. THOMAS' COMMENTARY |
|---|---|---|
| beatific vision of the Trinity. | Unity and substance. | Three methods:<br>—*Rationabiliter*<br>—*Disciplinabiliter*<br>—*Intelligibiliter*.<br>Use of Imagination.<br>How and in what manner we know God.<br>Speculative science and knowledge of God. |

The translator here wishes to express gratitude to the librarians of the Catholic University of America for the use of the Vives, Mandonnet, and Vedrine-Bandel-Fournet (French-Latin) editions of the opuscula of St. Thomas, as well as for other references used in making this translation.

Acknowledgment is also gratefully made to the editors of the Loeb Classical Library, Harvard University, for permission to reprint portions of the translation of *The Theological Tractates* of Boethius, translated by H. F. Stewart and E. K. Rand.

Special thanks are due to the Dominican Fathers of The College of St. Albert the Great, Oakland, California, for the use of the Parma edition of St. Thomas' works and for generous assistance in the task of correcting and revising the translation.

# COMMENTARY OF THE ANGELIC DOCTOR, ST. THOMAS AQUINAS, ON THE BOOK OF BOETHIUS, *DE TRINITATE*

### ST. THOMAS' INTRODUCTION

"I will seek her out from the beginning of her birth, and bring the knowledge of her to light" (Wisd. 6:24).

The natural intuition of the human mind, burdened by the weight of a corruptible body, cannot fix its gaze in the prime light of First Truth, in which all things are easily knowable; whence it must be that, according to the progress of its natural manner of cognition, the reason advances from the things that are posterior to those that are prior, and from creatures to God. "For the invisible things of Him, from the creation of the world, are clearly seen, being understood by the things that are made" (Rom. 1:20) and "For by the greatness of the beauty and of the creature, the Creator of them may be seen, so as to be known thereby" (Wisd. 13:5); and this is what is said in Job 36:25: "All men see Him, everyone beholdeth afar off."

For creatures, through whom God can be known by the natural light of reason, are at an infinite distance from Him. But since, in those who look at a thing from a great distance, vision may readily be deceived, therefore those striving to attain to a knowledge of God from creatures fell into many errors: wherefore it is said: "The creatures of God are . . . a snare to the feet of the unwise" (Wisd. 14:11), and: "They have failed in their search" (Ps. 63:7); and therefore God has provided for the human race another safe road of cognition, bestowing upon the minds of men, by faith, a knowledge of

## ST. THOMAS' INTRODUCTION

Himself. Therefore, it is said: "The things also that are of God no man knoweth, but the Spirit of God: but to us God has revealed them by His Spirit" (I Cor. 2:11): and this is the Spirit by whom we are enabled to be believers: "Having the same spirit of faith, as it is written: 'I believed, for which cause I have spoken' (Ps. 115:10); we also believe, for which cause we speak also" (II Cor. 4:13).

Therefore, as the principle of our cognition is naturally the knowledge of created things, obtained by means of the senses, so the principle of supernatural cognition is that knowledge of First Truth conferred upon us, infused by faith; and hence it follows that in advancing one proceeds according to a diverse order. For philosophers, who follow along the way of natural cognition, place knowledge about created things before knowledge about divine things: natural science before metaphysics: but among theologians the procedure is in reverse order, so that study of the Creator comes before that of creatures.

This order, therefore, Boethius followed: intending to treat of those things which are of faith, he took as the starting point of his study that highest origin of things, namely, the Trinity of the one, simple God. Whence it is that the above-quoted words are applicable to him: "I will seek her out from the beginning of her birth, and bring the knowledge of her to light."

In these words, as regards the present opusculum, which he addressed to Symmachus, a patrician of Rome, three things can be noted: namely, the matter, the mode, and the purpose.

The matter of this work is the Trinity of Persons in the one, divine Essence, that Trinity which has its source in the primal nativity in which divine wisdom is eternally generated by the Father. "The depths were not as yet, and I was already conceived" (Prov. 8:24), and: "This day have I begotten thee" (Ps. 2:7).

This nativity is the beginning of every other nativity, as it is the only one involving perfect participation in the nature of the generator: but all others are imperfect according as the one generated receives either a part of the substance of the generator, or only a similitude: from this it follows that from the aforesaid nativity, every other is derived by a kind of imitation; and thus: "Of whom all paternity in heaven and in earth is named" (Eph. 3:15); and on this account the Son is called the first-born of every creature (Col. 1:15) so that the origin of nativity and its imitation might be designated, but not according to the same meaning of generation; and therefore it is aptly said: "I will seek her out from the beginning of her birth." "The Lord possessed me in the beginning of his ways" (Prov. 8:22); for not only of creatures is the aforesaid nativity the beginning, but even of the Holy Spirit, who proceeds from the Generator and the Generated.

But in saying this, he does not say: "I will seek out the beginning of nativity," but "from the beginning" signifies that his search is not limited by initiation of this kind of nativity, but that, beginning from this, he proceeds to others, for his doctrine is divided into three parts. The first part, concerning the Trinity of Persons, from the procession of whom every other nativity and procession are derived, is contained in that book which we possess at hand, so far as anything can be known about the Trinity and Unity.

But in another book which he wrote to John, a deacon of the Roman Church, we find what he says about the mode of predication which we employ in the distinction of Persons and unity of essence; and this book begins: "I inquire whether the Father."

The second part, which is about the procession of good creatures from a good God, is in a book that is written to the same John (*De hebdomadibus*), and this begins: "You ask of me."

The third part is about the separation of creatures through

Christ. This is divided into two parts: For first, there is set forth the faith which Christ taught by which we are justified, in that book entitled *De fide Christiana*, which begins: "The Christian faith." In the second part, an explanation is given of what must be held about Christ: namely, how two natures are united in one person. This discussion of the two natures and the one person in Christ is also in a book written to the same John, which begins: "You, indeed, solicitously."

Now the mode employed in treating of the Trinity is twofold, as St. Augustine says in *I De Trinitate*, namely, through truths known on the basis of authority, and through those known by reason, both of which modes Augustine combined, as he himself says.

Some of the holy Fathers, as Ambrose and Hilary, employed but one mode of explanation: namely, by setting forth those truths founded upon authority. But Boethius chose to proceed according to the other mode; namely, according to reasoned arguments, presupposing what had been concluded by others on the grounds of authority. Hence also the method of his work is indicated in what he says: "I shall investigate," in which an inquiry of reason is signified. In Ecclus. 39:1 we read: "Wisdom," namely, knowledge of the Trinity; "of all the ancients," that is, which the ancients affirmed solely on the grounds of authority; "the wise man will seek out," that is, he will investigate by reason.

Wherefore, in the preface he speaks of "An investigation carried on for a very long time."

The purpose of this work is: that hidden things may be made manifest, so far as that is possible in this life.

"They that explain me shall have life everlasting" (Ecclus. 24:31); and therefore, he says: "I will bring the knowledge of her to light" (Wisd. 6:24). "The depths also of rivers he hath searched, and hidden things he hath brought forth to light" (Job 28:11).

## BOETHIUS' PREFACE

The problem which has been for so long a time the subject of my investigation—to the extent that the divine light has deigned to enkindle the feeble spark of my mind—now arranged according to a reasoned plan and consigned to writing, I have taken pains to offer and share with you, prompted as much by desire for your judgment as by zeal for my task.

In this matter it is possible to understand what my intention is whenever I entrust my thought to pen, both because of the difficulty of the matter and because it is only to you men that I am addressing it.

Indeed, I am not prompted by any desire for fame or for empty popular applause; but if there is any exterior reward, it can be no other than to hope for a judgment in keeping with the matter.

For, wherever I have directed my gaze, apart from you, I have encountered, on the one side, stolid indifference or, on the other, sly envy, so that I would appear to offer insult to matters pertaining to divine things by putting them before such monsters of men to be trampled under foot by them rather than to be acknowledged. On this account I restrain my pen by brevity, and truths gleaned from the deepest teachings of philosophy I veil over by the signification of new words, so that they may speak only to me and to you; if you, indeed, will direct your attention to them. But, as for others, I so disregard them that those who are unable to grasp the meaning of my words shall seem unworthy to read them.

Only so much ought one require of me as the intuition of human reason can approximate about the sublime truths of the Godhead. For in the case of other arts, the same limit is

## BOETHIUS' PREFACE

also established, namely, that which by the way of reason one can attain. Now, medicine does not always effect the cure of the patient. But no blame will be placed upon the physician if he has omitted none of the things which he ought to have done; and the same is true in other matters.

Moreover, in proportion to the difficulty of a problem, the pardoning of error ought to be the more easily granted. You must also determine this: whether the seeds of speculation, gathered from the writings of the blessed Augustine, have in my work borne fruit.

Now, therefore, let us undertake at this point the discussion of the proposed question.

## ST. THOMAS' COMMENTARY

To this work the author prefixes a preface, in which he does three things: First, he briefly indicates the causes of the work, in doing which he inclines his hearer to accept what he says. Secondly, he adds an excuse or explanation in which he gains the good will of his hearer, where he says: "I restrain my pen." In the third place, he points out that the source of his work and, in a certain way, its teaching, is the doctrine of St. Augustine, and in doing this he renders his hearer attentive, when he says: "You must also determine this: whether the seeds of speculation, gathered from the writings of blessed Augustine, have in my work borne fruit."

He likewise sets forth in the first part the four causes of his work.

1) First, the material cause, when he says: "the problem which has been for so long a time the subject of my investigation," that is, about the Trinity of Persons of the one God; and in these words he implies both the difficulty of the matter, because he has carried on the investigation for a very long time, and also the diligence of the study with which he has for so long a period investigated it, as "investigation" is understood by us, although it can also be understood to mean investigation by many; because from the beginning of the existence of the Church, this question has especially continued to challenge the cleverest minds of Christians.

2) Secondly, he indicates the proximate or secondary efficient cause when he says: "the feeble spark of my mind." Moreover, he speaks also of the first or principal cause when he adds: "that the divine light has deigned to enkindle."

Now the proximate cause of this investigation is, indeed, the intellect of the author, which is rightly termed a spark.

"For fire," as Dionysius says (XV *Coel. hier.*), "especially serves to signify properties of the divinity: at once by reason of its subtlety, of its light, and also by reason of its place and motion."

These things, in the highest degree, pertain to God, in whom exist the culmination of simplicity and of immateriality, perfect charity, almighty power, and highest majesty.

To the angels, "fire" (as indicative of intellect) may be applied in a middle sense, but to human minds, with only a more restricted meaning; for by union with a body, its purity is lessened, its light is obscured, its power weakened, and its upward motion retarded: wherefore the efficacy of the human mind is rightly compared to a spark.

Hence it would not be able to investigate the truth of this question unless light were cast upon it by the divine light; and thus the divine light is the principal cause; but the human mind, a cause in the secondary order.

3) Thirdly, he treats of the formal cause when he says: "arranged according to a reasoned plan," and he indicates the mode of treatment under three headings.

a) First, since he proceeds by argumentation, he therefore says, "arranged according to a reasoned plan." For a question discussed even over a long period according to probable reasons but still with doubt is, as it were, without form, not yet laying claim to the certitude of truth; and hence it is said to possess form when reasonable proof is added, through which certitude regarding the truth may be attained: in this process, intellect gives us vision of the truth, because what we believe, we owe to authority; but what we understand, we owe to reason, as Augustine says.

b) In the second place he discusses the mode of treatment, since he treats of this matter not only in words, but has incorporated it in writing, he says: "I entrust my thought to pen." In so doing, he has made provision against the weaknesses of memory.

c) Thirdly, since he has written, not after the manner of one imparting doctrine to another present with him, but as to one absent, by means of a letter.

Thus Aristotle also composed his books in different ways: some addressed to those who in his presence listened to him, and these books are called *Auditus,* as one such book is, entitled, *De naturali auditu;* but certain others he wrote to those absent, as we find in *I Ethic.* that the books *De anima* were so written, where the names of discourses addressed to those at a distance are given, as the Greek commentator says.

Accordingly, he adds: "I have taken pains to offer and share with you, prompted by desire for your judgment," as if addressing an expert and asking his opinion in this matter. Thus, he continues: "prompted as much by desire for your judgment as by zeal for my task." Because he had been zealous for ascertaining the truth, he had ordered the aforesaid question according to reasonable arguments; and because he was desirous of the judgment of Symmachus, he presented to him the work thus arranged in orderly fashion.

4) In the fourth place, he refers to the final cause when he says: "What my intention is," that is, what end I am striving for in regard to the above-mentioned problem: "Whenever I entrust my thought to pen" concerning the aforesaid or certain other matters, "it is possible to understand" for two reasons: "because of the difficulty of the matter" and also "because it is only to you men that I am addressing it."

This book, therefore, he has not written in order to read it to the many, which would be with hope of popular acclaim, but rather, for one wise man alone; wherefore, he continues: "I am not prompted by any desire for fame or for empty popular applause," as are the poets who recite their verses before the foolish crowds in the theater, because such applause is often altogether without reason. Thus he puts aside any unworthy end and establishes one that is honorable, implying a principal purpose, which is interior, namely, knowledge of divine truth, and, explicitly pointing out a secondary end, that is, the judgment of a wise man, when he says: "If there is any exterior reward," as if he would say: It is an interior reward that principally urges me on, but if there is any that is exterior, this can be none other than to wait and to hope for a judgment like to the matter, that is, proportionate to it: By way of exterior return I ask for nothing except what is fitting in a matter of such importance, in regard to which I have stated that a judgment of it should be neither stolidly indifferent nor the bitter one of an envious critic, but only that pronounced in good will by a wise man. Accordingly, he adds: "Wherever I have directed my gaze apart from you, that is, to whomsoever I have looked, except to you alone, I have encountered on the one side, stolid indifference"; that is, lack of comprehension, "on the other side, sly envy," that is, ill will, sly only in condemnation, so that he who treated of these things, would seem to offer insult to divine treatises, that is, by inordinately explaining them "to such monsters of men." Men are called monsters who, though in human body, bear within them the heart of a beast, since vice has made them like to beasts in their affections; hence these things "would be trampled under foot by them, rather than acknowledged," because they do not so much seek to know, but—because of their envy—to revile whatever is said; wherefore, "Give not that which is holy to dogs, neither cast ye your pearls before swine, lest perhaps they trample them under their feet" (Matt. 7:6). Therefore, that I should not do otherwise than this, "I restrain my pen by brevity."

This is the second part of the preface, in which he adds an explanation of his manner of writing. And first, he explains the difficulty of the task. In the second place, he excuses its imperfection. "Only so much ought one require of me as the intuition of human reason can approximate about the sublime truths of the Godhead." He refers also to a threefold difficulty which purposely he attached to it.

The first is by reason of the brevity of his writing; wherefore, he says, "I restrain my pen by brevity," according to that saying of Horace: "While I labor to be brief, I become obscure."

The second arises from the subtlety of the reasoning which he introduces; thus he says: "truths gleaned from the deepest teachings of philosophy," which are those doctrines abstracted from the senses, the principles and conclusions which metaphysics and logic make use of.

The third difficulty arises from the newness of the words used; wherefore he says: "I veil over by the signification of new words." These words are called "new" either with reference to the matter, because others treating of this same question did not employ the same vocabulary, or with reference to those who read them, because they are unaccustomed to such terms.

These three difficulties he adds to the fourth which he had previously mentioned: that is, the difficulty of the subject; consequently, in regard to those things written in this book, the meaning is clear only to the wise, to such men as the author himself and the one to whom he has addressed it. But others who cannot comprehend it are excluded from the reading of it. For things which are not understood are not read with pleasure. And because his reason for so writing is connected with preceding statements, he introduces it with "therefore," which is a sign of a conclusion. The meaning is clear.

"Only so much ought one require of me as the intuition of human reason can approximate about the sublime truths of the Godhead." Here he excuses a defect of the work, because, indeed, one ought not demand from him in this task any more certitude than that which the human reason, in mounting up to the divine, is capable of; a position which he justifies by reference to matters of less importance in other arts, in which only such an end is established for each craftsman as he can accomplish, one such as human reason allows. A physician does not always, indeed, effect a cure, but if he omits nothing which he ought to do, he will be without blame; and the same is true in regard to other arts. Therefore in this work, where the matter is difficult, going beyond the experience of human nature, the greater leniency ought to be granted if he does not solve the question with perfect certitude.

Then, when he says: "You must also determine this: whether the seeds of speculation, gathered from the writings of the blessed Augustine, have in my work borne fruit," he adduces whose authority he follows in his work, namely, Augustine. Not that he says only those things that are to be found in the books of Augustine, but because those things which Augustine said regarding the Trinity—namely, that the divine Persons are equal in an absolute sense and are distinguished according to relationships—he accepts as seeds and principles, which he uses in resolving this difficult question; and so this explanation of truth by means of many considerations of reason is the fruit springing forth from those seeds found in the writings of Augustine himself; but whether they are acceptable and productive, he leaves to the judgment of him to whom he writes, thus coming directly to the proposed question.

## QUESTION I

## CONCERNING THE KNOWLEDGE OF DIVINE THINGS

Here there occurs a twofold question: concerning the knowledge of divine things, and concerning the manifestation of them.

In regard to the first, four things are asked:

1. Whether the human mind in order to attain to a knowledge of truth requires a new illumination of divine light.
2. Whether it can attain to an idea of God.
3. Whether God is the first object known by the mind.
4. Whether the human mind is capable of arriving at a knowledge of the divine Trinity by natural reason.

### Article 1

#### WHETHER THE HUMAN MIND IN ORDER TO ATTAIN TO A KNOWLEDGE OF TRUTH REQUIRES A NEW ILLUMINATION OF DIVINE LIGHT

**Objections.** 1. It seems that the human mind in attaining to any knowledge whatever requires a new illumination of divine light. "Not that we are sufficient to think anything of ourselves as of ourselves, but our sufficiency is from God" (II Cor. 3:5); but there can be no perception of truth of any kind whatever without thought; therefore the human mind cannot know any truth unless it is illuminated by a new light from God.

2. It is easier to learn any truth from another than to discover it for oneself: wherefore, those who know things by their own efforts are preferred to those who are able to learn

## QUESTION I

from other men, according to I *Ethic.;* but man is not able to learn from another unless his mind is interiorly taught by God, as Augustine says in his book, *De magistro,* and Gregory in *Hom. Pentec.;* therefore neither can anyone discover truth of himself unless his mind is illuminated by God with a new light.

3. As the eyes of the body are related to corporeal things which they behold, so is the intellect related to the intelligible truth which it perceives, as is evident in III *De anima;* but the bodily eye cannot see corporeal things unless it is illuminated by the material sun; therefore neither can the intellect behold the truth unless it is illuminated by the light of the invisible sun, which is God.

4. Those acts are said to be in us (as our own) for the exercise of which we possess within ourselves principles that are sufficient; but in us there is not the power to know truth altogether [or absolutely] for there are many who labor to learn the truth and who, nevertheless, are unable to do so; therefore we have not in us sufficient principles for knowing truth and so it must be that to arrive at knowledge of it we require aid from outside ourselves, and so the conclusion is like the foregoing.

5. The operation of the human mind depends more upon the divine light than does the operation of sensible or inferior beings upon the light of the material heaven; but inferior bodies, although they have forms which are principles of their natural operations, are, nevertheless, incapable of perfecting these operations unless they are aided by the influence of the light of the stars; wherefore Dionysius (*De divi. nom.*, chap. 4) says that the light of the sun contributes to the generation of visible bodies and that it moves them to life and nourishes them and causes them to grow; therefore its natural light, which is, as it were, its form, would not suffice to make truth visible to the human mind unless another light, namely, the divine, supervened to assist it.

6. In all causes that are ordered to one another essentially, and not accidentally, no effect proceeds from a second cause unless through the operation of a first cause, as is established in the first proposition of *De causis;* but the human mind is ordained beneath the uncreated light according to an order that is essential and not accidental; therefore the operation of the human mind which is its proper effect, namely, the cognition of truth, cannot proceed from it unless by reason of the operation of the first uncreated light: its operation, however, seems to indicate nothing other than illumination; therefore, etc.

7. As the will is related to willing well, so the intellect is related to right understanding: but the will cannot will well unless it is aided by divine grace, as Augustine says; therefore neither can the intellect know the truth unless illuminated by divine light.

8. That for which our powers do not suffice is wrongly ascribed to our strength: but it is reprehensible that anyone should ascribe knowledge of the truth to his own ability, since indeed we are even commanded to ascribe it to God, according to this saying of Ecclus. 51:23: "To Him that giveth me wisdom, will I give glory"; therefore our powers do not suffice for knowledge of truth, and so the conclusion is as before.

**Sed contra.** The human mind is divinely illuminated by its natural light, according to the saying of Psalm 4:7: "The light of Thy countenance, O Lord, is signed upon us." Thus, therefore, if this created light is not sufficient for the knowing of truth, but there is required a new illumination, according to the same reasoning this superadded light would not suffice either, but would require still another light, and so on to infinity, which cannot be encompassed; and so it would be impossible to know any truth. Therefore one must stand firm in reliance upon the first light, namely, that the

# QUESTION I

mind by its natural light, without the superaddition of any other, can see the truth.

Again, as it suffices for what is actually visible that it should be proportionate to the sight in order to move it, so it suffices for what is intelligible that it should be proportionate to the intellect in order to move it: but our mind possesses within itself the power of making things intelligible in act, namely, the active intellect, and what is intelligible is proportionate to it; therefore it does not require another new illumination in order to know truth.

Moreover, as corporeal light is related to bodily vision, so is the intellect related to intelligible vision. But any corporeal light at all, even though it is weak, renders something corporeally visible, at least itself; therefore, the light of the intellect also, which is connatural to the mind, suffices for the understanding of some truth.

Furthermore, all things that are artificially made depend upon the cognition of some truth since the principle of them is knowledge; but it is certain that products of art do exist in which, according to Augustine, the free will is able [to act] by itself, as in building houses and the like; therefore man is sufficiently capable of knowing some truth without a new divine illumination.

**Response.** It must be said that between potencies that are active and those that are passive there is this difference: passive potencies cannot enter on the act of their proper operation unless they are moved to do so by their own active agents, just as the senses experience no sensation unless moved by some sensible object; but active potencies are capable of operation without being moved by another, as is evident in the case of the potencies of the vegetative soul: but as regards the intellect, a twofold potency is found, an active potency, that is, the active intellect, and a passive potency, that is, the possible intellect.

Now, there are certain philosophers who maintained that the possible intellect alone is a faculty of the soul, while the active intellect is a separate substance; and this is the opinion of Avicenna. According to this opinion, it follows that the human soul would not be capable of entering upon its proper operation, which is knowledge, unless illuminated by an exterior light, namely, by the light of that separate substance which they call the active intellect.

But because the words of the Philosopher (III *De anima*) seem to proclaim more convincingly that the active intellect is a potency belonging to the soul—and with this the authority of Scripture agrees, which declares that we are distinguished by that intellectual light to which the Philosopher compares the active intellect—therefore it is held that there is in the soul, fitting it for intelligible operation, that is, for undertaking the cognition of truth, a potency which is active and another which is passive. Wherefore, as some powers which are naturally active, when conjoined with those which are their passive complements, suffice for the carrying on of their natural operations, so also the soul of man, having in itself an active and a passive potency, is sufficient for perception of the truth.

Since, however, the power of any created thing is but finite, its efficacy will be limited to certain determined effects. Consequently it cannot attain to certain other effects unless new power is added to it; but there are some intelligible truths to which the efficacy of the active intellect does extend, as, for example, those first principles which man naturally knows, and those truths which are deduced from them; and for such knowledge no new light of intelligence is required, but the light with which the mind is naturally endowed suffices.

But there are other truths to which the aforesaid first principles do not extend; e.g., the truths of faith and things that exceed the faculty of reason, such as knowledge of future contingent events, and the like; and such things the human mind cannot know unless it is divinely illuminated by a new light, superadded to that which it naturally possesses.

For, although it does not require the addition of new light for knowledge of those things to which reason naturally extends, it does require divine operation: for over and above that operation by which God created the natures of things—giving to each its proper form and ability, by which they are able to exercise their proper operation— He also operates in things the works of Providence, directing and moving the capabilities of all things to their proper acts. For in this way the whole universe of creatures is subject to the divine governance, as instruments are subject to the direction of the workman and as natural qualities are subject to the power of the nutritive soul, as is said in II *De anima*. Therefore, as the work of digestion is accompanied by a natural heat, according to the measure which the digestive function imposes upon heat, and as all the inferior powers of the body operate according as they are directed and moved by virtue of the heavenly bodies, so all the active created powers are governed and moved by the Creator.

Thus, therefore, in all cognition of truth, the human mind requires the divine operation. In the realm of naturally known truths, however, it requires no new light, but only the divine motion and direction; for the knowledge of other (supernatural) truths it needs also a new illumination. And because it is of such things that Boethius speaks, he says: "To the extent that the divine light has deigned to enkindle the feeble spark of my mind."

**Answers to objections.** 1. Although we are in no way sufficient of ourselves, as from ourselves, to know anything without the operation of God, yet it is not necessary that for every operation of ours a new light should be given to us.

2. In matters of natural cognition God teaches us interiorly in this way: that He is the cause of the natural light

which is in us, and He directs it to the truth; but in other (supernatural) matters He further teaches us by the infusion of a new light.

3. The eye of the body, when illuminated by the light of the material sun, does not respond to a light which is in any way natural (i.e., intrinsic) to itself, by means of which it makes things to be actually visible; even as is the case with the mind when it is illuminated by the uncreated Light; and therefore the eye always requires an exterior light, but not the mind.

4. Where there is pure light of intellect, as in the angels, it makes evident without difficulty all things known in the natural order, so that in them there is cognition of all objects naturally intelligible to them: in us, however, this light is obscure, being overshadowed as it were by reason of conjunction with the body and with corporeal powers, and on this account it is hindered so that it cannot freely and naturally behold that truth which is itself knowable, as is said in the Book of Wisdom (9:15): "For the corruptible body is a load upon the soul; and the earthly habitation presseth down the mind that museth upon many things." From this it follows that on account of the impediment (of the body) it is not in our power to know truth altogether in its fullness. But each one possesses more or less the power to know in proportion to the purity of the intellectual light which is in him.

5. Although inferior bodies have need of superior bodies for their operation, to the extent that they must be moved by them; nevertheless, for the perfect accomplishment of their proper functions, they do not need to receive from these superior bodies any new forms. And in like manner it is not necessary that the human mind, which is moved by God, should be endowed with any new light in order to understand those things which are within its natural field of knowledge.

6. As Augustine says (*VIII super Gen. ad litteram*), as the

air is illuminated by the presence of light, but straightway grows dark if the light should be removed, so the mind is illuminated by God, and so also it is God who continually causes the natural light in the soul, not one kind now and another kind at another time, but the same (natural light); for He is the cause not only of its coming to be, but of its continued existence in us. In this way, therefore, God continually operates in the mind since He causes and governs the natural light in it, and thus the mind does not carry on its own function without the operation of the First Cause.

7. The will never can will the good without divine incitement: nevertheless it can will the good without infusion of grace, though not meritoriously. And likewise the intellect, without divine influence, is incapable of knowing any truth whatever; it can, however, know without infusion of new light, though not those truths which exceed natural cognition.

8. From the very fact that God causes the natural light in us by conserving it and directing it to seeing, it is manifest that perception of the truth must be ascribed principally to Him, just as the producing of a work of art is ascribed to the artist rather than to the thing produced.

## Article 2

WHETHER THE HUMAN MIND CAN ARRIVE AT AN IDEA OF GOD

**Objections.** 1. It seems that in no way can God be known by us. For that which in the highest degree of our knowledge remains unknown to us, in no manner is knowable: but in the most perfect degree of our cognition we are not united with God, except as with One who is, as it were, unknown, as Dionysius says (*Theologia mystica,* chap. 1); therefore God is in no way knowable by us.

2. Anything that is known is known through some other form; but, as Augustine says, God escapes (by transcending)

every form of our intellect; therefore in no way is He knowable by us.

3. Between the knower and the thing known must be some kind of proportion, as in the case of any potency and its object; but between our intellect and God there can be no proportion, as there can be none between the infinite and the finite; therefore our intellect can in no way know God.

4. Since potency and act are reduced to the same genus, inasmuch as they divide all classes of being, no potency can be in act which is outside its own genus: just as the senses are incapable of knowing intelligible substance; but God is outside every genus; therefore He cannot be known by any intellect that is in a genus; but our intellect is of this kind; therefore, etc.

5. If that which stands first is done away with, everything consequent upon it is likewise put aside: but what is first intelligible about a thing is its quiddity; hence that which a thing is, is said to be the proper object of the intellect (III *De anima*); and what is serves as a medium of demonstrating whether it exists, and all the other conditions of the thing. But concerning God, we are unable to know what He is, as Damascene says. Therefore, we can know nothing of God.

**Sed contra.** But on the contrary is the saying of Rom. 1:20: "For the invisible things of Him, from the creation of the world, are clearly seen, being understood by the things that are made: His eternal power also and divinity."

According to Jer. 9:24: "But let him that glorieth glory in this, that he understandeth and knoweth Me"; but this would be empty glory unless we were able to know Him; therefore we can know God.

Nothing is loved unless it is known, as is evident from Augustine (II *De Trinitate*); but we are commanded to love God; therefore we are capable of knowing Him, since the impossible is not enjoined by precept.

## QUESTION I

**Response.** I answer: It must be said that there is a twofold way in which anything is known. One manner is through its proper form, as the eye sees a stone through the species of the stone. Another way is through some other form similar to it, as a cause is known through the similitude of its effect, just as man is known through the form of his image.

Moreover, through its own form a thing is also known in two ways. One way is the following: when knowledge is through the form which is the thing itself, as with God who eternally knows His own essence, and as an angel knows itself. According to another mode, knowledge is through a form which is other than the thing: either when the form has been abstracted from a thing—in which case the form is more immaterial than the thing itself, as is the form of a stone abstracted from the stone itself—or when the form is impressed on the intellect by a thing, as occurs when the thing is more immaterial than the similitude by which it is known; thus, as Avicenna says, we know intellectual beings through their impression in us.

Therefore, since our intellect has, in our present state of wayfaring, a determined relation to forms abstracted from sensible things (since it is dependent upon phantasms in the same way as sight is upon colors, as is said in III *De anima*), it cannot know God in this life through that form which is His essence; though it is in this way that He is known by the blessed in heaven.

No similitude, however, of whatever kind impressed by Him upon the human intellect, would suffice to make His essence known, since He infinitely transcends every created form; consequently God cannot be made accessible to the mind through created forms, as Augustine says. Nor, in this present state, can God become known to us even through the species of things which are purely intelligible, which have in a certain way a likeness to Him, because our intellect is connaturally related to phantasms, as has been said. Therefore it remains certain that it is only through the forms of His effects that He is known.

There are, moreover, two kinds of effects: those which adequate the power of a cause, and through such an effect the power of a cause is fully known, and consequently the essence of the cause; and another kind of effect which is not completely equal to its cause. Through this latter kind of effect it is not possible to comprehend the power of the agent, and consequently not its essence either; but regarding the cause it can be known only that it exists. Thus the knowledge of an effect stands as a principle whereby the existence of its cause is known, just as does the quiddity of the cause when it is known through its own form. Now, it is according to this second mode that every effect stands in relation to God; and hence we are not able in this life to attain to any knowledge of Him, except that He is.

Nevertheless, of those knowing that He is, one will know Him more perfectly than another, because a cause is more perfectly understood from its effect the more perfectly the relation of the cause to its effect is apprehended. And in this relation of an effect not reaching in equality to its cause, three things are noted: namely, the progression of the effect from its cause; secondly, the consequent similitude of the effect to its cause; and thirdly, the failure on the part of the effect to attain to a perfect likeness of its cause. Thus the human mind grows in the knowledge of God, even though it cannot attain to a knowledge of what He is, but only to a knowledge that He is, in three ways.

Thus, in the first place, God is known as His productiveness and efficacy are more perfectly known. Secondly inasmuch as He is known as the Cause of the nobler of His effects, since those creatures which display being of a higher mode in their resemblance to Him manifest His eminence more than others. In the third place, He is better recognized as differentiated from all those things which appear in His effects.

## QUESTION I

Hence, in *De divinis nominibus*, Dionysius says that God is known inasmuch as He is the cause of all things, by His transcending eminence in comparison to all things, and by denial (of all created imperfection).

Moreover, in the attempt to arrive at some knowledge of God, the human mind is greatly assisted when its natural light is fortified by a new illumination: namely, the light of faith and that of the gifts of wisdom and of understanding, by which the mind is elevated above itself in contemplation, inasmuch as it knows God to be above anything which it naturally apprehends. But because even this new light does not suffice to penetrate to a vision of His essence, it is said to be, in a certain way, turned back upon itself by His excellent light; and this is what is said in Gregory's gloss regarding the statement in Gen. 32:30 ("I have seen God face to face"): "When the vision of the soul is directed to God, it is reflected back upon itself, overwhelmed by the brilliance of His immensity."

**Answers to objections.** 1. It is answered: God as an unknown is said to be the terminus of our knowledge in the following respect: that the mind is found to be most perfectly in possession of knowledge of God when it is recognized that His essence is above everything that the mind is capable of apprehending in this life; and thus, although what He is remains unknown, yet it is known that He is.

2. It may be said: From the fact that the divine essence escapes any form of our intellect, evidently it is not possible to know what He is, but only that He exists.

3. It is answered: Proportion is nothing other than the mutual relation of two things associated by something in respect to which they either agree or differ. Now, agreement may be of two kinds.

In one way, things may be associated as belonging to the same genus of quantity or quality, as is the relation of one surface to another or of one number to another inasmuch as one excels the other or is equal to it, or even as heat is related to heat; and according to this mode of relation there is no possible proportion between God and creature, since there is no agreement in any genus.

In another way beings are said to be related when they are associated in a certain order; and in this way there is proportion between matter and form, between the maker and the thing made. This also is the kind of proportion required between knower and knowable, since what is knowable is, in a certain way, the act of the knowing power. Such, too, is the proportion of a creature to God: that of caused to its cause, and of knower to the knowable; but according as the excellence of the Creator transcends the creature, there is no proportion of the creature to the Creator which makes it possible to receive from Him an influx proportionate to His complete power, or to know Him perfectly, even as He perfectly knows Himself.

4. It may be said: The intellect and the intelligible object are of one genus, as potency and act. God, however, although not in the genus of intelligible things, as if comprehended under a genus or participating in its nature, nevertheless is related to this genus as its principle. For His effects are not outside every genus of intelligible beings; wherefore, even here, He can be known through His effects, and in heaven, through His essence. Moreover, a thing seems to be called "intelligible" more by negation than by affirmation; for a thing is said to be intelligible inasmuch as it is either immune from matter or separated from it. Hence, negations may be stated in regard to divine things with truth; though affirmations are inadequate in expressing agreement, as Dionysius says (*Coel. hier.*, chap. 2).

5. It may be answered: When a thing is known, not through its own form, but through an effect, the form of that effect takes the place of the form of the thing itself, and

# QUESTION I

therefore from the effect it is possible to know whether the cause exists.

## Article 3

### WHETHER GOD IS THE FIRST OBJECT KNOWN BY THE MIND

**Objections.** 1. It seems that the first object known or perceived by the mind must be God Himself. For, that in which all other things are known and through which we form judgments of what we know from all other things, is the first thing known by us, just as light is known by the eye prior to what is seen by the light; and as principles are understood before conclusions: but all things are known in the First Truth, and through that Truth we judge of all things, as Augustine says in *De Trinitate* and in *De vera religione;* therefore the First Truth is first known by us.

2. When there are many ordered causes, the influx of the first cause into the thing caused is prior to that of the second cause, and it is the last to leave the effect, as is said in *Liber de causis:* but since human knowledge is caused by things, the knowable or the intelligible is the cause of the mind's intellection; therefore the first intelligible is the first to influence it: but the influence of the intelligible on the mind, as such, is that it be understood; therefore God is the first object known by our intellect, since He is the first intelligible.

3. In all cognition, in which those things that are prior and simpler are first known, what is first and simplest is known first: but in human cognition those things that are first experienced are things prior to others and simpler, as is evident, since being is that of which first the human mind forms a concept, as Avicenna says; being, moreover, is first among created things; therefore also, God first comes to the knowledge of the human mind, since He is absolutely first and most simple being.

4. That end which is the last in attainment is the first in

intention: but God is the last end of the human will, to whom all other ends are ordained; and He is, therefore, the first in intention. But this could not be unless He were known; therefore God must be the first object of knowledge.

5. That which requires no preliminary preparation in order to be fitted to the need of the workman is the first chosen for his task, rather than that which needs some labor in order to be made ready, just as one making a bench selects wood already cut rather than uncut wood: but sensible things need to be abstracted from matter by the active intellect before they can be understood by the possible intellect. God, on the other hand, is by His very nature altogether separate from matter: therefore He is understood by the possible intellect prior to sensible things.

6. Those things that are naturally known, and that cannot be thought of as non-existing, are what first occur to our cognition: but an idea of the existence of God is naturally implanted in all minds, as Damascene says. Neither is it possible to think of God as non-existent, as Anselm states; therefore God is the first being known by us.

**Sed contra.** On the contrary, according to the Philosopher, everything known by us takes its origin from sense knowledge: but God is absolutely remote from sense experience; therefore He is not first known by us, but is known last.

Again, according to the Philosopher, those things that are posterior, according to nature, are first known as far as we are concerned; and those things which are less knowable in themselves are better known as far as we are concerned. But created things are posterior and less knowable by nature than is God Himself; therefore, by us, He is known after creatures.

Again, what is promised as an ultimate reward does not come first, preceding everything done to deserve it: but knowledge of God is promised to us as the ultimate reward of all cognition and action; therefore God is not the first object known by us.

## QUESTION I

**Response.** I answer that it must be said: There are those who declare that the first object known by the human mind even in this life is God Himself, who is first truth and the one through whom all other things are known. But this is evidently false, since to know God through His essence constitutes the beatitude of man; wherefore it would follow that every man would be blessed.

Moreover, since in the divine essence all things said of it are one, no one would err in regard to anything he said concerning God—a thing which from experience is evidently false; furthermore, since things first in the comprehension of the intellect ought to be most certainly known, the intellect would be certain that it knew them; but it is clear that this is not the case in the proposition (as to knowing God).

This position is also repugnant to the authority of Scripture (Exod. 33:20): "Man shall not see Me and live."

Hence there are others who say that the divine essence is not the first thing known by us in this life, but the influx of its light is, and in this way God is the first object known by us.

But this claim cannot be held; for the first influx of divine light in the mind is the natural light by which the power of intellectual life is constituted. This light, however, is not at first known by the mind; neither by cognition by which is known what this light is, since much investigation is required to know the essence of the intellect; nor by cognition by which is known whether such a light exists; for we do not perceive that we possess intellect, except inasmuch as we perceive that we understand, as is clear from the Philosopher's words in IX *Ethic.* For no one knows that he understands anything, save inasmuch as he understands something intelligible. From this it is evident that cognition of an intelligible object precedes cognition by which one knows that he himself understands, and consequently precedes the cognition by which he knows that he possesses an intellect; and so the influx of the natural light of intelligence cannot be the first thing known by us;

and much less can any other kind of influx of light be the first thing known. Therefore it must be said that "the first thing known to man" is a phrase which can be understood in two ways: either according to the order of diverse potencies, or according to the order of objects in some one potency.

According to the first way, since all the knowledge of our intellect is derived from sense experience, what is made known to us by our senses is known prior to what is known by the intellect; and this is the singular, or the sensible-intelligible.

According to the other meaning, that is, according to the order of objects in any one potency, the proper object of each potency is what is first knowable by it. Since, however, in the human intellect there is an active potency and a passive one, the object of the passive potency, namely, the possible intellect, will be that which is in act through the active potency, that is, through the active intellect, since to the passive potency there must correspond that which activates it.

The active intellect, however, does not render intelligible separate forms, which are of themselves intelligible, but those forms which it abstracts from phantasms; and hence forms of this latter kind are those which our intellect knows. And among these forms, the ones that first come to be abstracted by the intellect hold the place of priority. These, furthermore, are the forms that comprehend more notes—either after the manner of a total universal or after the manner of an integral whole—therefore the more universal things are first known to the intellect; a composite is known before its component parts, and a definition before the parts of the definition.

In this respect there is a certain imitation of the intellect found in the sense powers, which also receive as their objects things which in a certain way are abstracted from matter. For even in the case of the senses, singular things of a more general nature are the first known, as "this body" is known sooner than "this animal."

## QUESTION I

Thus it is evident that God and other separate substances cannot in any way be the first objects of our intellection, but are understood from other things, as is said in Rom. 1:20: "For the invisible things of Him, from the creation of the world, are clearly seen, being understood by the things that are made."

**Answers to objections.** 1. It may be said: From the words of Augustine and from other similar sayings, it is not to be understood that the uncreated truth itself is the proximate principle by which we know and judge of things, but that through the light conferred upon us, which is a similitude of that truth, we have cognition and judgment. Nor would this light have any efficacy except from the First Light: just as in methods of demonstration second principles would have no certitude unless founded upon the truth of first principles. Nevertheless it should not be thought that even this (natural) light is the first thing known by us. For we do not know other things by means of it, as if it were a medium for cognition of the knowable, but because (as agent) it makes other things knowable. Wherefore it could not itself be known unless it were contained among knowable things; even as light could not be seen by the eye unless manifested in color itself.

2. It may be answered: In the case of a plurality of ordered causes, the influx into the ultimate effect is not always of the same nature. Therefore it need not be that the first intelligible so influence our intellect as to be Himself an object of our knowledge; but it is only necessary that as cause He bestow the power of intellection. Or it may be said that although in the order of intelligible things God is first absolutely, yet He is not first in the order of things that are intelligible to us.

3. It may be said: Although those things which are first in the genus of things abstracted by the intellect from phantasms are first known by us, as *ens* and *unum*, nevertheless it does

not follow that those which are first absolutely (*simpliciter*), which are not contained in the genus of any proper object, should be classed with the former [i.e., things abstracted from phantasms].

4. Answer is made: Although God is the last end in attainment and first in the intention of the natural appetancy, it is not necessary that He be first in the cognition of the human mind, which is ordained to its end, but first in the mind of the One ordaining it, as is the case in other things which by natural appetancy tend toward their own end. Nevertheless the end is known from the beginning and intended in a certain general way, inasmuch as the mind desires its own well-being and welfare, which is possible to it only on condition that it (ultimately) possess God.

5. It may be answered: Although a process of abstraction is not required for the understanding of separate substances, they are not intelligible through the light of the active intellect; wherefore they are not the first objects of knowledge as far as our intellect is concerned.

6. It may be said: The existence of God, considered in itself, is a thing knowable in itself, since His essence is His existence; and in this way Anselm stated the matter.

Nevertheless, to us, who do not behold His essence, it is not self-evident that He exists; though cognition of it may be said to be innate inasmuch as it is through principles which are innate in us that we are easily able to perceive that God exists.

## Article 4

### WHETHER THE HUMAN MIND IS CAPABLE OF ARRIVING AT A KNOWLEDGE OF THE DIVINE TRINITY THROUGH NATURAL REASON

**Objections.** 1. It appears that the human mind is sufficiently capable of attaining to a knowledge of the divine Trinity through natural reason. Whatever belongs to being inasmuch as it is being ought especially to be found in first being: but a trinity does belong to being inasmuch as it is being, since such is found in everything, in this way: that all things have species, mode, and order, as Augustine says; therefore it is possible to know by natural reason that in God there is a Trinity.

2. No perfection can be wanting in God: but three is the number of every perfect thing, as is said in I *De coelo et mundo:* therefore Trinity must be attributed to God, and thus the conclusion is like that of the previous argument.

3. All inequality is reducible to prior equality, as multitude is reducible to unity: but between God and first created being there is inequality; there must, therefore, be some preceding equality, but this could be no other than that of a plurality; therefore there must be some plurality in the Divine Being.

4. Anything that is equivocal is reducible to what is univocal: but the issuing forth of creatures from God is equivocal; it is needful, therefore, to presume as prior to it a univocal procession, by which God proceeds from God, by reason of which a Trinity of persons ensues.

5. Without companionship, there can be no joy in the possession of any good: but in God there is from all eternity a most joyful possession of good; therefore, He possesses eternal companionship; but this could be no other than the companionship of divine persons, since no creature is eternal. Therefore, it is necessary to suppose a plurality of persons in the Deity.

6. It is possible to know from natural reason that God is intelligent; but from the fact that He is intelligent it follows that He conceives the Word, since this is common to every intelligence; therefore by natural reason it is possible to know of the generation of the Son and, in the same way, of the procession of love (between Father and Son: the Holy Ghost).

7. Richard of St. Victor in his *De Trinitate* says: "I believe without any doubt that in the case of whatever things are necessary there cannot be wanting reasons to explain them, not only probable arguments, but necessary ones"; but that God is three and one is a necessary truth, since He is eternal; therefore in proof of this there are necessary arguments of reason, and so the conclusion is as the previous one.

8. The Platonists had no knowledge of God except through reason: but they held that there were at least two persons: namely, the Father and the Mind generated by the Father, and this Mind contained the ideas of all things—a truth which we claim in regard to the Son; therefore by natural reason a plurality of persons can be known.

9. The Philosopher at the beginning of *De coelo et mundo* says: "Through this same number (three) we ourselves are accustomed to call upon God the Creator"; and so the conclusion is the same.

10. In this life we can in no way know what God is but only that He is: but there is a way in which we know that God is three and one, since we know it by faith; therefore this truth does not pertain to a quidditative knowledge of God, but only to an entitative knowledge. But by natural reason we can know God entitatively; therefore it is possible by natural reason to know that God is three and one.

**Sed contra.** Faith is of things that are not apparent to reason, as is clear from Heb. 11:1; but that God is three and one is an article of faith; therefore reason does not suffice for knowing this.

Again, natural reason has its efficacy from first principles of natural cognition: but that God is three and one cannot be deduced from principles naturally known, for these are derived from sense experience, and in sensible things there is found nothing like to three *supposita* of one essence; therefore God cannot be known as three and one from reason.

Moreover, according to the words of Ambrose: "It is impossible for anyone to know the secret of generation; the mind fails; the voice is silent; not only mine, but even that of the angels"; therefore natural reason does not suffice for knowledge of divine generation, and consequently for knowledge of the Trinity of persons.

**Response.** I answer that the truth that God is three and one is altogether a matter of faith; and in no way can it be demonstratively proved. For, although certain reasons can be found (by way of demonstration *ad hoc*), they are not necessary, or even very probable except to one who believes it. This is evident from the fact that in this life we know God only from His effects, as previous statements have proved. Hence, according to natural cognition, we can know nothing of God except what we can derive concerning Him from viewing the relationship of effects to Him. Thus there are things that designate His causality and His eminence over creatures and that deny in Him any of the imperfections found in effects. The existence of a Trinity of persons, however, cannot be perceived from a consideration of divine causality, since causality is common to the whole Trinity. Nor can it be known from His lacking any imperfection. Therefore in no way can it be demonstratively proved that God is three and one.

**Answers to objections.** 1. It may be said: Those things which are many among created beings are in fact one in God: and therefore, although in every creature there is found a certain kind of trinity, it cannot be necessarily concluded from this that there is such a trinity in God, except logically, and this kind of plurality is not sufficient to prove a distinction of persons.

2. It may be answered: The perfection of the number three is found in God according even to the unity of His essence, not because His essence is subject to numeration, but because in it there is contained virtually the perfection of every number, as is said in the *Arithmetica* of Boethius.

3. It may be said: Apart from any distinction of persons, there is equality in the Divinity, inasmuch as Its wisdom is equal to Its power. Or it can be said that in regard to equality there are two points of consideration, namely, plurality of *supposita*, among whom equality exists, and unity of quantity, which is the cause of equality. The reduction of inequality to equality, therefore, does not occur by reason of the plurality of *supposita*, but by reason of the cause; for just as unity is the cause of equality, so inequality is the cause of plurality. Hence it must be that the cause of equality precedes the cause of inequality, but not that any kind of inequality is preceded by some kind of equality: otherwise it would be necessary in an order of numbers that there should be something before unity and duality, which are unequals; or that in unity itself there should be found plurality.

4. It must be said: Although anything equivocal is reducible to what is univocal, it is not necessary that equivocal generation should be reduced to univocal generation, but that it should be reduced to a generator which is univocal in itself. Now, in natural things we see that equivocal generations are prior to univocal because equivocal causes have an influx extending to the total species, whereas univocal causes have not, their influence extending only to one individual; and thus they are quasi-instruments of equivocal causes, just as inferior bodies are of superior.

5. It is answered: It is not possible for man to have a joyous life without companionship because he has not within himself that which makes him all-sufficient; whereas, for the same reason, animals that are self-sufficient require no association with others for preservation of life, but are solitaries. God, however, is supremely self-sufficient; wherefore, even though there were no distinction of persons, infinite joy would still be His.

6. It may be said: In God, intellect and object of intellect

## QUESTION I

are the same; and therefore, from the fact that He is intelligent, it need not be supposed that in Him there is any concept really distinct from Himself, as is the case with us: Trinity of persons, however, requires real distinction.

7. It may be answered: Understanding of this passage is clarified by that which follows: "Although they (these truths) are of such kind as to escape all our endeavors." All things that are necessary in themselves, therefore, are either known in themselves or are knowable through other things: yet not in such a way that they are necessarily apparent to us. Therefore we cannot, even as a result of all our industry, discover necessary arguments of reason sufficient to prove all necessary truths.

8. It may be said: The position of the Platonists affords no argument as regards the truth of this matter, even though it appears to do so according to words. For they did not hold that this Mind was of the same essence with God the Father, but that it was another substance proceeding from the first, and separate; and they also supposed that there was a third substance, the Soul-of-the-World, as is evidenced by Macrobius. And because all these separate substances they called "gods," it came about that they called upon or spoke of three gods, as Augustine says in *De civitate Dei* (chap. 10); because they did not hold that there was anything like to the Holy Ghost, as there was to the Father and the Son. For the Soul-of-the-World is not the *nexus* of the other two, according to their doctrine, as is the Holy Spirit between the Father and the Son; therefore they are said to have lacked the third sign, that is, knowledge of the Third Person. Or it may be said, as the more common explanation has it, that they knew two persons according to the things appropriated to power and wisdom, but not according to the things proper to them. But goodness, which is appropriated to the Holy Spirit especially, has as its effects things which they did not know.

9. It may be said: Aristotle did not have any intention

of saying that God should be worshiped as three in one, but that He was honored by the ancients by the number three in their sacrifices and prayers because of the perfection of three as a number.

10. It may be answered: All things in God are of one, simple essence; but those things that in Him are one, are many in our intellect; and on this account our intellect can apprehend one of these things without the other. Therefore in this life we are able to understand the quiddity of none of these things, but only their existence; and thus it happens that one of them may be known to exist and not another: just as one might know that there is wisdom in God, but not know that there is also omnipotence; and likewise it is possible, by natural reason to know that God exists, but not that He is a Trinity, and one God.

## QUESTION II

## CONCERNING THE MANIFESTATION OF KNOWLEDGE OF DIVINE TRUTH

Here four questions are proposed:
1. Whether divine truths ought to be treated of by the method of inquiry.
2. Whether there can be any science of divine truths which are founded upon faith.
3. Whether in the science of faith, which is concerning God, it is permissible to employ arguments of the natural philosophers.
4. Whether divine truths ought to be veiled by new and obscure words.

*Article 1*

WHETHER DIVINE TRUTHS OUGHT TO BE TREATED OF BY THE METHOD OF INQUIRY

**Objections.** 1. It seems that it is not permissible to investigate divine things by the arguments of reason. In Ecclus. 3:22, it is said: "Seek not the things that are too high for thee"; but divine truths are, in a special way, too high for man, and particularly those truths which are of faith; therefore it is not permissible to inquire into them.

2. Punishment is not inflicted except for some fault; but, as it is said in Prov. 25:27, "He that is a searcher of majesty shall be overwhelmed by glory"; therefore, it is not right to search out those things which pertain to divine majesty.

3. Ambrose says: "Abandon arguments where faith is sought." But in regard to divine truths, especially those con-

cerned with the Trinity, faith is required; therefore in this matter it is not permissible to inquire into truth by arguments of reason.

4. Ambrose, in speaking of divine generation, says: "Supernal mysteries are not to be scrutinized: one may know that the Son was begotten; but how He was begotten should not be analyzed." Accordingly, for the same reason it is not permissible to make rational investigation of those truths which pertain to the Trinity.

5. Gregory in his *Homily for Easter* (chap. 8) says: "Faith has no merit where human reason affords proof"; but it is wrong to lose the merit of faith; therefore it is not right to investigate matters of faith according to methods of reason.

6. All honor ought to be given to God: but divine mysteries are honored by silence; wherefore Dionysius says at the close of *Coel. hier.*: "Honoring by silence the hidden truth which is above us"; and with this there agrees what is said in Psalm 64, according to the text of Jerome: "Praise grows silent before Thee, O God," that is, silence itself is Thy praise, O God; therefore we ought to refrain ourselves in silence from searching into divine truths.

7. No one is moved to infinity, as the Philosopher says in I *De Coelo et mundo*, because all motion is on account of the attaining of an end [terminus], which is not to be found in infinity; but God is infinitely distant from us. Since, therefore, investigation is a kind of motion of reason toward that which is being searched out, it appears that divine truths ought not to be investigated.

**Sed contra.** On the other hand, it is said (I Pet. 3:15): "Being ready always to satisfy everyone that asketh you a reason of that (faith and) hope which is in you"; but this could not be done unless we inquired reasonably into those things which are matters of faith; therefore investigation according to methods of reason into the truths of faith is necessary.

Again as is said in Titus 1:9, it pertains to a bishop that he be capable of exhorting in sound doctrine and of overcoming those contradicting it: but he cannot do this without use of argumentation; therefore one ought to employ the arguments of reason in matters of faith.

Again Augustine says in I *De Trinitate:* "With the help of God our Lord, we shall begin to discuss according to reason that for which they [our adversaries] seek explanation: that the Trinity is one God." Therefore man can inquire about the Trinity according to methods of reason.

Also Augustine says in his argument against Felician: "Since without too much disagreement you recognize these two things—since you do not disregard the foregoing argument and the word of authority—I present the matter to follow in such a way that you yourself may accept it as proof"; that is, I shall make use of arguments from reason and authority; and thus the conclusion is like the previous one.

**Response.** I answer that it must be said that, since the perfection of man consists in his union with God, it is right that man, by all the means which are in his power and in so far as he is able, mount up to and strive to attain to divine truths, so that his intellect may take delight in contemplation and his reason in the investigation of things of God, according to the saying of Ps. 72:28, "It is good for me to adhere to my God." Hence also the Philosopher in X *Ethic.* opposes the saying of those who maintained that man ought not concern himself about divine things, but only about such as are human, saying: "One ought to be wise in regard to man, however, not according to those treating of human affairs alone, as a mortal knowing only mortal things; but, inasmuch as it is fitting for a mortal man to do so, he ought to do all things according to the best of those powers that are in him."

In a threefold manner, however, it is possible for man to err on this point:

First, by presumption, since one might enter upon such

investigation as if he could attain a perfect comprehension, and it is this kind of presumption that is denounced in Job 11:7: "Peradventure thou wilt comprehend the steps of God, and wilt find out the Almighty perfectly?" And Hilary says: "Do not involve yourself in the hiddenness and mystery of this inconceivable nativity; do not overwhelm yourself, presuming to comprehend the loftiest of intelligible things, but understand that it is incomprehensible."

In the second place, error arises if, in matters of faith, reason has precedence of faith and not faith of reason, to the point that one would be willing to believe only what he could know by reason, when the converse ought to be the case: wherefore Hilary says: "While believing [in a spirit of faith], inquire, discuss, carry through your speculation."

In a third way error results from undertaking an inquiry into divine things which are beyond one's capacity. Wherefore it is said in Rom. 12:3, "Not to be more wise than it behoveth to be wise, but to be wise unto sobriety and according as God hath divided to every one the measure of faith." All men, indeed, have not been accorded the same measure; wherefore a thing is beyond the capacity of one which is not beyond that of another.

**Answers to objections.** 1. It may be said: Those things are said to be too high for man which exceed his capacity, not those things which are of greater dignity according to nature: for the more man fixes his gaze upon things loftier by nature, in accordance with his capacity, the more it is to his advantage; but in the consideration of things which in the least exceed his capacity, he easily falls into error. Therefore the gloss on this same passage says: "Heretics are produced in two ways: namely, when men, beyond their proper capacity, entering upon inquiry concerning the Creator or creatures, fall into errors and depart from the truth."

2. Answer may be made: To search out is, as it were, to press one's investigation to the very end; but this would be

unlawful and presumptuous if one should so investigate divine truths as though he could attain to complete comprehension as his goal.

3. It is answered: Where faith is sought for, those arguments which are in opposition to faith and those which seek to have precedence over it are cast aside, but not those which in due manner follow it.

4. It may be said: It is not lawful in this world to inquire into divine mysteries in such a way that one would have the intention of comprehending them, as is evident from the words that follow: "It is lawful to know that He was begotten," etc. For he undertakes an unlawful mode of inquiry who seeks to know what the nature of this nativity is, since in regard to divine things we are able to know what they are not, but not what they are.

5. It may be answered: Human reasoning may be spoken of in two ways: in one way, it may be regarded as demonstrative, forcing the intellect to believe; and this kind of reasoning cannot be possessed in regard to those truths which are of faith; but it is possible to possess this kind of reasoning in refuting those arguments which would destroy faith or assert the impossible. For, although reason cannot demonstrate those things which are of faith, neither can these same truths be demonstratively disproved. Moreover, if this kind of reason could lead to a proving of those things which are of faith, it would deprive man of the merit of faith, because then assent would not be voluntary, but necessary.

Persuasive reasoning, however, derived from certain likenesses to those things which are set forth by faith does not void the meaning of faith, since it does not make these truths to be apparent, for there can be no resolution of them to those first principles discernable by the intellect. Nor does it take away the merit of faith, because it does not force the intellect to comprehend truth, but assent remains voluntary.

6. It may be said: God is honored by silence, but not in

such a way that we may say nothing of Him or make no inquiries about Him, but inasmuch as we understand that we lack ability to comprehend Him. Wherefore in Ecclus. 43: 32–34, "Glorify the Lord as much as ever you can, for He will yet far exceed, and His magnificence is wonderful. Blessing the Lord, exalt Him as much as you can: for He is above all praise. When you exalt Him put forth all your strength, and be not weary: for you can never go far enough."

7. Answer may be made: Since God is infinitely distant from creatures, no creature is so moved unto God as to be made His equal, either in receiving from Him or in knowing Him. Therefore, by reason of the fact that God is infinitely distant from creatures, there is no terminus to the motion of creatures; but every creature is moved to this: that he may be more and more like to God, so far as this is possible: and so also the human mind ought always be moved more and more to a knowledge of God, according to the measure that is proper to it. Therefore Hilary says: "He who in pious spirit undertakes the infinite, even though he can in no wise attain it, nevertheless profits by advancing."

*Article 2*

WHETHER THERE CAN BE ANY SCIENCE OF DIVINE TRUTHS WHICH ARE MATTERS OF FAITH

**Objections.** 1. It appears that there can be no science of those divine truths which are matters of faith. For wisdom is distinguished from science; but wisdom treats of divine truths; therefore science cannot do so.

2. As is said in 1 *Poster.*, in every science one must suppose a quidditative knowledge of the subject; but in regard to God, it is impossible for us to know in any way what He is, as Damascene says; therefore it is not possible to possess any science of God.

3. It pertains to every science to consider the parts and passive potencies of its subject; but, since God is simple form [absolute act], He has not any parts that can be distinguished, nor in Him can there be any passive potencies; therefore there can be no science about God.

4. In any science, reason precedes assent, for it is demonstration which in the sciences makes one assent to what is knowable; but in regard to those truths which are of faith, the converse ought to prevail, namely, assent on account of faith ought to precede reason, as has been said; therefore, of divine truths, especially of those which are known by faith, there can be no science.

5. Every science proceeds from self-evident principles which every man accepts upon first hearing, or from principles in which he has faith because of those first principles; but the articles of faith which are first principles in matters of faith, are not principles of this same kind, since they are not *per se nota* nor can they be resolved by demonstration to those that are, as has been said; therefore, there can be no science of divine truths held by faith.

6. Faith is not of those things that are apparent: but science is of things that are apparent, because through science those things that are treated of come to be clearly seen; therefore, concerning divine truths that are held by faith there can be no science.

7. Understanding is the principle of every science, because from the intellection of principles one comes to scientific knowledge of conclusions: but in those things that are of faith, intellection is not the beginning, but the end, for, as is said in Isa. 7:9, "If you will not believe, you shall not understand"; therefore there can be no science of divine truths held by faith.

**Sed contra.** But on the contrary is what Augustine says in XII *De Trinitate:* "To that science only do I attribute any value by which faith is well served, which leads to, produces, defends, and strengthens happiness"; therefore there is a science of the truths of faith.

Also, Wisd. 10:10: "She gave to him the science of the saints" [Douay Version: "knowledge of holy things"], that is, of the truths of faith, because no other science can be here meant except that by which saints are distinguished from sinners, which is the science of faith.

Also the Apostle in speaking of the knowledge of the faithful, says in I Cor. 8:7: "But there is not knowledge in everyone"; and thus we come to the same conclusion as before.

**Response.** I answer that, since the essence of science consists in this, that from things known a knowledge of things previously unknown is derived, and this may occur in relation to divine truths, evidently there can be a science of divine things.

But knowledge of divine truths can be thought of in two ways. In one way, as on our part, such truths are not knowable except from created things, of which we have a knowledge derived from sense experience. In another way, on the part of the nature of these things themselves, they are, in themselves, most knowable; and although they are not known by us according to their essences, they are known by God and by the blessed according to their proper mode; and so science of divine things must be considered in a twofold manner. One is according to our mode of knowledge, in which knowledge of sensible things serves as the principle for coming to a knowledge of divine; and it was in this way that the philosophers handed down a traditional science of divine things, calling first philosophy a divine science. The other mode is according to that of divine things themselves as they are understood in themselves. This is, indeed, a mode of knowledge which we cannot possess perfectly in this life; but there is for us, even in this life, a certain participation and assimilation to such a cognition of divine truth, inasmuch as through the faith which is infused into our souls we adhere to the very First Truth on account of Itself. And as God, since He knows Himself, knows in a way that is His own, that is, by simple intuition, not by discursive thought, so we, from those truths that we possess in adhering to First Truth, come to a knowledge of other truths, according to our own mode of cognition, namely, by proceeding from principles to conclusions. Wherefore, those truths that we hold in the first place by faith are for us, as it were, first principles in this science, and the other truths to which we attain are quasi-conclusions. From this it is evident that this science is of a higher order than that which the philosophers traditionally termed divine, since it proceeds from higher principles.

**Answers to objections.** 1. It may be said: Wisdom is not distinguished from science as opposed to it, but as related to science by adding to it. For wisdom is, indeed, as the Philosopher says in VI *Ethic.*, the head of all the sciences, regulating all others inasmuch as it treats of highest principles: on this account it is also called "the goddess of sciences" in I *Metaph.*; and much more is this true of that wisdom which is not only about highest principles, but from highest principles. Moreover, the function of wisdom is to order, and therefore this highest science, which orders and rules all others, is called wisdom; just as in mechanical arts we call those men wise who direct others, as the architects: but the name of "science" is also left to others that are inferior, and accordingly science is distinguished from wisdom as a property from a definition (i.e., as properties flow necessarily from an essence, so do the other sciences from wisdom).

2. It may be said: As has been previously declared, since causes are known through their effects, the knowledge of an effect substitutes for the quidditative knowledge of the cause;

this is necessarily required in those sciences treating of things that cannot be known through themselves: thus, for us to have a science of divine things, it is not necessary that we first have a quidditative knowledge of God. Or, again, it can be said that what we know God is not, takes the place, in divine science, of a cognition of what He is: for as one thing is distinguished from others by what it is, so God is here known by that which He is not.

3. It may be answered: In science the parts of a subject are not to be understood only as subjective or integral parts; but the parts of a subject are all those things of which knowledge is required in order to have cognition of the subject, since all things of this sort are not dealt with in a co-science except inasmuch as they are related to the subject. Those also are called passive potencies which can be proved in regard to anything, whether they are negations or relations to other things. And many such things can be proved in regard to God, both from naturally known principles and from principles of faith.

4. It may be answered: In any science whatever there are certain things that serve as principles, and others as conclusions. Hence the reasoning process set forth in the sciences precedes the assent given to a conclusion, but follows upon assent to principles, since it proceeds from them. Now, it is true that the articles of faith are in this science rather principles than conclusions, but they must be defended against those opposing them, as the Philosopher (IV *Metaph.*) proves against those denying first principles: for they may be made clearer of understanding by certain similitudes, by inducing results of opposing naturally known principles, but they cannot be proved by demonstrative reasoning.

5. It must be said: Even in those sciences handed down to us by human tradition, there are certain principles in some of them which are not universally known, but which presuppose truths derived from a higher science, just as in sub-

ordinate sciences certain things taken from superior sciences are assumed and believed to be true; and truths of this kind are not *per se nota* except in the higher sciences. This is the case with the articles of faith; for they are principles of that science leading to knowledge of divine things, since those truths which are *per se nota* in the knowledge which God has of Himself, are presupposed in our science; and He is believed as the one manifesting these truths to us through His messengers, even as the doctor believes from the word of the physicist that there are four elements.

6. Answer is made: The evident truths of a science proceed from the evident truth of principles. Wherefore a science does not make clear the truth of its principles, but makes clear that of its conclusions: and in this same way the science of which we now speak does not make evident the things of which we have faith, but on the basis of them, it makes other things evident with the same certitude as that belonging to their first principles.

7. It may be said: Understanding is always the first principle of any science, but not always the proximate principle; rather, it is often faith which is the proximate principle of a science, as is evident in the case of the subordinate sciences; since their conclusions proceed from faith in truths accepted on the authority of a superior science as from a proximate principle, but from the understanding of scientists in the superior field who have intellectual certitude of these created truths as from their ultimate principle. So likewise the proximate principle of this divine science is faith, but the first principle is the divine intellect to the revelation of which we give the assent of faith; but faith is in us that we may attain to an understanding of those things we believe; in the same way that a scientist in an inferior field, if he should gain knowledge of a higher, would then possess understanding and science of truths which previously were accepted only on faith.

## Article 3

WHETHER IN THE SCIENCE OF FAITH, WHICH IS CONCERNING GOD, IT IS PERMISSIBLE TO USE THE RATIONAL ARGUMENTS OF THE NATURAL PHILOSOPHERS

**Objections.** 1. It seems that in regard to those truths that are of faith it is not right to employ the rational arguments of the natural philosophers, for, according to I Cor. 1:17, "Christ sent me not to baptize, but to preach the gospel: not in wisdom of speech"; that is, "in the doctrine of the philosophers," as the gloss says. And concerning the line (I Cor. 1:20), "Where is the disputer of this world?" the gloss says: "The disputer is he who searches into the secrets of nature; such men God does not accept as preachers." And on the line (I Cor. 2:4), "And my speech and my preaching was not in the persuasive words of human wisdom," the gloss says: "Although the words were persuasive, they were not so because of human wisdom, as is the word of pseudo-apostles."

From all these lines it is evident that in matters of faith it is not lawful to employ philosophical reasoning.

2. On that line (Isa. 15:1), "Because in the night Ar of Moab is laid waste," the gloss says: "Ar, that is, the adversary, namely, secular science, which is the adversary of God"; therefore, etc.

3. Ambrose says: "The deepest mysteries of faith are free from the reasonings of the philosophers"; therefore, when a matter of faith is dealt with, the reasonings and words of the philosophers ought not to be used.

4. Jerome relates in a letter to Eustochium that in vision he was beaten, according to divine justice, because he had read the books of Cicero, and that those standing by besought that leniency might be granted on account of his youth, and that afterward the extreme penalty should be exacted if he read again the books of the Gentiles; where-

fore, calling upon the name of God, he exclaimed: "If ever I shall possess secular books, if ever I read them, I shall have denied Thee"; therefore it is not lawful to use them in treating of divine things.

5. In Scripture, secular wisdom is often represented by water, but divine wisdom by wine. Now, according to Isa., chap. 1, the innkeepers are upbraided for mixing water with wine; therefore the doctors are blameworthy for their mingling of philosophical doctrine with sacred Scripture.

6. Jerome says, in his gloss on Osee, chap. 2, "With heretics we ought not to have even names in common." But heretics use the arguments of philosophers to destroy faith, as is maintained in the gloss on Prov., chap. 7 and Isa., chap. 15; therefore Catholics ought not to use such in their discussions.

7. Every science has its proper principles, and thus also sacred doctrine has those that belong to it, namely, the articles of faith; but in other sciences the process is not valid if principles are taken from a different science, but each ought to proceed from its own principles, according to the teaching of the Philosopher (I *Poster.*); therefore the method is not permissible in sacred doctrine.

8. If the doctrine of anyone is repudiated in any respect, the authority of his teaching will not be valid in proving anything; wherefore Augustine says that, if in sacred doctrine we discover some falsity, the authority of that teaching is destroyed for confirming anything in regard to faith; but sacred doctrine repudiates the doctrine of the philosophers in many ways, because many errors are found among them; therefore their authority has no efficacy in proving anything (regarding sacred doctrine).

**Sed contra.** But on the contrary, the Apostle (Titus 1:12) makes use of a verse from the poet Epimenides, saying, "The Cretans are always liars, evil beasts," etc.; and (I Cor. 15:33) he employs the words of Menander: "Evil communications corrupt good manners"; and in Acts 17:28 are the words of Aratus, "For we are also his (i.e., God's) offspring." Therefore it is licit for other doctors of divine Scripture also to make use of the arguments of the philosophers.

Again, Jerome, in a letter to Magnus, a famous orator of Rome, having enumerated many doctors of Scripture, such as Basil and Gregory, adds: "All these have so intermingled in their books the teachings and the sayings of the philosophers that one knows not which to admire first in them, their secular erudition or their knowledge of the Scriptures." But this they would not have done had such been illicit or useless.

Also Jerome in a letter to Pammachius about the death of Paula says: "If you have become enamored of the captive woman, secular wisdom, and captivated by her beauty, cut her hair and her finger nails, cut away the enticement of her tresses and the adornments of her words, bathe her with prophetic niter, and, lying with her, say: 'His left hand under my head, and his right hand shall embrace me' (Cant. 8:3), and many children will the captive woman give to thee, and from the Moabite, Israelites will be born to thee." Therefore with fruitful results some make use of secular wisdom.

Again Augustine (II *De Trinitate*) says: "I shall not be without zeal in seeking out knowledge of God, whether through Scripture or creatures"; but knowledge of God through creatures is given in philosophy; therefore it is not unfitting that in sacred doctrine one should make use of philosophical reasoning.

Again Augustine (Book II, *De doctrina Christiana*) says: "If the philosophers have by chance uttered truths helpful to our faith, they are not only not to be feared, but rather those truths ought to be taken from them as from unjust possessors and used to our advantage." Thus the conclusion is as before.

Also on the saying in Dan. 1:8, "But Daniel purposed in his heart," the gloss says: "If anyone ignorant of mathematics should write in opposition to the mathematicians, or knowing nothing of philosophy should argue against the philosophers, would he not be derided?" But doctors of sacred Scripture must at times argue with philosophers; therefore it is needful that they make use of philosophy.

**Response.** I answer that it must be said that gifts of grace are added to those of nature in such a way that they do not destroy the latter, but rather perfect them; wherefore also the light of faith, which is gratuitously infused into our minds, does not destroy the natural light of cognition, which is in us by nature. For although the natural light of the human mind is insufficient to reveal those truths revealed by faith, yet it is impossible that those things which God has manifested to us by faith should be contrary to those which are evident to us by natural knowledge. In this case one would necessarily be false: and since both kinds of truth are from God, God would be the author of error, a thing which is impossible. Rather, since in imperfect things there is found some imitation of the perfect, though the image is deficient, in those things known by natural reason there are certain similitudes of the truths revealed by faith. Now, as sacred doctrine is founded upon the light of faith, so philosophy depends upon the light of natural reason; wherefore it is impossible that philosophical truths are contrary to those that are of faith; but they are deficient as compared to them. Nevertheless they incorporate some similitudes of those higher truths, and some things that are preparatory for them, just as nature is the preamble to grace.

If, however, anything is found in the teachings of the philosophers contrary to faith, this error does not properly belong to philosophy, but is due to an abuse of philosophy owing to the insufficiency of reason. Therefore also it is possible from the principles of philosophy to refute an error of this kind, either by showing it to be altogether impossible, or not to be necessary. For just as those things which are of faith cannot be demonstratively proved, so certain things contrary to them cannot be demonstratively shown to be false, but they can be shown not to be necessary.

Thus, in sacred doctrine we are able to make a threefold use of philosophy:

1. First, to demonstrate those truths that are preambles of faith and that have a necessary place in the science of faith. Such are the truths about God that can be proved by natural reason—that God exists, that God is one; such truths about God or about His creatures, subject to philosophical proof, faith presupposes.

2. Secondly, to give a clearer notion, by certain similitudes, of the truths of faith, as Augustine in his book, *De Trinitate*, employed many comparisons taken from the teachings of the philosophers to aid understanding of the Trinity.

3. In the third place, to resist those who speak against the faith, either by showing that their statements are false, or by showing that they are not necessarily true.

Nevertheless, in the use of philosophy in sacred Scripture, there can be a twofold error:

In one way, by using doctrines contrary to faith, which are not truths of philosophy, but rather error, or abuse of philosophy, as Origen did.

In another way, by using them in such manner as to include under the measure of philosophy truths of faith, as if one should be willing to believe nothing except what could be held by philosophic reasoning; when, on the contrary, philosophy should be subject to the measure of faith, according to the saying of the Apostle (II Cor. 10:5), "Bringing into captivity every understanding unto the obedience of Christ."

**Answers to objections.** 1. It may be said: From all these words it is shown that philosophical doctrine ought not to be used as if it had first place, as if on account of it one believed by faith; nevertheless the fact is not disproved that doctors

## QUESTION II

of sacred learning may employ philosophy, as it were, secondarily. Wherefore, on the saying (I Cor. 1:19), "I will destroy the wisdom of the wise," the gloss adds: "This he does not say because the understanding of truth can be worthy of God's anger, but because the false prudence of those who trusted in their erudition is worthy of reproof."

Nevertheless, in order that all that is of faith might be attributed not to human power or wisdom but to God, God willed that the primitive preaching of the apostles should be in infirmity and simplicity; though, on the other hand, with the later advent of power and secular wisdom, He manifested by the victory of the faith that the world is subject to God as much by wisdom as by power.

2. It may be said: Secular wisdom is said to be contrary to God in so far as it is an abuse of wisdom (i.e., erroneous) as when heretics abuse it, but not in so far as it is true.

3. It may be answered: The sacred deposit of the truth of faith is said to be free from philosophical doctrine inasmuch as it is not confined by the limits of philosophy.

4. It may be said: Jerome was so influenced by certain books of the Gentiles that he contemned, in a way, sacred Scripture: wherefore he himself says: "If I began to read it while turning over the words of the Prophets in my own mind, their crude expression filled me with distaste." And no one will deny that such was reprehensible.

5. It may be said: No conclusive argument can be drawn from figurative speech, as the Master (Peter Lombard) says.[1] Dionysius also says in his letter to Titus that symbolic theology has no weight of proof, especially when such interprets no authority. Nevertheless it can be said that when one of two things passes into the nature of another, the product is not considered a mixture except when the nature of both is altered. Wherefore those who use philosophical doctrines in sacred Scripture in such a way as to subject them

[1] VI *Distinc.*, Bk. I.

to the service of faith, do not mix water with wine, but change water into wine.

6. It may be said: Jerome is speaking of those arguments that were invented by heretics to give support to their errors; but such doctrines do not belong to philosophy; rather they lead only to error; and consequently on their account the truths of philosophy ought not be shunned.

7. Answer may be made: Sciences which are ordered to one another are so related that one can use the principles of another, just as posterior sciences can use the principles of prior sciences, whether they are superior or inferior: wherefore metaphysics, which is superior in dignity to all, uses truths that have been proved in other sciences. And in like manner theology—although all other sciences are related to it in the order of generation, as serving it and as preambles to it—can make use of the principles of all the others, even if they are posterior to it in dignity.

8. It may be said: Inasmuch as sacred doctrine makes use of the teachings of philosophy for their own sake, it does not accept them on account of the authority of those who taught them, but on account of the reasonableness of the doctrine; wherefore it accepts truth well said and rejects other things: but when it uses these doctrines to refute certain errors, it uses them inasmuch as their authority is esteemed by those whose refutation is desired, because the testimony of an adversary has in that case greater weight.

## Article 4

### WHETHER DIVINE TRUTHS OUGHT TO BE CONCEALED BY NEW AND OBSCURE WORDS

**Objections.** 1. It seems that in the science of faith divine truths ought not to be veiled over by obscurity of words, for it is said in Prov. 14:6, "The learning of the wise is easy."

## QUESTION II

Therefore these truths ought to be presented without obscurity of words.

2. According to Ecclus. 4:28, "Hide not thy wisdom in her beauty," and Prov. 11:26, "He that hideth up corn (the gloss says that preaching is here meant) shall be cursed among the people." Therefore the words of sacred doctrine ought not to be hidden.

3. The text of Matt. 10:27, "That which I tell you in the dark (gloss, in mystery) speak ye in the light (gloss, openly)." Therefore the obscure truths of faith ought to be made more manifest, rather than hidden by the difficulties of words.

4. The doctors of truths of faith are debtors to wise and unwise, as is evident from Rom. 1:14: therefore they ought so to speak that they may be understood by great and small, that is, without obscurity of words.

5. Wisd. 7:13, "Which I have learned without guile, and communicate without envy"; but those who hide do not communicate; therefore they seem guilty of envy.

6. Augustine in IV *De doctrina Christiana* says: "Those explaining sacred Scripture ought not to speak in such a way that they themselves need explanation as of the same authority; but in all their sermons they ought to strive primarily and especially to be understood, and to declare these truths with as much clarity as possible so that he would be very dull who would not comprehend them."

**Sed contra.** But on the contrary is that which is said in Matt. 7:6, "Give not that which is holy to dogs," on which the gloss comments: "A hidden thing is more eagerly sought for, a thing concealed appears more worthy of veneration, that which is a long time sought for is held more dear." Since, therefore, sacred writings ought to be regarded with the greatest veneration, it seems that it is expedient they be discussed with obscurity of speech.

Again, Dionysius (I *Eccles. hier.*) says: "Do not reveal to another every holy thing in praise of God, except those forms of praise generally ordained; that is, those divine rites by which all the sacraments are surrounded should not be revealed except to those like yourself"; but if they were written in conspicuous words, they would be apparent to all; therefore the secrets of faith are to be concealed by obscuring words.

Also it is said in Luke 8:10, "To you it is given to know the mystery of the kingdom of God" (that is, to have understanding of the Scriptures, as is evident from the gloss); "but to the rest in parables." Therefore one ought by obscurity in speech conceal some sacred truths from the multitude.

**Response.** I answer that the words of a teacher ought to be so moderated that they result to the profit and not to the detriment of the one hearing him. Now, there are certain things which on being heard harm no one, as are the truths which all are held responsible to know: and such ought not to be hidden but openly proposed to all. But there are others which, if openly presented, cause harm in those hearing them; and this can occur for two reasons: in one way, if the secret truths of faith are revealed to infidels who oppose the faith and so come to be derided by them. On this account it is said in Matt. 7:6, "Give not that which is holy to dogs." And Dionysius (II *Coel. hierar.*) says, "Listen reverently to these words, to this doctrine given for our instruction by the divinity of divinities, and hide these holy teachings in your minds, shielding them from the unclean multitude so that you may keep them as uniform as possible."

Secondly, if any subtleties are proposed to uncultivated people, these folk may find in the imperfect comprehension of them matter for error; wherefore, in I Cor. 3:1 it is said: "And I, brethren, could not speak to you as unto spiritual, but as unto carnal. As unto little ones in Christ, I gave you milk to drink, not meat." And therefore also, on Exod. 21:33, "If a man open a pit," the gloss of Gregory says: "He who in sacred eloquence now understands lofty things should cover over these sublime truths by silence when in the presence of those who do not comprehend them, lest through some scandal of mind he cause the loss of some little one among the faithful or of an infidel who otherwise might have come to believe. Those truths, therefore, ought to be hidden from those to whom they might do harm; but a distinction can be made as regards speaking, since these same truths may be privately revealed to the wise, though publicly silence is kept regarding them."

Thus, Augustine (IV *De doctrina Christiana*) says: "Where certain truths are, by reason of their own character, not comprehensible, or scarcely so, even when explained with every effort on the part of the speaker to make them clear, these one rarely dwells upon with a general audience, or never mentions at all: but in writing, the same distinction cannot be adhered to, because a book, once published, can fall into the hands of any one at all, and therefore some truths should be shielded by obscuring words so that they may profit those who will understand them and be hidden from the simple who will not comprehend them."

And by this procedure no harm is done to anyone, because those who understand are held by that which they read, but those who do not understand are not compelled to continue reading. And therefore Augustine says in the same place: "In books which are so written that they somehow keep a hold on the attention of the reader who understands them, but cause no harm to the one who does not understand them and so is unwilling to read further, there is no failure in duty on the part of the author as long as we bring these truths, even though they are so difficult of comprehension, to the understanding of some."

**Answers to objections.** 1. It is answered: The authority quoted is not relevant to the proposition. For it is not to be understood that the teaching of prudent men be "easy" in the active sense; that is, that they easily teach everything; but in the passive sense: that such men are easily taught, as is evident from the gloss.

2. It may be answered: These authorities speak of hiding truths which ought to be made manifest; wherefore it is previously said in Ecclus. 4:28, "Refrain not to speak in the time of salvation." By this, however, there is no denial of the fact that there are mysteries which ought to be concealed by obscuring words.

3. It may be said: The doctrine of Christ ought to be taught publicly and openly to this extent: that the truths expedient for each one to know be made clear. Things that are not expedient, however, need not be publicly taught.

4. It may be answered: The doctors of sacred Scripture are not debtors to the wise and to the foolish in such a way that they must propose the same truths to both, but that they propose to each what is to the advantage of each.

5. It may be said: Subtle truths are not concealed from the multitude on account of envy, but rather out of due discretion.

6. It may be answered: Augustine is here speaking of explanations made orally to the people, not of those transmitted in writing, as is evident from what follows.

## Lectio I[1]

#### BOETHIUS' TEXT

There are many who claim as theirs the dignity of the Christian religion; but that form of faith has supreme authority, and has it exclusively, which, both on account of the universal character of the rules and doctrines affirming its authority, and because the worship in which they are expressed has spread throughout the world, is called catholic or universal. The belief of this religion concerning the Trinity is as follows: The Father is God, the Son is God, the Holy Spirit is God. Therefore, Father, Son, and Holy Spirit are one God, not three Gods.

The nature of Their Unity is such that there is no difference. Difference cannot be avoided by those who add to or take from the Unity, as for instance the Arians, who by graduating the Trinity according to merit, break it up and convert it to Plurality. For the essence of plurality is otherness; apart from otherness plurality is unintelligible.

In fact, the difference between things is to be found in genus or species or number. In as many ways as things are the same, in the same number of ways they are said to be diverse. Sameness is predicated in three ways: by genus; e.g., a man and a horse, because of their common genus, animal. By species; e.g., Cato and Cicero, because of their common species, man. By number; e.g., Tullius and Cicero, because they are numerically one. Similarly difference is expressed by genus, species, and number.

But a variety of accidents brings about numerical difference; three men differ neither by genus nor species, but by their accidents, for if we mentally remove from them all other accidents, still each one occupies a different place which cannot possibly be regarded as the same for each, since two bodies cannot occupy the same place, and place is an accident. Wherefore it is because men are plural by their accidents that they are plural in number.

[1] *Lectio I*, inserted after Question II (Parma ed., p. 364), is Part I of Boethius' *De Trinitate*, given verbatim in its entirety. The translation of it here given is adapted from that of H. F. Stewart and E. K. Rand, *The Theological Tractates of Boethius*, Loeb Classical Library Edition (Harvard University Press, 1936).

## ST. THOMAS' COMMENTARY

Hereupon, after the Prooemium, Boethius begins his treatise *De Trinitate personarum, et Unitate divinae essentiae:* and this book is divided into two parts. First, he discusses those things which pertain to the unity of the divine essence, making opposition to the Arians. Secondly, he treats of those things which pertain to the Trinity of persons, in opposition to Sabellius, beginning: "In as many ways as things are the same, in the same number of ways they are said to be diverse."

The first part is also divided into two sections. In the first, he proposes the doctrine of the Catholic faith in regard to the unity of the divine essence. Secondly, he investigates the truth of the doctrine proposed when he says: "Come, therefore, let us begin." In the first section he treats of two things. First, he represents the condition of that faith whose doctrine he intends to explain. Secondly, he sets forth the doctrine of the faith he has described concerning this proposition, saying: "The belief of this religion concerning the Trinity."

He describes this religion in a twofold manner, namely, by comparison with heretical cults, which it excels, and also in its own name since it is called catholic or universal. He says, therefore, that there are many, that is, many sects of diverse heresies, who make unlawful claims, since they unduly attribute to themselves the honor of the Christian religion, that is, the honor which ought to be paid to it: namely, that all others should be subject to it. I John 5:4: "This is the victory that overcomes the world, our faith." Or, again, they claim the dignity which belongs to the Christian religion in that it manifests the glory of God by believing those truths which have been divinely revealed.

"But that form of faith has supreme authority, and has it exclusively." Here he adds the two things that make it distinct both according to truth and according to reputation. Now according to the truth of the matter, heretics are not Christians, since they cut themselves off from the teachings of Christ, and in this respect the Catholic faith alone is valid. But according to appearances and in the opinion of men, heretics are called Christians because they do indeed still, at least in word, confess the name of Christ; and according to this aspect, the Catholic faith is not the only one, but holds the place of greater authority.

That this religion is the more common and the more widely diffused is understood when he says, "is called catholic or universal." Now this is the same thing; for *catholic* in the Greek means the same as the Latin *universal*. For the use of this name, he assigns two reasons, saying: "On account of the precepts of its universal rules," for the precepts which the Catholic religion sets forth are not to be observed by one race alone, but by all: and in this respect it differs especially from the Law of Moses which gave precepts to one people alone. Likewise even individual heresies propose rules that are accommodated to their own members only; while the Catholic faith, having the care of all, gives its precepts to all: not to the unmarried alone, as do the Manichaeans, but also to the married; not to the innocent alone, as do the Novatians, but to sinners as well, for whom that sect would make salvation impossible. Wherefore he adds: "the authority of this religion is evident because of its universal rules," on account of which all ought to be subject to it.

Or they may be called universal rules since there is in them no falsity or any admixture of evil, neither in any essential article or accidentally. Then he adds another reason, saying: "Because the worship in which they are expressed has spread throughout the world," a thing which is evidently in accord with that saying of Ps. 18:5: "Their sound hath gone forth into all the earth: and their words unto the ends of the world."

Hereupon he next sets forth the doctrine of the Catholic

faith concerning the question proposed: "The belief of this religion concerning the Trinity." Concerning this, he does three things: First, he presents the teaching of the Catholic faith on the unity of the Trinity. Secondly, the reason for this opinion: "The principle of this unity." Thirdly, he shows the fitness of the reason, saying: "Now the essence of plurality."

Moreover, he proposes the opinion of Catholic faith in a certain argumentative form, because faith is called "the evidence of things that appear not" (Heb. 11:1). In the same argument, indeed, from the fact that divinity is attributed equally to each of the Persons, he concludes that of all three the name "God" is predicated not plurally, as taken together, but individually.

Next he assigns the reason for this belief. First, he states the reason; and secondly, he explains it by its contrary where he says: "Difference cannot be avoided by those who add to or take from the Unity."

Therefore he says: "The nature of Their Unity is such that there is no difference," namely, the Unity of Deity in the three Persons, as confessed by the Catholic faith. From this the conclusion following upon the foregoing words is that Deity without difference is attributed to each of the three Persons; and this reasoning he explains by its contrary saying: "Difference cannot be avoided by those who add to or take from the Unity (of the Deity)": that is, who hold that one Person is greater or less than the others, as the Arians, who make the Father greater than the Son. Wherefore he continues: "As for instance the Arians, who by graduating the Trinity, break it up"; that is, by graduating the Trinity according to dignity, since they make the Son subject to the Father, and the Holy Spirit to both Father and Son, and so "convert it to Plurality"; that is, produce diversity by dividing the Deity among the Persons. For from division there follows plurality. Conversely, Catholics who confess an equality of the Persons, an equality without difference, make profession of consequent Unity.

Next, he shows that the foregoing reasoning is valid, saying: "For the essence of plurality is otherness," and first he points out the necessity possessed by this reasoning. Secondly, what in the demonstration itself had been supposed is made clear: "In fact, the difference between three or more things lies in genus or species or number." Regarding the first point he does two things. First he shows that otherness is the principle of plurality, understanding by "otherness" any difference by which things can be constituted among themselves as other. And he prefers to say "otherness" rather than "separateness" because not only substantial differences constitute plurality, since they make another thing, but accidental differences also constitute plurality, since they make for otherness: they make a thing other. Now otherness follows upon separateness; but the converse is not true. And the reason for the deduction of the Arians follows from this supposition. For if otherness is the principle of plurality, and positing a cause posits its effect, then supposing in them that otherness is by augmentation and diminution, plurality of divinity would follow.

Secondly, he proposes that otherness is properly the principle of plurality, because, except for it, understanding of plurality is impossible; and according to this principle is the Catholic explanation of divine unity: for if a proper cause is taken away, so also is the effect. If, therefore, in the three Persons there is no otherness of Deity, there will be no plurality, but unity.

Next, he proves what was supposed, namely, that otherness is the proper principle of plurality, when he says, "In fact, the difference between three or more things." And the reason is that in all things that differ in genus or species or number, there is some otherness or difference which is the cause of plurality or diversity. But all plural things, whether three or more, are diverse either generically, specifically, or numerically; therefore some kind of otherness is the principle of all plurality.

In explaining this, he does three things. First, he states the minor; secondly its proof, beginning, "In as many ways as things are the same, in the same number of ways they are said to be diverse." This is [the demonstration of] the proof: In as many ways as things are said to be the same, in the same number of ways they are said to be diverse. But things are said to be the same in three ways, namely, in genus, species, and number. Therefore things are said to be diverse in the same number of ways. The first is supposed from what is stated in I *Topic.*, that as much is said of one of two opposites as is said of the other: and from the saying of X *Metaph.*, that the same and different are opposites.

The second is made clear by examples and supposes what is said in I *Topic.*

Thirdly, he proves the major in regard to that point which might be held in doubt, saying: "But a variety of accidents brings about numerical difference." That the diversity of those things which are diverse according to genus or species must have as principle some otherness, is evident from the name itself. For from the fact that things are of different genera it is evident that a different, or other, genus belongs to each; and if they differ in species, it is because they are contained under other species. But in the case of things which are said to be diverse numerically, it is not evident from the name itself that otherness is the principle of plurality. Furthermore, it might rather appear to be the converse according to the name and that plurality, which is designated by number, might be the principle of diversity, since things numerically different are different according to the same name employed when difference is by genus or species: Therefore, to prove the major of his syllogism, he shows that this difference by which things are said to differ numerically is produced by a certain kind of otherness or variety. He proves this by the fact that in three men who agree in genus and species, but who differ numerically, there is found accidental otherness, just as between man and ox there is specific otherness and between man and stone generic otherness. Wherefore, as man and ox differ specifically, so two men differ accidentally.

And because some one might be able to say that accidental variety is not the cause of numerical plurality since, if accidents are done away with—either removed actually, as when separable, or by the mind and in thought, as when inseparable—substance still remains, since accident is that which can be present or absent without corruption of the substance: therefore he forestalls this objection, saying that, although all accidents might indeed be separated from a substance by the mind, nevertheless the diversity of one accident could in no way, even by the mind, be separated from diverse individuals, namely, diversity of place. For two individuals cannot be in the same place either according to fact or according to any fiction of the mind, since this cannot be understood or imagined. Wherefore he concludes that from the fact that men are plural in number they are plural by reason of accidents; that is, they are for this reason diversified; and with this is terminated the teaching of this part of the treatise.

## QUESTION III

## CONCERNING THOSE THINGS THAT PERTAIN TO THE KNOWLEDGE POSSESSED BY FAITH

This question is twofold. First, there is consideration of those things that pertain to the communion of faith: secondly, of those that pertain to the cause of plurality.

In regard to the first, four questions are asked:

1. Whether faith is necessary for mankind.
2. How faith is related to religion.
3. Whether the true faith is aptly called Catholic or universal.
4. Whether this is the confession of the true faith: that Father, Son, and Holy Spirit each is God, and that the Three are one God without any difference owing to inequality.

*Article 1*

### WHETHER FAITH IS NECESSARY FOR MANKIND

**Objections.** 1. It seems that faith should not be considered necessary for mankind. As is said in Eccles. 7:1, "What needeth a man to seek things that are above him?" This is to say, there is no need. But those things that are believed by faith are above man, as exceeding his reason; otherwise his reason, which is the cause of science, would suffice. Therefore it was not necessary for man that, over and above the truths of reason, he should be taught those of faith.

2. God established human nature as something perfect when He created it. Deut. 32:4, "The works of God are perfect." But from the ability bestowed upon the human mind according to its original condition, man cannot attain to those

## QUESTION III

things which must be known by faith; otherwise he would be able to possess scientific knowledge of them, a knowledge which is caused by the fact that conclusions are resolved into naturally known principles. Since, therefore, a thing is called perfect if it lacks nothing that it ought to possess, as is said in V *Metaph.*, it seems that man does not require faith.

3. Every wise man makes choice of the shorter way to reach a goal: but it would appear exceedingly difficult for a creature to believe truths which are above reason and, in the case of men, extremely dangerous, since many fall away from the state of salvation because they do not believe; therefore it seems that God, who is all-wise, ought not to have established faith as the way of salvation for men.

4. Whenever there is acceptance of knowledge without judgment, the road to error is easy; but we have in ourselves no ability by which we are able to judge of the things which we accept by faith, since our natural judgment does not extend to truths of this kind, as they exceed reason; therefore evidently the road to error is an easy one for us, and so it would appear rather harmful than useful for man that he should be directed to God by the way of faith.

5. As Dionysius says, it is an evil for man to exist apart from reason; but man in adhering to faith departs from reason, and in this he is even accustomed to despise reason; therefore it seems that such a way is evil for men.

**Sed contra.** But on the contrary, it is said in Heb. 11:6, "Without faith it is impossible to please God"; but it is supremely necessary for man that he be pleasing to God, since otherwise he can neither do nor possess any good; therefore faith is most necessary for man.

Again, it is most necessary for man to know the truth, since beatitude is joy in knowing the truth, as Augustine says; but faith establishes believers in truth and establishes truth in them, as Dionysius says (*De div. nom.*, chap. 7); therefore faith is most necessary for man.

Again, that without which human society cannot be conserved is especially necessary for man, since man is a political animal, as is said in VIII *Ethic.;* but without faith human society cannot be preserved, since it is requisite that one man believe in the promises of another and in his testimony and the like, for this is necessary if they are to live together; therefore faith is most necessary for mankind.

**Response.** I answer that it must be said that faith has something in common with opinion, and something in common with knowledge and understanding, by reason of which it holds a position midway between opinion and understanding or science, according to Hugh of St. Victor. In common with understanding and knowledge, it possesses certain and fixed assent; and in this it differs from opinion, which accepts one of two opposites, though with fear that the other may be true, and on account of this doubt it fluctuates between two contraries. But, in common with opinion, faith is concerned with things that are not naturally possible to our understanding, and in this respect it differs from science and intellection.

That a thing should not be apparent to human understanding can arise for two reasons, as is said in II *Metaph.:* namely, because of lack of knowability in things themselves, and because of lack of intellectual ability on our part.

1. It may be due to lack on the part of things, as in the case of singular and contingent things which are remote from our senses, like the deeds and words and thoughts of men; for these are of such a nature that they may be known to one man, but unknown to others. And since among men dwelling together one man should deal with another as with himself in what he is not self-sufficient, therefore it is needful that he be able to stand with as much certainty on what another knows, but of which he himself is ignorant, as upon the truths which he himself knows. Hence it is that in human society faith is necessary in order that one man give

# QUESTION III

credence to the words of another, and this is the foundation of justice, as Tullius says in his book, *De officiis.* Hence also it is that no lie is without sin, since every lie derogates from that faith which is so necessary.

2. The truth of things may also not be evident because of defect on our part, as in the case of divine and necessary things which, according to their own nature, are most knowable. Wherefore, to understand them, we are not capable of immediate intellection, from the very beginning, since it is in accordance with our nature to attain from things less knowable and posterior in themselves, to knowledge of those that are themselves more knowable and prior. But since from none of those things that we know last do we have any knowledge of those that we know first, it is needful for us even at first to have some notion of those things that are most knowable in themselves; but this cannot be except by believing. And this is evident even in the order of the sciences; since that science which is concerned with highest causes, namely, metaphysics, comes last in human knowledge; yet in sciences that are preambles to it there must be supposed certain truths which only in it are more fully revealed; therefore every science has some suppositions that must be believed in order to carry on the process of learning.

Since, therefore, the end of human life is beatitude, which consists in the full cognition of divine truths, it is necessary that human life be directed to this beatitude by an initial possession of divine truths by faith, truths which man can hope to know fully in the ultimate state of human perfection.

Certain of these truths that must be known can be attained by reason even in this life: however, although knowledge of them is possible and even possessed by certain men, nevertheless faith is necessary for five reasons, which Rabbi Moses enumerates:

1. First, on account of the depth and subtlety of the matter, by which divine truths are hidden from human under-

standing. Therefore, lest any man be without some knowledge of them, provision is made that through faith, at least, he know divine truths. Therefore, in Eccles. 7:25 it is said: "It is a great depth, who shall find it out?"

2. Secondly, on account of the weakness of the human intellect from the beginning. For perfection of knowledge does not belong to the human intellect except at the end; therefore, that it should at no time lack a knowledge of God, it requires faith by which it may accept divine truths from the very beginning.

3. Thirdly, because of the many preambles that are required for a knowledge of God according to reason. For this there is needed knowledge of almost all the sciences, since cognition of divine things is the end of them all. But few indeed would comprehend these preambulatory truths or investigate them completely. Therefore, lest large numbers of men should be left without knowledge of divine things, the way of faith has been provided by God Himself.

4. In the fourth place, many men on account of their natural constitution are unfitted for perfect intellectual investigation according to reason; therefore, that these might not lack knowledge of divine truths, the way of faith has been provided.

5. In the fifth place, because of numerous occupations with which men are busied, it would be impossible for all of them to discover, by way of reason, necessary truth in regard to God, and on this account the way of faith has been established, both as regards things that might in some way be known and as regards those that required revelation in order that they be believed.

But in the case of certain divine truths, for a complete understanding of them the human mind in no way suffices, but full knowledge of them is to be awaited in that future life when there will be complete beatitude: such is the truth of the Trinity and the unity of one God; and man is led to knowledge of this, not in accordance with anything due his nature, but by divine grace alone. Therefore it is necessary that, for a perfection of knowledge of this kind, certain suppositions be proposed which must be believed at first, and from these one is directed into full cognition of those truths which at the outset he held on faith, even as in other sciences also, as has been said. Hence in Isa. 7:9 it is said, according to one translation: "Unless thou hadst believed, thou wouldst not understand." And suppositions of this sort are those that must be believed by all, since in this life they are neither known nor understood by any one.

**Answers to objections.** 1. It may be said: Although matters of faith considered according to man's natural powers are above him, they are not above man when he is illuminated by divine light; hence it is not necessary for man that he seek out such truths by his own power, but it is necessary for him to know them by divine revelation.

2. It may be said: God, in the first creation of things, established man as perfect in accordance with the perfection of his nature, and this consisted in the fact that man had all things due to his nature. But over and above that due to nature there were added afterward to the human race certain other perfections owing their source to divine grace alone, and among these was faith, as is evident from Eph. 2:8, where it is said of faith that it is "the gift of God."

3. It may be said: For anyone striving to attain beatitude it is necessary to know in what he ought to seek this beatitude, and in what way. But this, indeed, can be done in no easier way than through faith, since investigation by reason cannot attain to such knowledge except after a previous knowledge of many other things, things not easy to know. Nor can one attain to such knowledge without danger, since human investigation, because of the weakness of our intellect, is prone to error; and this is clearly shown by reference to those philosophers who, in attempting to find out the pur-

pose of human life by way of reason, did not find in themselves the true method, and so fell into many and shameful errors; and so greatly did they differ among themselves that scarcely two or three among them all were in agreement on any one question; yet, on the other hand, we see that by faith many peoples are brought to the acceptance of one common belief.

4. It may be said: Whenever there is acceptance of a truth, by whatever mode of assent, there must be something which moves the mind to assent: just as the naturally possessed light of the intellect causes assent to first principles, and the truth of those first principles causes assent to conclusions made from them; while in other ways we assent to things of which we have an opinion, though, if motives were a little stronger, they would incline us to belief, in so far as faith is said to be opinion. But that which inclines the mind to assent to the first principles of understanding or to conclusions known from these principles is a sufficient induction which forces assent, and is sufficient to judge of those things to which the mind gives its assent. On the other hand, whatever inclines one to form an opinion, even though with a good amount of conviction, is not that sufficient form of induction whereby assent is forced, nor by reason of it can there be perfect judgment of the things to which assent is given. Therefore also in faith by which we believe in God, not only is there acceptance of the truths to which we give assent, but also something which inclines us to that assent; and this is the special light which is the habit of faith, divinely infused into the human mind. This, moreover, is more sufficient for inducing belief than any demonstration, for, though from the latter no false conclusions are reached, still man frequently errs in this: that he thinks something is a demonstration which is not. The light of faith is also more sufficient than the natural light of reason by which we assent

to first principles, since this natural light is often impeded by bodily infirmity, as is evident in the case of the insane. But the light of faith, which is, as it were, a kind of impression of the First Truth in our minds, cannot fail, any more than God can deceive us or lie; therefore this light suffices for making judgment.

This habit of faith, nevertheless, does not move us by way of intellectual understanding, but more by way of the will; therefore it does not make us comprehend those truths which we believe, nor does it force assent, but it causes us to assent to them voluntarily. And thus it is evident that faith comes in two ways: namely, from God by reason of the interior light which induces assent, and also by reason of those truths which are proposed exteriorly and take their source from divine revelation. These latter are related to the knowledge which is of faith as things known by the senses are to knowledge of first principles, because in both cases there is a certain determination given to cognition. Therefore, as cognition of first principles is received by way of sense experience, and yet the light by which those principles are known is innate, so faith comes by way of hearing, and yet the habit of faith is infused.

5. It may be said: To live in accordance with reason is the good of man inasmuch as he is man. Now, to live apart from reason, according to one meaning, can be understood as a defect, as it is in those who live according to sense; and this is an evil in man. But in another way, it may mean to live above reason as when, by divine grace, a man is led to that which exceeds reason: and in this case, to live apart from reason is not an evil in man, but a good above that which is human. And such is the cognition of truths of faith, although faith itself is not in every way outside reason; for it is the natural reason which holds that assent ought to be given to truths declared by God.

## Article 2

#### WHETHER FAITH SHOULD BE DISTINGUISHED FROM RELIGION

**Objections.** 1. It seems that faith ought not to be distinguished from religion, because, as Augustine says in *Ench.*, "God is to be worshiped by faith, hope, and charity"; but worship of God is an act of religion, as is evident from the definition of Tullius, which says: "Religion is that which offers to a superior nature, which men call divine, worship and ceremony"; therefore faith pertains to religion.

2. Augustine says in *De vera religione:* The true religion is that by which the one God is honored and known with a most unsullied piety or purity." But to know God is a thing which belongs to faith; therefore, faith is contained under religion.

3. To offer sacrifice to God is a function or act of religion, but this pertains to faith, as Augustine says in IV *De civ. Dei:* "True sacrifice is any work done in order that we may adhere to God in holy association"; but the first adherence of man to God is by faith; therefore faith pertains principally to religion.

4. In John 4:24 it is said: "God is a Spirit, and they that adore Him, must adore Him in spirit and in truth." Now, God is adored more when one submits his intellect to Him than when a bodily prostration is made; but through faith the intellect is submitted to God, since it subjects itself entirely in assenting to the truths revealed by God; therefore faith pertains especially to religion.

5. Every virtue having God as its object is a theological virtue: but religion has God as its object, since it is nothing else than the offering of due reverence to God; therefore it is a theological virtue. But it appears to belong more to faith than to any of the others, since only those are said to be outside the Christian religion who are outside [i.e., without] faith; therefore religon seems to be the same as faith.

## QUESTION III

**Sed contra.** On the contrary is what Tullius says in II *Veteris Rhetoricae,* where he makes religion a part of justice, which is a moral virtue. Therefore, since faith is a theological virtue, religion is of a genus other than that of faith.

Again, religion consists also in activity regarding the neighbor, as is evident in Jas. 1:27: "Religion clean and undefiled before God and the Father is this: to visit the fatherless and widows in their tribulation"; faith has no act except that which is referred to God; therefore religion is altogether distinct from faith.

Again, those are commonly called "religious" who are bound by special vows, but they are not the only ones called "the faithful." Since, therefore, one of the faith and a religious are not the same thing, faith and religion are not the same.

**Response.** I answer that it must be said that, as is evident from Augustine (X *De civ. Dei), theosebia,* which the worship of God is called, includes as pertaining to it in the same way, religion, piety and latria, since all have as their purpose the worship of God. Reverence paid to anything, however, seems to be nothing else than a due operation performed with regard to it; and consequently men are said to cherish in various ways their fields, their parents, their country, and other like things because different works are fitting to each. But God is not "cherished" in this same way: that any operation of ours would be of benefit or assistance to Him, as in the case of the above-mentioned instances; but it implies only that we submit ourselves to Him and show ourselves to be His subjects. Therefore this reverence which is absolutely divine is designated by the name of *theosebia.* But religion implies a certain "binding back" according to which man obliges himself in some manner to this worship of God; wherefore Augustine says in his book, *De vera religione:* "The word 'religion' is thought to be derived from the *religare* ('to bind back'), or from *recte eligere* ('to choose rightly')," as is said in

IV *De civ. Dei.* For it is by proper choice that a person binds himself to do something that must be done. We must also re-elect those things which by negligence we have lost, as he also says. Therefore it is that those who consecrate their whole lives and themselves to the service of God by certain vows are called religious; but piety regards the mind of the worshiper, that it be not insincere or moved by desire of gain.

Since also a certain divine veneration, as it were, is due to those above us, even the acts of kindness which are done for the unfortunate are in a way sacrifices to God, according to the last part of the Epistle to the Hebrews (13:16): "And do not forget to do good and to impart: for by such sacrifices God's favor is obtained." Hence it is that the name of piety and of religion are transferred to works of mercy, and especially to benefits done to parents and country. But *latria* implies a reverence that is of obligation, or worship in its essence; and this is so because we are, indeed, the subjects of Him whom we honor, not after the manner in which one man is said to be the servant of another, because of some accidental debt to him, but because all that we are we owe to Him as our Creator. Therefore *latria* is not any kind of service, but that by which man acknowledges his subjection to God. Thus, therefore, religion consists in an operation by which man honors God by submitting to Him; and this operation ought to be in harmony with Him who is honored and with the one offering homage.

Now since He who is reverenced is a spirit, He cannot be approached by the body, but only by the mind; and so worship of Him consists chiefly in acts of the mind by which the mind itself is ordained to God. These acts are principally those of the theological virtues; and in accordance with this, Augustine says that God is worshiped by faith, hope, and charity, to which are added also the acts of the gifts ordained toward God, such as those of wisdom and of fear.

But because we who honor God are also possessed of

bodies and receive our knowledge through bodily senses, there is the necessity that certain physical actions accompany the worship of God, not only that we may render service to God with our whole being, but also that by these bodily actions we may arouse in ourselves and in others acts of the mind ordained to God. Wherefore Augustine says in his book, *De cura pro mortuis habenda:* "Those who pray make the members of their bodies conform to their acts of supplication when they genuflect, extend their hands, or prostrate themselves upon the ground, or perform any other visible action; and although it is their invisible will and the intention of the heart that is known to God, it is not unseemly that the human soul should so express itself, but rather by so doing man stirs himself to pray and to lament his sins the more humbly and fervently."

Hence, all acts by which man subjects himself to God, whether they are acts of mind or of body, pertain to religion. But because those things that are rendered to the neighbor on account of God are rendered to God Himself, it is evident that they also pertain to this same subjection in which religious worship consists; and so to one diligently considering the matter it is apparent that every good act pertains to religion. Hence Augustine says (*loc. cit.*): "True sacrifice is every work done that we may adhere to God in holy companionship; however, in a certain order." First and foremost, those acts of the mind ordained to God pertain to the worship which we are speaking of. Secondly, there are acts of the body intended to arouse reverence of mind or to give expression to it, such as prostrations, sacrifices, and the like. Thirdly, there also pertain to divine worship all other acts ordained to the neighbor for the sake of God.

Nevertheless, as magnanimity is a certain special virtue, although it uses the acts of all virtues, since it bestows a grandeur in the exercise of them all and so regards its object under a certain special aspect; so also religion is a special virtue in the acts of all the virtues, considering a special aspect of its object, namely, that which is due to God; and thus it forms a part of justice. There are, moreover, special acts assigned to religion, which pertain to no other virtue, such as prostrations and the like, in which the worship of God consists secondarily.

From this it is evident that acts of faith pertain, indeed, materially to religion, as do the acts of other virtues, and the more so inasmuch as acts of faith are the first motions of the mind toward God; but formally faith is distinguished from religion, as regarding another aspect of its object. Faith agrees with religion also because faith is the cause and principle of religion. For no one would elect to manifest reverence to God unless by faith he held that God was the Creator, Ruler, and Rewarder of human actions.

Nevertheless religion is not a theological virtue: for it has as its matter all acts, as those of faith or of any other virtue inasmuch as these are offered as due to God; but it has God as its end. For to worship God is to offer acts of this kind as due to God.

From what has been said, the response to all the objections is evident.

*Article 3*

WHETHER THE CHRISTIAN RELIGION IS APTLY CALLED CATHOLIC OR UNIVERSAL

**Objections.** 1. It seems that the Christian religion ought not be called Catholic, because knowledge must be proportionate to the knowability of a thing. Now an indefinite thing is not known in any way at all: but faith is a knowledge of God who is neither universal nor particular, as Augustine says in his book, *De Trinitate;* therefore this religion cannot be called universal.

2. One can have only singular knowledge about singular things; but by faith we hold the truth of certain singular facts,

as the Passion and Resurrection of Christ, and the like; therefore the Christian faith cannot be called universal.

3. From what is common to many, it is not permissible to impose a name as proper to any one of them, since a name is given in order that a thing may be known as distinct: but every school or sect proposes certain things that must be universally held by all its followers, or certain doctrines that must be universally affirmed as true; therefore the Christian religion has no special right to be called Catholic.

4. Idolatry extends to every corner of the earth; but the Christian religion has not yet been brought to all the regions of the world, since there are yet some barbarians who do not know the faith of Christ; therefore these idolatrous sects, rather than the Christian religion, deserve the name of Catholic.

5. What does not include all should not be called universal; but the Christian religion is not accepted by many; therefore it is inaptly called universal or Catholic.

**Sed contra.** On the contrary is that which Augustine says in *De vera religione:* "The Christian religion must be held by us, and the communication of that Church which is catholic and which is called Catholic, not only by its own members, but even by its enemies."

Again, universal and common appear to be the same; but the Christian faith is called the common faith by the Apostle (Titus 1:4): "To Titus, my beloved son according to the common faith"; therefore it is rightly called Catholic.

Again what is universally proposed to all should in a special way be called universal; but the Christian faith is universally proposed to all, as is evident in the last chapter of Matthew (28:19), "Teach ye all nations," etc.; therefore it is deservedly called Catholic or universal.

**Response.** I answer that it must be said that faith, just as any other cognition, has a twofold matter: namely, that in which it exists (the believers themselves) and that about which it is concerned (the truths believed); and as regards both types of matter, the Christian religion can be called Catholic.

*As regards the believers* it is Catholic because the Apostle (Rom. 3:2) asserts that that is the true religion which was given testimony to by the law and the prophets. Since, however, in the times of the prophets various tribes offered worship to different gods, only one nation, the people of Israel, gave due honor to the true God, and so there did not exist that one universal religion which was foretold to them by the Holy Spirit, that worship of the true God which would be paid by all. Therefore Isaias (45:24) says: "For every knee shall be bowed to Me, and every tongue shall swear." And this prophecy has, indeed, been fulfilled by faith and the Christian religion.

Therefore deservedly is that faith called Catholic since it has been accepted by men of every condition. And thus, those who have fallen away from this faith and this religion which has been so universally foretold and received, and who have become divided into various sects, are not called Catholics, but as it were, having been cut off from the communion of the faithful, they are called heretics.

*As regards the truths* proposed for belief in the Christian religion, there is also found truth that is catholic. Now, there were various arts and ways in ancient times according as there was vision, or belief in the vision of the human mind among men. For certain men placed the good of man in corporeal things alone, either in riches or in honors or in pleasures. Some others placed this good in the soul alone, as in moral or intellectual virtues. Certain others, as Augustine says in his book, *De civ. Dei,* thought that gods ought to be honored because of the corporeal blessings of this life; but others, on account of blessings to be realized after death. Porphyry also relates that it was believed among certain peoples of the earth that the imaginative part of the soul would be cleansed, but not the whole soul; and he said, as Augustine tells in X *De civ. Dei*, that there had not yet been found a single sect that possessed a universal way for liberty of spirit. Now this way, as Augustine says in the same place, is the Christian religion.

This religion teaches that God is to be honored not only on account of eternal, but also because of temporal benefits; that He rules man not only in spiritual ways but also in all that concerns him bodily, and that He promises beatitude for both soul and body. Hence His regulations are called universal, as pertaining to the whole life of man and as extending to all that in any way affects man.

For these two reasons, therefore, the name "universal" is given to the Christian religion, as Boethius in the text makes clear.

**Answers to objections.** 1. It may, therefore, be answered: Although God is in Himself neither universal nor particular, yet He is the universal cause and end of all things, and thus knowledge which is held concerning Him is universal since it extends to all things.

2. It may be said: Faith holds these particular facts as universal remedies for the healing and the liberation of the whole human race.

3. Answer may be made: Other sects claim for themselves what is proper to the Christian faith, but they cannot vindicate this claim; therefore, the name of universality does not properly belong to them.

4. It may be said: Idolatry was no one form of religion, but differed among various peoples, since they set up for themselves various gods to be worshiped. Nor again, were those forms of idolatry accepted by all nations, since they were rejected by those who honored the true God, and even by the philosophers of the Gentiles, who said that certain religious ceremonies ought to be observed since they were commanded by law, but not because they could be known

to please the gods, as Seneca said, according to Augustine in *De civ. Dei*.

5. It may be answered: The Christian religion is not called Catholic on account of individual nations who adhere to it, but on account of the body of individual men from all conditions of mankind who adhere to it.

## Article 4

### WHETHER IT IS A TRUE ARTICLE OF FAITH, THAT THE FATHER, SON, AND HOLY SPIRIT ARE ONE GOD

**Objections.** 1. It seems that it is not the confession of the Catholic faith that Father, Son, and Holy Spirit are one God: because, as Boethius himself says, upon inequality there follows plurality of gods. But the Catholic Scripture, which is the head of the Catholic religion, as Augustine says in *De vera religione*, states that there is inequality between Father and Son, as is evident from what is said in the person of the Son in John 14:28: "The Father is greater than I." Therefore what is said is not the confession of the Catholic religion.

2. I Cor. 15:28 says: "And when all things shall be subdued unto Him, then the Son also Himself shall be subject unto Him that put all things under Him, that God may be all in all." And so the conclusion is like the former.

3. Prayer is not made except by an inferior to a superior: but the Son prays for us. Rom. 8:34, "Christ Jesus . . . who also maketh intercession for us." Likewise of the Holy Spirit it is said in the same place (8:26), "The Spirit Himself asketh for us with unspeakable groanings." Therefore the Son and the Holy Spirit are inferior to the Father according to the confession of the Catholic faith, and so the conclusion is the same.

4. John 17:3 gives the words of the Son addressing Him-

## QUESTION III

self to the Father: "That they may know Thee, the only true God, and Jesus Christ, whom Thou hast sent." Therefore the Father alone is the true God, and not the Son and the Holy Spirit. Therefore they seem to be creatures, and so the same conclusion is reached.

5. In I Tim. 6:15, the Apostle says: "Which in His times He shall show, who is the Blessed and only Mighty, the King of kings, and Lord of lords. Who only hath immortality and inhabiteth light inaccessible." Therefore all these titles belong only to the Father, and so the conclusion is as before.

6. In Mark 13:32 it is said: "But of that day or hour no man knoweth, neither the angels in heaven, nor the Son, but the Father." Therefore the Father's knowledge is greater than that of the Son. Consequently His essence also is greater, and thus the conclusion is the same.

7. Matt. 20:23 says: "To sit on My right or left hand, is not Mine to give to you, but to them for whom it is prepared by My Father." Therefore the power of the Son is not equal to that of the Father.

8. In Col. 1:15, it is said of the Son that He is "the firstborn of every creature." But this comparison would not be made unless of beings of one genus; therefore the Son is a creature.

9. In Ecclus. 24:14 it is said in the person of divine Wisdom, "From the beginning, and before the world, was I created." Thus the conclusion is the same.

10. He who is revealed is less than he who reveals; but the Son is revealed by the Father, as is evident in John, chap. 12; therefore, the Son is less than the Father.

11. The one sending is greater than the one sent. But the Father sends the Son, as is clear from Gal. 4:4, "God sent His Son," etc. And He also sends the Holy Spirit, according to John 14:26, "The Paraclete, the Holy Ghost, whom the Father will send in My name." Therefore the Father is

greater than the Son and the Holy Spirit. And thus the aforesaid doctrine does not seem to be in accordance with the Catholic faith.

**Sed contra.** But on the contrary it is said in John 1:1, 3: "In the beginning was the Word, and the Word was with God, and the Word was God. . . . All things were made by Him," etc. From this it is to be held that the Son is eternal, for otherwise He could not have been in the beginning: and that He is equal to the Father, for otherwise He would not be God: and that He is not a creature, for otherwise all things would not have been made by Him.

Again, since the Son is truth, He could not lie concerning Himself. But the Son said that He was equal to the Father (John 5:18): "He also said God was His Father, making Himself equal to God." Therefore He is equal to the Father.

Again, Phil. 2:6 says: "He thought it not robbery to be equal with God." But it would have been robbery if He thought that was so which was not. Therefore He is equal to God.

Again, John 10:30, "I and the Father are one." And John 14:11, "I am in the Father, and the Father in Me." Therefore one is not greater than the other.

Again, Rom. 9:5: "And of whom is Christ, according to the flesh, who is over all things, God blessed forever." Therefore no one is superior to Him; and thus He is not less than the Father.

Again, I John 5:20, "And we know that the Son of God is come: and He hath given us understanding that we may know the true God, and may be in His true Son. This is the true God and life eternal." Therefore He is not less than the Father.

Again, it is shown that the Holy Spirit is the true God, and equal to the Father by what is said in Phil. 3:3, according to the Greek text. "We are the circumcision, who serve God the Spirit" [Douay: "who in spirit serve God"], and in regard to this service, that of *latria* is understood, as is evident in the Greek. And such honor is due to no creature. Deut. 6:13 and Matt. 4:10: "The Lord thy God shalt thou adore, and Him only shalt thou serve." Therefore, the Holy Spirit is not a creature.

Again, the members of Christ cannot be the temple of anyone who is less than Christ: but our bodies, which are members of Christ, according to the Apostle, are temples of the Holy Ghost, as is said in I Cor. 6:19. Therefore the Holy Spirit is not less than Christ, or less than the Father; and thus it is true, as the author says, that this is a doctrine of the Catholic religion.

**Response.** I answer that it must be said that the position of the Arians, which establishes inequality among the divine persons, is not a confession of the Catholic religion, but rather an impiety of the Gentiles, as is thus evident.

Among the Gentiles all immortal substances are called gods. Among these, moreover, they hold, or rather the Platonists hold, that there are three principal persons, as is made clear by Augustine in *De civitate Dei* (Bk. X), and by Macrobius on the *Somnium Scipionis,* namely, the God, who is the Creator of all things, whom they call also the Father, since all things have their source in Him; and, secondly, a certain inferior substance, whom they call the Paternal Mind or the Paternal Intellect, who contains the ideas of all things, and who is made by God the Father, they say; and thirdly, after Him they suppose a Soul-of-the-World, a spirit who is, as it were, the life of the whole world. And these three substances they name as their chief gods, and as the three principles by which souls are purified.

Origen, moreover, following the teachings of the Platonists, thought that after the same manner the doctrine of the true faith ought to be interpreted, because it is said, "There are three who give testimony in heaven" (I John 5:7). And so, as the Platonists supposed that there were three principal substances, Origen held that the Son was a creature and less than the Father, in that book which is entitled *Periarchon* ("Concerning the Principles"), as is made clear by Jerome in a certain epistle regarding the errors of Origen. And since Origen himself taught at Alexandria, Arius drank in his error from the things he wrote. On this account Epiphanius says that Origen was the father and font of Arius.

Therefore the position of the Christian and Catholic faith regarding the Trinity differs as much from the position of Arius as does the error of the Gentiles, which, in calling creatures gods, rendered to them the service of divine praise. This the Apostle (Rom. 1:25) criticizes when he says, "They worshiped and served the creature rather than the Creator."

**Answers to objections.** 1. It may be said: As Augustine states in II *De Trinitate,* passages found in the Scriptures in regard to the Father and the Son are threefold.

a) First, some show a certain unity of substance and equality of persons, as, "I and the Father are one" (John 10:30).

b) Other passages show the Son to be less because of His having the form of a servant, according as He made Himself less, as is said in Phil. 2:7, "He emptied Himself, taking the form of a servant."

c) Certain things are also said that show Him to be neither less nor the equal of the Father, but only that the Son is from the Father, as in John 5:26, "As the Father hath life in Himself, so He hath given to the Son also to have life in Himself."

The first authoritative passages are used by Catholics in making a defense of the truth. But those of the second and third kind are employed by heretics in confirmation of their error, though in a vain attempt. For the things that are stated of Christ according to His human nature should not be referred to His divinity; otherwise it would follow that His death, which is recorded of Him according to His humanity, would be according to His divinity. Likewise, neither is it shown that the Son is less than the Father, although the Son is from the Father, because the Son has from the Father all that the Father possesses, as is held in John, chap. 16, and Matt., chap. 11. Wherefore no inequality of divinity can be asserted because of the order of origin.

When, therefore, it is said, "The Father is greater than I," this is said of the Son according to His human nature and not according to His divine nature, as Augustine maintains; or, as Hilary says, according to His divine nature in such a way that "greater" does not imply inequality (because the Son is not less than the Father, inasmuch as to Him is given a name above all names); but it implies dignity of a principle inasmuch as it is from the Father that the Son possesses that by which He is the equal of the Father.

2. It may be said: All things the Father not only subjected to the Son, but the Son Himself made them subject to Himself, according to the saying of Phil. 3:21: "According to the operation whereby also He is able to subdue all things unto Himself," i.e., according to the Divinity which is equal in Him to that of the Father. Wherefore, when it is said that Christ will be subject, this does not imply relation of the Son to the Father according to Divinity, but rather the relation of the human nature of the Son to the Divinity of the Father, which Divinity is common to the whole Trinity.

And when the divine nature shall be perfectly known, then it will be apparent that especially according to His human nature He is subject to the divine nature; but not with such a subjection as that which certain heretics claim who say that the very human nature which was assumed by the divine nature is transmuted into it, but rather that He is less than the Father by reason of His humanity. This is made especially clear by the fact that He will deliver His kingdom, that is, the faithful, to the Father, not claiming them for Himself, but leading them to the vision of the Father, a vision in which His own Divinity also will be seen.

3. It may be answered: According to Augustine (III *De Trinitate*), inasmuch as the Son prays He is less than the Father; but inasmuch as He obtains hearing with the Father, He is the equal of the Father.

But the Holy Spirit is said to intercede for us inasmuch as He causes us to make intercession, and renders our prayers efficacious.

4. It may be said: According to Augustine (VI *De Trinitate*), the statement that there is one only true God must not be interpreted to refer to the Father alone, but as including Father, Son, and Holy Ghost simultaneously; and they are said to be the one true God because no being outside the Trinity is true God. Wherefore, it must be in this way that one understands: "That they may know Thee, the only true God, and Jesus Christ whom Thou hast sent" (John 17:3). For there is one only true God, and no mention is here made of the Holy Spirit, because, since He is the nexus of the other two Persons, He is understood by mention of the other two.

5. It may be answered: According to Augustine (I *De Trinitate*), this saying is not to be understood of the Person of the Father alone, but of the entire Trinity. For the whole Trinity is blessed and powerful, and the whole Trinity shows forth the Son. Even if He did say: "He shall show, who is the Blessed and only Mighty," etc., this would not indicate that the Son is separate from the Father, or that the Father is considered as being separated from the Son, because it is said in Ecclus. 24:8, in the person of the Son, who is the Wisdom of God, "I alone have compassed the circuit of heaven." This is said, therefore, because in those things which pertain to the essence of God, Father and Son are altogether one, and hence what is said of one of them by diction which may be exclusive does not imply any mutual separation, but only their separation from creatures.

6. It may be said: The Son knows "that day and hour,"

## QUESTION III

not only according to His divine nature, but even according to His human nature, since His soul knows all things. Hence He is said not to know that day, as Augustine explains in I *De Trinitate,* because He does not make it known to us; wherefore He said to those questioning Him: "It is not for you to know the times," etc. (Acts 1:7). And in the same way the Apostle says in I Cor. 2:2, "I judged not myself to know anything among you," because he was unwilling to disclose lofty things to them since they lacked capacity to understand.

Or this may be understood as regarding the Son, not in His character as head of the Church, but in the person of His members, since the Church, as Jerome says, is without knowledge of these truths. However, in saying that the Father alone knows them, it is evident that the Son also knows them, according to the aforesaid reason.

7. Answer may be made: As Augustine says in I *De Trinitate,* the verse: "It is not Mine to give to you," etc., must be understood to mean that it is not in the power of human nature to give this, so that He may be known to grant it by reason of the fact that He is God and equal to the Father.

8. It may be said: According to Augustine, I *De Trinitate,* many heretics, not understanding this point of apostolic doctrine, broke out into insult of the Son of God, saying and declaring that He was a creature, having little regard for the import of words. For He is said, indeed, to be the first begotten, but not the first created, so that He might be believed to have been begotten, according to His divine nature, and to be first on account of His perpetuity. Moreover, although the Son belongs to no genus of creatures, yet, as Basil holds, He has something in common with creatures: namely, the fact that He received from the Father that which He has; but this possession is superior to that of creatures, since through His own nature He possesses what He receives from the Father. On this account there can be noted

a certain order between the generation of the Son and the production of creatures.

9. It may be said: This saying and all sayings similar to it, which are read in regard to the wisdom of God, ought to be referred to the wisdom of creatures, such as the angels, or to Christ Himself according to His human nature. Thus His wisdom is said to be "from the beginning," or "at the beginning of creation," as if from eternity it predestined that creation should belong to Him.

10. Answer may be made: As Augustine says in II *De Trinitate:* From the fact that the Father will glorify the Son, it does not follow that the Son is inferior to the Father; otherwise He would be less than the Holy Spirit, because the Son says of the Holy Spirit in John 16:14: "He shall glorify Me." Now, this glorification refers not to the Person of the Son, but to the fact that in the knowledge of men He will be glorified, since the Spirit will make Him known; or it may be referred to the body which He had assumed and to the glory of the Resurrection.

11. It may be said: The Son and the Holy Spirit are said to be "sent" by the Father, not that they now are where they had previously not been; but that they are now there in a certain manner in which they had not previously been: that is to say, as regards a certain effect in creatures. Wherefore, when the Son and the Holy Spirit are said to have been sent by the Father, no inequality in the Trinity is revealed, but an order of origin, by which one Person is from another. Therefore the Father is not "sent," because He is not from another in such a way that He has from another His efficacy in relation to any of His effects; and it is in this way that a divine Person is "sent."

## QUESTION IV

## CONCERNING THOSE THINGS THAT PERTAIN TO THE CAUSE OF PLURALITY

Inquiry is made of those things that pertain to the cause of plurality. And this inquiry involves four questions:
1. Whether otherness is the cause of plurality.
2. Whether variety of accidents produces diversity according to number.
3. Whether two bodies can be, or can be thought of as being, simultaneously in the same place.
4. Whether difference of location exerts some influence as to difference according to number.

### Article 1

#### WHETHER OTHERNESS IS THE CAUSE OF PLURALITY

**Objections.** 1. It seems that the cause of plurality cannot be otherness. For as is said in the *Arithmetica* of Boethius, all things whatever of the sum-total of beings that have been established in nature seem to have been formed by reason of numbers. For this was the principal exemplar in the mind of the builder of the universe: and this is in agreement with what is said in Wisd. 11:21, "Thou hast disposed all things in weight and in number and in measure" [Douay: "Thou hast ordered all things in measure and number and weight"]. Therefore plurality or number is first among created things, and no cause of it is to be sought for.

2. As said in the book *De causis*, the first of created things is being; but being is divided at first by one and many; hence nothing can exist as prior to multitude except being

and unity. Therefore it does not seem to be true that anything else should be its cause.

3. Plurality either includes all genera according as it is distinguished from unity, which is convertible with being: or it is itself in the genus of quantity, according as it is distinguished from that unity which is the principle of number. But otherness is in the genus of relation, and relations are not causes of quantities, but rather the converse is true. Much less, then, is relation the cause of what is in every genus, because in that case it would be the cause of substance; therefore otherness can in no way be the cause of plurality.

4. For contrary things there are contrary causes: but identity and otherness or diversity are opposites; therefore they have opposite causes. But unity is the cause of identity, as is evident in V *Metaph.;* therefore plurality or multitude is the cause of diversity; and consequently otherness is not the cause of plurality.

5. The principle of otherness is accidental difference; for differences of this kind, according to Porphyry, make a thing other. But accidental difference is not found in all things in which there is plurality; in fact, in some cases there is no difference of any kind. Certain things, such as simple forms, cannot be subjects of accidents; and there are other things that agree in no way, so that they cannot be called different, but diverse, as is evident by the words of the Philosopher in X *Metaph.* Therefore otherness is not the cause of all plurality.

**Sed contra.** But on the contrary is what Damascene says, that division is the cause of number; but division consists in diversity or otherness; therefore diversity, or otherness, is the principle of plurality.

Again, Isidore says that number is called, as it were, the master of numeration, that is, of division; and so the conclusion is like the first.

## QUESTION IV

Again, plurality is not constituted except by recession from unity; but there is no loss of unity except by division, since a thing is said to be one in that it is undivided, as is evident from X *Metaph.;* therefore division constitutes plurality, and thus the conclusion is as before.

**Response.** I answer that it must be said, as the Philosopher states in X *Metaph.*, that a thing is said to be plural (many) from the fact that it is divisible or has been divided. Wherefore anything that is the cause of division ought to be regarded as a cause of plurality.

Now, the cause of division cannot be considered the same in posterior and composite beings as in those that are first and simple. For in posterior and composite things, the cause of division which is, as it were, the formal cause of division by reason of which division comes about, is diversity found in more simple and primary beings, as is made clear in the case of division according to quantity. For one part of a line is divided from another part by the fact that they have each a different place, which is, as it were, the formal difference of a thing of continuous quantity having position. It is also evident in the division of substances. For man is different from an ass because he has diverse constitutive differences: but the diversity by which posterior, composite beings are divided according as prior and simpler beings are, presupposes plurality of these same primary and more simple beings. For the reason why man and ass have diverse differences is that rationality and irrationality are not one and the same thing, but differ in many ways. Nor can it be said endlessly that the plurality of one thing is owing to another diversity in another prior and simpler cause, because thus we would go on to infinity. Therefore it is necessary in some other way to assign a cause of plurality and division in prior and more simple beings.

Now, there are some beings of this kind divided in themselves. Nevertheless it cannot be that being is divided from being, inasmuch as it is being: for nothing is divided from being except non-being. Likewise also from this-being, this-being is not divided, unless in this-being there is included negation of the same being. Wherefore in primary termini of thought negative propositions are immediately, as it were, negations, one of the other, in the intellect. For the first thing caused constitutes plurality with its cause, which does not reach to it [so as to be identical with it]. And according to this, certain philosophers hold that plurality is caused in a certain order from one and the selfsame thing; so that from one thing proceeds, at first, one being, which with its cause constitutes a plurality, and from this plurality, now two things can proceed, one according to the thing itself, and the other according to its conjunction to a cause. But we are not forced to say this, since one thing might be able to imitate the first in some way in which the second would fail to agree with it; and this defect could be imitated in another; and so there can be found many effects of the first cause in any number of which there is both negation of the cause and negation of the effects in the same way, or according to distance separating one from the other.

So, therefore, it is evident that the first reason or principle of plurality or division is from affirmation and negation, as the order of origin of such plurality is understood, because first there must be understanding of being and non-being, by which first divisions are constituted, and by this, there are the many.

Hence, just as first being, inasmuch as it is undivided, is immediately recognized as one, so after division of being and non-being there is immediate recognition of the plurality of first simple beings. The nature of diversity, moreover, follows upon plurality according as there remains in it the virtue of its cause, that is, the opposition of being and non-being. Therefore one of many diverse things is said to be re-

QUESTION IV

lated to another because it is not that other. And since a second cause does not produce its effect except by virtue of a first cause, therefore the plurality of first causes does not make division and plurality in secondary, composite beings unless there remains in that plurality the virtue of prime opposition, which is between being and non-being, by reason of which it has the nature of diversity; and thus the diversity of first causes produces the diversity of second.

According to this, it is true, as Boethius says, that otherness is the principle of plurality. Indeed, otherness is to be found in things because there is diversity among them. However, although division precedes plurality of first causes, diversity does not; because division does not require the being of things divided among themselves, since division is by affirmation and negation, but diversity does require each to be a distinct being; wherefore it presupposes plurality. Hence it is in no way possible that the cause of the plurality of first beings should be diversity, unless diversity is employed as meaning division.

Boethius, therefore, is speaking of the plurality of composite beings, as is evident from the fact that he presents a proof involving those things that are diverse according to genus or species or number, and these kinds of diversity exist only in composite beings. For anything which is in a genus must be composed of genus and difference. Those, therefore, who declare the Father and Son to be unequal make declaration of composition, at least according to reason, inasmuch as they say the Father and Son agree in this, that they are God, but differ in the fact that they are unequal.

**Answers to objections.** 1. It may be said: In these words, number is shown to be prior to other created things, such as the elements and other such beings; but it is not prior to other notions, such as affirmation and negation or division and the like. Moreover, not every kind of number is prior to all created beings, but only number which is the cause of each thing, namely, God Himself, who, according to Augustine, is Number, giving species to every creature.

2. It may be answered: Plurality, commonly speaking, immediately follows upon being; but this is not necessarily true of all plurality, and so it is not unfitting that the plurality of posterior beings should be caused by the diversity of those that are prior.

3. It may be said: As one and many are not properly of one genus, so neither are the same and the diverse, but they are *passiones* of being inasmuch as it is being, and hence there is no difficulty if the diversity of certain beings causes the plurality of others.

4. It may be said: Some kind of plurality precedes all diversity, but diversity does not precede all plurality, yet some kind of diversity precedes certain plurality. Hence two things are equally true: namely, that, commonly speaking, multitude produces diversity, as the Philosopher says; and that diversity in composite things produces plurality, as Boethius here declares.

5. It may be answered: Boethius is using "otherness" in place of "diversity," which is constituted by certain differences, whether they are accidental or substantial. But those beings that are diverse yet not different are first beings, and Boethius is here not speaking of them.

## Article 2

### WHETHER VARIETY OF ACCIDENTS PRODUCES DIVERSITY ACCORDING TO NUMBER

**Objections.** 1. It seems that variety of accidents cannot be the cause of plurality according to number. For the Philosopher says in V *Metaph.* that those things are numerically one in which the matter is one; therefore they are numerically

## QUESTION IV 105

plural in which the matter is plural; therefore variety of accidents does not produce diversity in number, but rather diversity of matter does so.

2. As the Philosopher says in IV *Metaph.*, the cause of the substance and of the unity in things is the same; but accidents are not the cause either of the substance or of the unity in the individual; consequently they cannot be the cause of numerical plurality.

3. All accidents, since accidents are indeed forms, are themselves communicable or common and universal: but nothing of this kind can be the cause of individuation in another, or a principle of individuation; therefore accidents cannot be principles of individuation. But certain things are diverse according to number inasmuch as they are divided in their own individuation; therefore accidents cannot be causes of diversity according to number.

4. As those things that are in a genus or a species differ according to their substance, and not only according to an accident, so also those things that differ according to number must do likewise; but certain things are said to be diverse in genus or in species by reason of what is in the genus of substance, and not according to their accidents; therefore, in like manner, things are said to be numerically diverse according to what is in the genus of substance, and not according to accidents.

5. If a cause is removed, so is its effect. Now it happens that every accident is removed from a subject either actually or by thought. If, therefore, an accident were the principle of plurality according to number and diversity, it would happen that the same things would sometimes be numerically one and sometimes diverse, either actually or by thought.

6. What is posterior is never the cause of what is prior. But among all accidents, quantity holds first place, as Boethius says in *Lib. praedicam.* Among quantities, however, number is prior since it is more simple and more abstract.

Therefore an accident cannot be the principle of plurality according to number.

**Sed contra.** On the contrary is the statement made by Porphyry, that a collection of accidents which are not to be found in another produces the individual. But what is the principle of individuation is the principle of numerical plurality; therefore accidents are the principle of plurality according to number.

Again, in the individual, there is found nothing except matter, form, and accidents. Diversity of form, however, does not produce diversity according to number, but according to species, as is said in X *Metaph.* Now, diversity of matter produces diversity of genus. For the Philosopher says in X *Metaph.* that those things differ in genus in which there is not common matter, or generation of one into the other (mutual generation). Therefore diversity according to number cannot be produced except by diversity of accidents.

Moreover, what is found as common in many things that are specifically different is not the cause of diversity according to number, because the division of genus into species precedes the division of species into individuals; but matter is found to be common in things that are different in species because the same matter is possessed by contrary forms, otherwise beings having contrary forms would not be transmuted one into the other; therefore matter is not the principle of individuation according to number, and neither is form, as has been noted at the beginning. Hence it remains that accidents are the cause of this kind of diversity.

Again, in the genus of substance there is found only genus and difference; but the individuals of one species differ neither in genus, nor by reason of substantial differences; therefore they do not differ except because of accidental differences.

**Response.** I answer: For the clarification of this question and of those other questions treated of in the text of Boethius, it is necessary to see what may be the cause of the threefold diversity spoken of in the text.

Now, since in the individual composite in the genus of substance there are only three things (matter, form, and the composite), it must be that in each of these things the causes of their diversities are to be found. Accordingly it must be evident that diversity of genus is reduced to diversity of matter; but diversity according to species is reduced to diversity of form; whereas diversity according to number is owing partly to diversity of matter, and partly to accidental diversity.

Since, moreover, genus is the principle for knowableness of a thing, inasmuch as it is the first part of a definition, though matter in itself is unknowable, it is not possible that from matter *in se* diversity of genus should be known, but only according to that mode by which it is knowable. Now, a thing is knowable in two ways. (1) In one way, by analogy, or by comparison, as is said in I *Physic.* Thus we say that this is matter or that matter is related to natural things as wood is to a couch. (2) In another way, a thing is known by the form because of which it has actual being. For everything is known inasmuch as it is in act, not according as it is in potency, as is said in X *Metaph.*

According to this aspect, diversity of genus derives from matter in two ways. (1) In one way, by analogous diversity in relation to form, and thus the first genera of things are distinguished according to matter. For what is in the genus of substance is referred to matter as to a part of itself; but what is in the genus of quantity has no matter as a part of itself, but is related to it as its measure, and quality is related as its disposition. And by means of these two genera (namely, quantity and quality), all other genera are diversely related to matter, which is a part of substance; hence substance has the nature of a subject and as such has a certain relation to accidents. (2) In another way, diversity of genus has its origin in matter inasmuch as matter is perfected by form. And since matter is pure potency, just as God is Pure Act, to say that matter is perfected by act (which is form) is to say nothing else than that in some way it shares in a certain similitude to First Act, imperfectly indeed, since what is composed of matter and form is midway between pure potency and pure act.

Moreover, matter does not receive similitude to First Act in an altogether equal way, but in some things it is received imperfectly and in others more perfectly; thus, for example, some beings participate in a divine similitude inasmuch only as they subsist; others, in that they have knowledge; and still others, by possession of intellect. Therefore what is the similitude of First Act in any existing matter is its form. But in some beings this form causes it only to exist, in others to exist and to live, and so, in one and the same being, form may be the cause of other perfections. For what is the more perfect similitude has everything that less perfect similitudes have by way of perfections, and more besides. Something common, therefore, may be found in various similitudes, but possessed more imperfectly in some and more perfectly in others; just as matter may be subjected to both act and privation. And so matter, once taken together with this common element, is still material in regard to the aforementioned perfection and imperfection. From this material element it takes its genus, but its difference is from the perfection or imperfection of which we spoke above. For example, from this common material element (namely, having life), there is derived the genus "animated body"; but because of a superadded perfection there derives the difference "sensible," while, on the other hand, from imperfection there is derived the difference "insensible." Thus the diversity of such material things brings about diversity of genus, as that between animal and plant. On this account matter is said to be the principle of diversity according to genus, and in the same way, form is the principle of diversity according to species; because it is by reason of formal qualities which material things possess in addition to those which are the cause of their genus as material things, or by relation of form to matter, that the differences constituting species are derived.

However, it must be borne in mind that this "matter" whence genus is derived has in itself both form and matter. While the logician considers genus only according to its formal aspect, his definitions are said to be formal; but the natural philosopher considers genus from both aspects. Hence it sometimes happens that a thing shares in a logical genus in which it would not be classed according to the natural philosopher. Now, this happens when something by way of similitude to First Act is found in a material thing, and again in one without matter, and again in a being altogether different in matter. Thus it is evident that a stone which is in matter in such a way as to be potential to being, attains to something of similitude to First Act by being subsistent, and the sun also attains to the same similitude, though being in matter which is potential to place, but not any longer to being (having subsistent existence); and an angel likewise, although lacking any kind of matter. Hence the logician, finding in all these beings that from which a genus derives, places them all in the genus of substance; but the natural philosopher and the metaphysician, who considers the principles of things, not finding these all to be in material agreement, says that they differ in genus; as is said in X *Metaph.:* that corruptible and incorruptible differ generically and that those beings agree in genus whose matter is one and among which there is mutual generation.

Thus therefore it is evident in what way matter produces diversity in genus, and form produces diversity in species. But among individuals of the same species diversity should be considered, according to that laid down by the Philosopher (VII *Metaph.*); namely, that just as parts of genus and species are matter and form, so the parts of the individual are this matter and this form. Therefore, just as diversity of matter causes diversity in genus, or diversity of form causes diversity in species, absolutely, so this form and this matter produce diversity in number: but no form, as such, is of itself. I say, however, "no form, as such," because of the rational soul, which in a manner is this something of itself, but not merely inasmuch as it is a form. Intellect, in truth, since it is a form capable of being received into anything—as its matter, or as its subject—can naturally be attributed to many; a thing which is contrary to the nature of that which is this something; hence it is made a form by the fact that it is received in matter. But since matter, considered in itself, is indistinct, it is not possible that it would individuate a form received into it, except as it is distinguishable. For no form is individuated by the fact that it is received into matter, except in so far as it is received into this matter, or it is this distinct form, determined to this, and at this time.

Moreover, matter is not divisible except by quantity. Therefore the Philosopher says in I *Physic.*, that if quantity were removed, a substance would remain indivisible: hence matter is made to be this matter and is signate inasmuch as it exists under dimensions. Dimensions, however, can be considered in two ways.

1. In one way according to their termination, and I say that they are terminated according to limited measure and figure; and so, as complete beings, dimensions are classed in the genus of quantity, and thus they cannot be the principle of individuation: because such termination of dimensions may frequently vary in regard to the same individual, and in such case it would follow that the individual would not remain numerically the same.

2. In another way, dimensions may be considered without this certain determination, merely in the nature of dimension, although they never could exist without some kind of

determination; just as the nature of color cannot exist without determination to white or black; and according to this aspect dimensions are classed in the genus of quantity as imperfect. And by these indeterminate dimensions matter is made to be this signate matter, and thus gives individuality to a form, and thus also by matter there is caused the numerical diversity of things in the same species.

Therefore it is evident that matter, according as it is considered in itself, is not the principle of diversity, either according to species or according to number; but as it is the principle of generic diversity inasmuch as it is considered the subject of a common form, so it is the principle of numerical diversity inasmuch as it is considered as subject to indeterminate dimensions. Therefore also, since these dimensions are in the genus of accidents, diversity according to number is reduced to diversity of matter, or to accidental diversity, according to the nature of the aforesaid dimensions. Other accidents, however, are not principles of individuation, but they are the principle of knowing the individual to be distinct. In this way individuation is also attributed to other accidents.

**Answers to objections.** 1. It may be said: When the Philosopher says that those things are numerically one in which the matter is one, this must be understood of signate matter which is the subject of dimensions; otherwise it would be necessary to say that all generable and corruptible things are numerically one, since their matter is one.

2. It may be answered: Since dimensions are accidents, they cannot *per se* be the principle of the unity of an individual substance; but matter, inasmuch as it underlies such and such dimensions, is understood to be the principle of this unity and of this multitude.

3. It may be said: It is according to the nature of an individual thing that it be undivided in itself, and divided from other things by an ultimate division. No accident, how-

ever, has in itself the proper nature of division, unless it is quantity; therefore dimensions of themselves have a certain nature of individuation according to a determined place, inasmuch as place is a difference of quantity. Thus there is a twofold meaning of individuation: the one on the part of a subject, and this is the same for any accident; the other meaning, on the part of individuation itself, inasmuch as it has place, by reason of which, in abstracting from sensible matter, we may imagine this line and this circle. Hence it rightly pertains to matter to individuate all other forms, because it gives to this form, which of itself has the nature of individuation, that it also be terminated by those dimensions that are found in a subject now made complete; accordingly they are individuated by matter which is individuated by indeterminate dimensions conceived of as in matter.

4. It may be said: Things that differ numerically in the genus of substance, differ not only because of accidents, but also by reason of form and matter; but if it is asked how this form differs from that, the only reason can be that it is in other signate matter. Nor can there be found another reason why this matter is divided from that except by reason of its quantity. Hence matter subject to dimension is understood to be the principle of this kind of diversity.

5. It may be said: This reasoning relates to completed accidents which follow upon the existence of a form in matter; but not to those indeterminate dimensions which may be conceived of before the reception of the form in matter. For without these, a thing cannot be understood to be individual, any more than it can be conceived of without form.

6. It may be answered: Number, formally speaking, is prior to continuous quantity: but materially, continuous quantity is prior, since number is the result of the division of a continuum, as is said in IV *Physic*. In this way, division

# QUESTION IV

of matter, according to dimensions, causes numerical diversity. As to contrary reasons proposed, it is clear what must be conceded and what false conclusions have been deduced.

## Article 3

### WHETHER TWO BODIES CAN BE, OR CAN BE CONCEIVED OF AS BEING, SIMULTANEOUSLY IN THE SAME PLACE

**Objections.** 1. It seems that two bodies can be conceived of as being in the same place. For any proposition seems to be intelligible in which there is included no opposition of the predicate to the subject, since such a proposition contains nothing repugnant to understanding. But this proposition, "Two bodies are in the same place," is not a proposition repugnant to the intellect. Otherwise it could not happen miraculously, a thing evidently false regarding the body of our Lord, which came forth from the closed womb of the Virgin, and which entered into the midst of the disciples, the doors being shut. Now, even God cannot cause affirmation and negation to be simultaneously true, as Augustine says in answer to Faustus; therefore one can understand, or at least conceive of in his mind, that two bodies could be in the same place at the same time.

2. From glorified bodies there will be removed not the nature of corporeity, but only that of *corpulentia* (bodily mass). When this is removed, the possibility of being with other bodies in the same place is theirs by reason of the gift of subtlety, as is said by many. Therefore this condition does not follow the nature of corporeity, but that of *corpulentia,* of a certain mass. Therefore it is not impossible to conceive of two bodies being simultaneously in the same place.

3. Augustine, in commenting upon the Book of Genesis, speaks of light as holding first place among corporeal things; but light is simultaneously in the same place with air; there-

fore two bodies can be in the same place at the same time.

4. Any species of fire, as the Philosopher says in V *Topic.*, is a body; and so the conclusion is like the previous one.

5. In glowing iron, the fire and the iron are simultaneous; but each is a body; therefore it is possible for two bodies to be in the same place at the same time.

6. Elements in a compound are not corrupted; otherwise a compound would not follow the motion of a dominant element; but all four elements are bodies and are simultaneously in every part of the compound; therefore it is possible for two bodies to be simultaneously in the same place.

7. The fact that two bodies are not simultaneously in one place does not occur by reason of the matter of the bodies, since to matter in itself there is no due place; nor does it occur because of the form, for the same reason; nor is it because of dimension, since dimensions do not fill up place, as is evident from the fact that certain philosophers are accustomed to say that the place where there are only dimensions is a vacuum. Therefore this characteristic of a body must arise only from certain posterior accidents, which are not altogether common and which can be separated from the body; and so it seems that two bodies could be simultaneously in the same place.

8. According to the astrologers who follow Ptolemy, the six bodies of the planets move in epicycles, which are circles intersecting the spheres extrinsic to the planets. Therefore it must be that a body of a planet at some time would arrive at the place of section. But it cannot be said that at that place there is any vacuum, since nature does not suffer this; nor that the substance of the spheres is divisible, so that it might be thought of as giving way when the planetary body had reached it, as air gives way to a stone, for the heavens are most solid, being formed, as it were, of molten brass, as is said in Job, 37:18. Therefore it must be that the body of the planet is simultaneously in the same place as the body

## QUESTION IV

of the sphere; and so Boethius falsely says that two bodies cannot occupy one and the same place.

**Sed contra.** On the contrary is the fact that if two bodies are in one and the same place, they are the same in nature and in every respect; but any body, however large, can be divided into small bodies of any quantity, according to any number; therefore, it would follow that in the very smallest place there would be contained the largest body, a thing which appears to be absurd.

Again, it is impossible for there to be many straight lines between two given points. But this would follow if two bodies could be in the same place. For then, given two points in two opposite parts of space, there will be between them two straight lines assigned corporeally to two places. Now, it cannot be said that between these two points there will be no lines at all, or that a line of one location would be greater than the other, or that there could be any one line apart from those corporeally located between the two points of given location, for in that case the two lines would not be in a subject. Therefore it is impossible for two bodies to be simultaneously in the same place.

Again, it has been demonstrated in geometry that two circles are tangent only at one point: but if we posit two bodies being simultaneously in the same place, it would follow that two circles could be totally tangent. Therefore it is impossible that two bodies should be in the same place at the same time.

Again, whatever things are equal to one and the same thing are equal to each other; but since local dimension must be one with a localized body (since no dimension can be supposed without a subject), if two bodies could be simultaneously in the same place, it would follow that the dimensions of each body would be equal to the dimensions of the place; therefore it would follow that the bodies would be the same, but this is impossible.

**Response.** I answer that it must be said that in those things belonging to our world, all of which are judged to be corporeal, we see from sense experience that when one body arrives at any given place, any other body is expelled from that place; therefore it is experimentally evident that two such bodies cannot be in the same place.

There are, however, certain philosophers who declare that two bodies are not thus prohibited from simultaneous occupation of the same place on account of their corporeity, or on account of anything else which belongs to the nature of a body, as a body, for thus it would follow that it would be altogether impossible for two bodies to exist simultaneously [in the same place]. But they say that this prohibition is due only to their *corpulentia*. But whatever this *corpulentia* may mean—whether density or impurity or corruptibility which attends certain bodies, or even some special nature superadded to the general nature of corporeity—the prohibition can be on account of none of these things.

Now, there is to be found a double relation of a body to place. One is according as it has location in this or that determined place; and this relationship follows upon the specific nature of this or that body, just as heavy things, by the very nature of their gravity, hold a lower place, but light bodies, a higher place.

But another relationship prevails according as a body is said, absolutely, to be in place: and this relationship characterizes a bodily thing by the very nature of its corporeity, not because of anything additional. For according as a particular body is in place, it is commensurate with that place; but this is because it has dimensions that are equal and similar to the dimensions of the place; moreover, dimensions belong to every body by reason of its very corporeity. For, that many bodies should or should not be in the same place, has no relation to a determined place, but

## QUESTION IV 117

regards place absolutely; therefore it must be that the cause of this impediment should be referred to the nature of corporeity, by reason of which every body, inasmuch as it is a body, is destined to be in place.

And if the last sphere should not be in place, this is so only because nothing can be outside it, but not because it is lacking in the aforesaid aptitude to occupy place.

Hence there are others who concede that, absolutely, no two bodies can be in the same place at the same time, and they assign the reason for this to mathematical principles, which ought to be observed in all the natural sciences, as is said in III *Coel. et mun*. But this reason does not seem fitting, because it does not pertain to the objects of mathematics to be in place, except improperly and by similitude, as is said in II *De generatione*. Hence, the reason for maintaining this impediment should not be derived from mathematical principles, but from the principles of natural things, to which place is properly due. Furthermore, mathematical reasoning is sufficiently conclusive only in regard to its own matter. For, although mathematical truths are preserved in natural sciences, beings of the natural order add something over and above what is possessed by mathematical beings: namely, sensible matter; and because of this addition it is possible to assign as an explanation of something in the natural order what would not be assigned in explanation of an object of mathematics. For in mathematics no reason for diversity of two given lines can be assigned except because of their situation; wherefore, if diversity of situation is removed, there remains no plurality of mathematical lines, and likewise no diversity of surfaces or of bodies. On this account mathematical bodies cannot be both many and simultaneous, and in like manner neither can lines or surfaces.

But in regard to corporeal things in nature, it is possible to assign another and different reason for diversity: namely, that of sensible matter, even though diversity of situation were removed. Hence the reasoning which proves that two mathematical bodies cannot be simultaneously in the same place does not suffice for proving that two bodies in the natural order could not be simultaneous. And therefore the explanation of Avicenna must be accepted, which he uses in his *Sufficientia,* in the treatise *De loco.* In this explanation he assigns as reason of the aforesaid prohibition one which, by natural principles, is owing to the very nature of corporeity itself. For he says there can be no cause of this prohibition except that it pertains, first and *per se,* to a thing to be in place: but this means that it is destined by its nature to fill a place. Moreover, it does not pertain to a form to be in place, except accidentally; although certain forms are the principles by which a body is inclined to this or that place. Likewise neither does it pertain to matter, considered *per se,* to be in place, because, as so considered, it is understood apart from all genera, as is said in VII *Metaph.* Wherefore it must be that matter, according as it is subject to that by which it has primary relation to place, is the cause of this prohibition; but it is related to place inasmuch as it is subject to dimensions: hence it is by nature of matter subject to dimensions that many bodies are prohibited from being in the same place.

For, wherever the form of corporeity is found to be divided, there must be a plurality of bodies; but this division does not take place except by division of matter. Since division of matter is only by dimensions, because of which matter has situation, it is impossible that this matter should be distinct from that unless it is distinct according to situation. But this would not be the case if two bodies were posited as being in the same place; for then they would not be two bodies but one body, a thing which is impossible. Since, therefore, matter subject to dimensions is found in all corporeal things, it must be by reason of the very nature of corporeity that any two bodies are prohibited from being in the same place at the same time.

**Answers to objections.** 1. It may be said: A proposition may be called not-intelligible in two ways. In one way, it may be on the part of the one understanding, because of the deficiency of his intellect, as is the case in relation to this proposition: "In the three divine Persons there is one essence." In a proposition of this kind, there can be, indeed, no contradiction.

In another way, non-intelligibility may be on the part of the proposition, and this again for two reasons. In one way because it implies a contradiction, absolutely, as for example, "The rational is irrational"; and not even by a miracle can propositions of this sort be made true. In another way, because they imply a contradiction in a certain manner, as this proposition: "The dead man rose to life by his own (proper) power"; for, by the fact that he is said to be "dead," it is posited that he is destitute of every principle of life. Propositions of this kind can be made true by the miraculous operation of a superior power, and such is the case in regard to this proposition. For just as there can be found no natural cause of diversity for two bodies in the same place, so, by divine power, it is possible that two bodies be in the same place and that, although united in situation, their distinction be conserved, as does miraculously happen.

2. It may be said: Whatever may be this *corpulentia*, which is said to be removed from glorified bodies, nevertheless it is evident that corporeity will not be removed from them; therefore, neither will the cause which naturally prohibits any one of them from simultaneously occupying the same place with another; but only by a miracle is it possible that a glorified body be in the same place simultaneously with other bodies.

3. It may be answered: Light is not a body, but a certain quality, as Damascene says, and Avicenna also. But Augus-

tine gives light the same name as fire, as is evident from the fact that he speaks of light as contradistinguished from air, water, and earth.

4. It may be answered: The three species of fire spoken of by the Philosopher are to be understood in such a way that by "light" is understood fire existing in its proper matter, and granted also, as some say, that fire in its own proper sphere emits no light. For it does not belong to the nature of light to be luminous, but by participation in it other things become so. The same is true of fire: for, although in its own sphere it emits no light, nevertheless, by participation in it, other things become refulgent. By flame, however, is to be understood fire in the air; and by *carbo,* fire in terrestrial matter. In aqueous matter, however, fire cannot continue in such a way as to have the nature of fire, because water has qualities which are altogether opposed to fire.

5. It must be said: In iron which has become ignited there are not two bodies, but one body having indeed the species of iron, but certain properties of fire.

6. It may be answered: Although elements in a compound are supposed to remain according to their substantial forms, nevertheless it is not supposed that there are then many bodies *in act,* for otherwise no compound would be truly one; but while it is potentially many, it is one in act.

Nevertheless the opinion of the Commentator, III *Coel. et mun.,* seems the more probable. In rejecting the opinion of Avicenna, he says that the forms of elements neither remain in a compound nor are altogether corrupted, but that from them there comes to be one common or neuter form inasmuch as they comprise it, more or less. But since to give rise to a substantial form "more or less" seems an improbability, it appears that this saying ought to be understood in this way: that the forms of the elements are receptive of more or less (or comprise the form of the compound, more or less), not *secundum se,* but according as they remain in elementary qualities, as it were in their proper instruments. And thus it is said: Forms remain virtually in the qualities of the elements certain instrumental properties, as it were. Forms *secundum se*, do not remain, but only according as they remain virtually in their qualities, out of which there is made one, median, or common quality.

7. It may be said: Although dimensions of themselves cannot fill out a place, nevertheless a natural body, because of the fact that its matter is understood to be subject to dimensions, has the natural characteristic of filling a place.

8. It may be said: The opinion of Ptolemy regarding epicycles and eccentrics does not seem consonant with principles of natural philosophy which Aristotle holds; hence this opinion is not acceptable to the followers of Aristotle. If, however, it should be sustained, no necessity arises for supposing two bodies to be in the same place since, according to those who hold this opinion, the substances of heavenly bodies are distinguished as of three kinds: namely, the substance of the stars, which is luminous; the substance of the spheres, which is diaphanous and solid, but not divisible; and another kind of substance, which is between the spheres, and which is divisible and of resisting density, after the manner of the air, although this substance is incorruptible. And thus those who hold the theory of this third substance have no need to say that the substance of the spheres is divided or that two bodies occupy the same place simultaneously.

## Article 4

WHETHER VARIETY OF LOCATION HAS ANY INFLUENCE IN EFFECTING NUMERICAL DIFFERENCE

**Objections.** 1. It seems that variety of location effects nothing as regards diversity according to number. For the cause of diversity according to number is in those things which differ numerically; but place is outside things that are located; therefore diversity of place cannot be the cause of numerical diversity.

2. A thing is not complete in being unless it is distinct from others; but place comes after complete being; therefore motion to a place is the motion of that which is perfect according to substance, as is said in IX *Physic*. Therefore it is not possible that any cause of the distinction of bodies occupying space should be derived from place.

3. Numerical distinction is invariable as regards things that are distinct: but an invariable effect cannot proceed from a variable cause; therefore, since place varies in regard to that having location, it is not possible for diversity according to place to be the cause of numerical diversity.

4. If a cause is removed, so also is its effect: but it sometimes happens by a miracle that distinction of place is removed in respect to two bodies, as has been previously said; yet distinction according to number is not removed; therefore distinction according to place is not the cause of numerical diversity.

5. Diversity according to number is found not only in corporeal things, but even in incorporeal substances; but in these latter, diversity according to place cannot be the cause of numerical diversity, since incorporeal beings are not in a place, as Boethius himself says in his book, *De hebdomadibus;* therefore diversity according to place cannot be taken as the cause of diversity according to number, that is, as its cause by very reason of its nature, as he himself seems to say.

**Sed contra.** On the contrary is the fact that things differing according to number differ by reason of their accidents: but the diversity of no other accident is so inseparably related to diversity in number as is diversity of location; therefore diversity in place seems especially to influence diversity in number.

Again, diversity of location according to the species of things is concomitant with the diversity of bodies according to their species, as is evident in the case of heavy and light bodies. Therefore also diversity of places according to number is indivisibly concomitant with diversity of bodies according to number, and so the conclusion is the same as before.

Again, as time is the measure of motion, so place is the measure of a body: but motion is divided numerically according to time, as is said in V *Physic.;* therefore also what is corporeal is divided numerically according to place.

**Response.** I answer: It must be said that, as is evident from previous statements, diversity according to number is caused by division of matter existing under dimensions. Now, matter itself, according as it exists under dimensions, prohibits two bodies from being in the same place, inasmuch as in each of the two bodies there must be matter distinct in its situation. And thus it is evident that diversity according to number is caused by the same thing as diversity of location in diverse bodies. Hence diversity of location, considered in itself, is a sign of the diversity which exists according to number—just as is also true of other accidents, except the first indeterminate dimensions which have been previously discussed. But if diversity of place is considered according to its own cause, then it is clear that diversity of place is the cause of diversity according to number. Therefore Boethius says it is variety of accidents that produces diversity according to number. But if all other accidents are removed, numerical diversity still remains verifiable by reason of the diversity of things in place; since, indeed, no other of those accidents which appear as extrinsic to a complete being is so closely related to the cause of diversity according to number as is diversity of location.

**Answers to objections. 1–3.** To the first, second, and third objections it may be said: These reasons show conclusively that diversity of place is not the cause of diversity of individuals, *secundum se,* but this does not refute the fact that the cause of diversity of locations is the cause of diversity according to number.

4. It may be answered: All effects of second causes depend more on God than on secondary causes, since either with these second causes, or without them, He is able to produce miraculously whatever effects He wills.

5. It may be said: In corporeal substances diversity according to species follows diversity according to number, except in the case of the rational soul, which follows division of matter disposed for it. Here, however, Boethius is speaking of diversity according to number where the species is the same.

**Further answers.** 1. In contradiction to the first objection, it may be said: Variety of accidents, because of indeterminate dimensions, does not produce diversity in number after the manner of a cause, but this variety is said to produce a sign indicating numerical diversity; and diversity of place does this in a special way, inasmuch as it is the sign most closely related to numerical diversity.

2. To the second, it may be answered: Diversity of locations according to species is a sign of diversity of bodies according to their species, but not a cause of specific diversity.

3. To the third, it may be said: Although division of time is caused by division of motion, diversity, even diversity of time, is not the cause of diversity of motion, but a sign of it; and the same is true of location in its relation to a body.

## *Lectio II*

(INSERTED BY ST. THOMAS BETWEEN QUESTIONS IV AND V OF HIS COMMENTARY.)

### BOETHIUS' TEXT

Let us now begin a careful consideration of each several point, as far as it can be grasped and understood; for it has been wisely said, in my opinion, that it is a scholar's duty to formulate his belief about anything according to its real nature.

*Speculative science* may be divided into three kinds: physics, mathematics, and theology.

*Physics* deals with motion and is not abstract or separable; for it is concerned with forms of bodies together with their constituent matter, which forms cannot be separated in reality from their bodies. As bodies are in motion—the earth, for instance, tending downward, and fire tending upward—form takes on the movement of the particular thing to which it is annexed.

*Mathematics* does not deal with motion and is not abstract, for it investigates forms of bodies apart from matter, and therefore apart from movement, which forms being connected with matter cannot really be separated from bodies.

*Theology* does not deal with motion and is abstract and of things inseparable, for the divine substance is without matter or motion. In physics we are bound to use scientific concepts, in mathematics systematic concepts, in theology intellectual concepts; and in theology we will not let ourselves be diverted to play with imaginations, but will consider simply form.

## ST. THOMAS' COMMENTARY

Boethius has previously set forth the doctrine of the Catholic faith regarding the unity of the Trinity, and indicated the reason of this belief. Now he intends to proceed to an investigation of the aforesaid doctrine. Since, according to the opinion of the Philosopher in II *Metaph.*, inquiry into the method of a science ought to precede science itself, he therefore divides this section into two parts. In the first place Boethius points out the method proper for this kind of inquiry, which is concerned with divine things. In the second place he proceeds, according to the method he has indicated, to inquire into the proposition determined upon, where he says, "Which form, indeed."

The first part is again divided into two sections: first, he indicates the necessity of making clear the method of investigation. Secondly, he shows that the method of the present inquiry is suitable, saying: "Speculative science may be divided into three kinds." Therefore he says: "Wherefore it is certain that this is the doctrine of the Catholic faith regarding the unity of the Trinity, and the nature of that unity without difference."

Thereupon, he says by way of exhortation, "Let us now begin," that is, let us inquire more deeply, carrying our investigation to an examination of the intimate principle of things and of truth which is, as it were, veiled and hidden away from view. And that method which he deems fitting is indicated by the words: "Let us now begin a careful consideration of each several point, as far as it can be grasped and understood," that is, according to the mode by which understanding and apprehension are possible. Moreover, he uses the two words ("grasped" and "understood") because the method of any investigation ought to be in harmony both with things and with us. For if it is not suited to the matter, things will not be understood; and if it is not suited to us, we shall not be able to apprehend the matter; for example, divine things are such by their very nature that they cannot be known except by intellect. Wherefore, if anyone wished to follow another way and to use imagination instead, he would not be able to understand anything of them as a result of his consideration, because truths of this kind are not thus to be known. But if, on the other hand, one wished to know divine things so as to see them in themselves, and to comprehend them with the same certitude with which sensible things or mathematical demonstrations are comprehended, this too would be impossible; even things which are, in themselves, understandable in this way cannot be perfectly grasped because of the weakness of our intellect.

He also shows that the mode of inquiry used must always correspond to the kind of investigation undertaken, by reference to the authority of the Philosopher in I *Ethic.* when he says: "For it has been wisely said that it is a scholar's duty to formulate his belief about anything according to its real nature." So, in regard to a doctrine of faith, the same principle must be applied: for in all cases, equal certitude and demonstrative evidence cannot be demanded. And these are the very words of the Philosopher in I *Ethic.*: "It is the duty of the scholar to demand as much certitude in his investigation of each thing as the nature of that thing permits."

In the second place, when he says: "Speculative science may be divided into three kinds," he inquires into the method of his own investigation, testing its congruousness by distinguishing it from the methods employed in other sciences; and since method ought to correspond to the matter under investigation, he therefore divides this part of his consideration into two sections.

First, he distinguishes sciences according to the matter with which each is concerned. Secondly, he indicates the methods suitable for each kind of matter, beginning, "Physics deals."

In regard to the first point, he does three things. First, he shows what the objects of natural philosophy are. Secondly, he indicates the objects of mathematics. Thirdly, he speaks of the truths with which divine science is concerned, when he says: "Theology does not."

Therefore he says: "It has been wisely said that it is a scholar's duty to formulate his belief about anything according to its real nature." For, since there are three divisions of speculative science (or philosophy), and he calls it "speculative" to differentiate it from ethics, which is operative or practical; in each of these the method must be in conformity with the matter. The three divisions of speculative science indicated are physics or natural science, mathematics, and divine science or theology. While, I say, there are three divisions, natural philosophy, which is one of the three, "deals with motion and is not abstract," that is, it is concerned with things in motion and not abstracted from matter. This he proves by examples, as is evident in his treatise. When, however, he says: "Form takes on the movement of the particular thing to which it is annexed," his words should be understood as follows: that what is composite of matter and form, inasmuch as it is due the nature of a thing of this kind, has motion; or, in other words, a form existing in matter is the principle of motion. Therefore the consideration of things that are material and of things that are in motion is the same.

He then indicates the subject matter of mathematics, saying: "Mathematics does not deal with motion"; that is, it involves no consideration of motion or of movable things, and on this point it differs from natural philosophy. Mathematics, moreover, is said to be "not abstract"; that is, it considers forms which according to their existence are not abstract from matter, and in this respect it is in agreement with natural philosophy. He then explains how this is: Mathematics considers forms which are without matter and hence without motion, because wherever there is matter there is motion as is proved in X *Metaph*. For according as things have matter there will also be motion, and thus the speculations of a mathematician are without matter and without motion, although these forms, namely, those about which the mathematician speculates, "being connected with matter, cannot really be separated from bodies," according to their being [real existence]; but according to speculation, they can be considered as separable.

Then he indicates the objects of divine science, calling it, "theology," that is, the third division of speculative science, which is termed divine, or metaphysics, or first philosophy; and it deals with objects apart from motion, in which it agrees with mathematics and differs from natural philosophy. It also is "abstract," namely, from matter, and "inseparable"; and because of these two facts it differs from mathematics. For the objects of divine science are of themselves abstract from matter and motion, but those of mathematics are not thus naturally abstract, but separable in thought. The objects of divine science, however, are called "inseparable" because a thing is not separable unless there is some conjunction with matter. Hence the objects of divine science are not separable from matter by thought, but are abstract according to their very being; while the converse is true in the case of the objects of mathematics. This he proves by the fact that the substance with which divine science is principally concerned is that of God, and on this account it is called "divine."

In the next place, when he says, "In physics, then, we are bound to use scientific concepts, in mathematics systematic concepts, in theology intellectual concepts." He points out the methods that correspond to the aforesaid divisions. Here he treats of two things. First, he draws conclusions about the methods appropriate for each of the divisions named, and the disposition of this section is left open for discussion. Secondly, he describes the last mode, which is that proper to the present investigation, and indicates a twofold procedure: first, by the removal of that which is an impediment to speculation saying, "In theology we will not let ourselves be diverted to play with imaginations (that is, in such a way that in formulating judgments we follow the judgment of the imagination) but will consider simply form."

Secondly, he indicates the method which is the proper one when he says: "but will consider simply form" (apart from motion and matter), the nature of which he consequently explains in beginning his treatment of the proposed question.

## QUESTION V

## CONCERNING THE DIVISION OF SPECULATIVE SCIENCE

This question is twofold. First, concerning the division of speculative science which is assigned in the text of Boethius. Second, concerning the modes attributed to speculative science.

With regard to the first, four things are asked:

1. First, whether this division is suitable by which speculative sciences are divided into these three: natural science, mathematics, and divine science.

2. Second, whether natural philosophy is of those things that are in motion and matter.

3. Third, whether mathematics is a study of things viewed without motion and matter.

4. Fourth, whether divine science is concerned with those things that are without motion and matter.

### Article 1

WHETHER THE DIVISION IS SUITABLE BY WHICH SPECULATIVE SCIENCE IS DIVIDED INTO THESE THREE PARTS: NATURAL SCIENCE, MATHEMATICS, AND DIVINE SCIENCE

**Objections.** 1. It seems that speculative science is not suitably divided into these three parts. For the parts of speculation are those habits that perfect the contemplative part of the soul: but the Philosopher in VI *Ethic.* states that the soul's knowledge, which is the contemplative part of it, is perfected by three virtues; namely, wisdom, knowledge, and understanding; therefore the parts of speculative science are these three, and not those proposed in the text.

2. Augustine says (VIII *De civ. Dei*) that rational philosophy, which is logic, is classed under speculative philosophy, or contemplative philosophy; since, therefore, the proposed division makes no mention of logic, it seems to be an insufficient division.

3. Philosophy is commonly divided into the seven liberal arts, among which neither natural philosophy nor theology is included, but only rational philosophy and mathematics. Therefore natural philosophy and theology ought not to be made parts of speculation.

4. The science of medicine seems to be especially operative; nevertheless in it one part is considered speculative, and another practical; therefore, for the same reason, in all other operative sciences some part is speculative, and hence in this division mention should be made of ethics or moral philosophy, although it concerns action, on account of the part of it which is speculative.

5. The science of medicine is a part of philosophy, and there are other arts which are called mechanical, as the science of agriculture, alchemy, and the like. Since, therefore, these are sciences of operation, it does not seem that natural science ought to be classed absolutely under the speculative sciences.

6. The whole ought not to be divided in opposition to any of its parts; but theology seems to be the whole in respect to physics and mathematics, since the subjects of these latter are parts of theology, whose subject is being, of which a part is mobile being, which natural science considers, and another part quantity, which mathematics studies, as is clear from III *Metaph.;* therefore divine science ought not to be opposed in division to natural science and to mathematics.

7. Sciences are divided as are things, as is said in III *De*

# QUESTION V

*anima;* but philosophy concerns *being,* for it consists in knowledge of being, as Dionysius says in his *Epistola ad Polycarpum.* Since, therefore, being is, first of all, divided into potency and act, through one and many, through substance and accident, it seems that in the same manner the parts of philosophy ought to be distinguished.

8. There are many other divisions of being concerning which there are sciences more essential than those made on the basis of mobility and immobility, abstract and nonabstract: as, for example, corporeal and incorporeal, animate and inanimate, and others of the sort. Therefore the division of the parts of philosophy ought to be made on the basis of difference of the latter kind, rather than those here proposed.

9. That science upon which others are based ought to be prior to them; but all other sciences depend upon theology as upon their foundation because it belongs to it to prove the principles of the others; therefore divine science ought to be preordained to the others.

10. Mathematics is prior to natural science in the order of learning; hence children are able to learn mathematics easily, but not natural science, unless they have already made some progress, as is said in VI *Ethic.* Consequently the order in learning the sciences followed by the ancients is said to have been that first they studied logic, then mathematics, thirdly natural sciences, afterward moral philosophy, and finally divine science; therefore mathematics ought to precede natural science.

**Sed contra.** On the contrary, that this division suffices is proved by the Philosopher in VI *Metaph.,* where he says that there will be three parts of philosophy and of theory: mathematics, physics, and theology.

Moreover, in II *Physic.,* and commonly according to the Philosopher, three modes of knowledge are named, which also seem to be related to these three divisions.

Further, Ptolemy also in the beginning of the *Almagestus* makes use of the same division.

**Response.** I answer that it must be said that the theoretical or speculative intellect is to be distinguished from the operative or practical by this peculiar fact: that the speculative intellect has for its end the truth which it considers; the practical, on the contrary, ordains the truth considered in respect to some operation as to its end. Hence the Philosopher says (III *De anima*) that each science differs as to its end; and in II *Metaph.* it is said that the end of speculation is truth; the end of the operative or practical intellect is action. Since, therefore, the matter ought to be proportionate to the end, the matter of the practical sciences should be those things that can be made or done by our work, so that knowledge of them can be ordered to operation as to an end.

But the matter of the speculative sciences ought to be things that cannot be made by our effort; therefore the consideration of them is not ordained to operation as to an end; and according to the differences of these ends the speculative sciences ought to be distinguished.

Moreover, it must be noted that, while habits or powers are distinguished by their objects, they are not distinguished by any kind of difference at all in these objects, but in accordance with those things that belong *per se* to their objects as objects.

For, in regard to a sensible thing, in so far as it is viewed merely as sensible, it matters not whether it is an animal or a plant (it may chance to be either); hence, according to this, each is distinguished by the senses, not on the basis of animal or plant, but rather on the basis of color and of sound; therefore the speculative sciences ought to be divided according to differences of the things contemplated inasmuch as they are objects of speculation.

For the speculable, however, according as it is an object of a speculative power, something is required on the part

## QUESTION V

of the intellective power, and something on the part of the habit of knowledge (or virtue), by which the intellect is perfected.

On the part of the intellect, it is required that the object should be immaterial, because the intellect itself is immaterial; as regards the habit of science, it is required that it should be of necessary things, because science is of the necessary, as is proved in the first part of the *Posterior*. Moreover, any necessary thing, inasmuch as it is so, is immobile; because anything that is moved, inasmuch as it is of this order, is capable of existence or of non-existence, either absolutely or after some manner, as is said in X *Metaph*.

Therefore on the part of the object of speculation, as an object of speculative science, it is supposed that there is *per se*, separation from matter and motion, or from reference to them; therefore, according to the order of abstraction from matter and from motion, the speculative sciences are distinguished.

*First degree* of abstraction. There are certain objects of speculation which are dependent upon matter as to their existence, since they cannot exist except in matter, and these are distinguished because they depend on matter both really and logically, such as things whose definition posits sensible matter. Hence, they cannot be understood without sensible matter, as, for example, in the definition of man it is necessary to include flesh and bones; and with things of this kind physics, or natural science, is concerned.

*Second degree* of abstraction. But certain other things, although they depend upon matter as to their existence, do not so depend as far as the intellect is concerned; because in a definition of them sensible matter is not included, as in the case of lines and numbers with which mathematics deals.

*Third degree* of abstraction. But there are still other objects of speculation that do not depend upon matter for existence, because they can exist without matter: either they are never found in matter, as God and the angels, or they are sometimes in matter and in other cases not, as substance, quality, potency, act, one, and many, and things of this sort.

With these things theology treats, that is, divine science, because the most important of its objects is God. By another name, it is called metaphysics, that is, *transphysica*, because it is fitting for us to study it after physics, as it is natural for us to arrive at knowledge of the nonsensible by means of those things that are sensible.

It is also called first philosophy, inasmuch as other sciences, receiving their principles from it, follow upon it.

Moreover, it is not possible for there to be other things which, according to the intellect, are dependent upon matter, but not so with respect to their real existence; because the intellect, inasmuch as it is considered in itself, is immaterial; wherefore there is no fourth division of philosophy over and above those named.

**Answers to objections.** 1. *Sciences distinguished by objects.* It may be answered: The Philosopher in VI *Ethic.* considers the intellectual habits inasmuch as they are virtues of the intellect. They are called virtues by reason of the fact that they perfect the intellect in its operation. For a virtue is that which makes the one possessing it good and renders the work good, and therefore according as one is perfected in diverse ways by means of these diverse speculative habits, so the virtues are themselves diversified.

Now, there is one way in which the speculative part of the soul is perfected by the intellect which is due to the habit of principles, by which things are known of themselves; and another way by which conclusions are known as demonstrated from principles of this sort, whether demonstration proceeds from inferior causes as in science, or from the highest (ultimate), causes as in the case of wisdom.

Since, however, sciences are distinguished according as there are certain habits of the soul, it is fitting that they should be distinguished by their objects; that is, according to those things concerning which the sciences treat; and so there are distinguished here and in metaphysics three parts of speculative philosophy.

2. *Logic.* It must be said: The speculative sciences, as is clear in the beginning of the *Metaph.*, are those the knowledge of which is sought for their own sakes. However, the subjects with which logic is concerned are not studied that they may be known for themselves, but as certain means to the knowledge of other sciences. Therefore logic is not classed under speculative philosophy as one of its principal parts, but as if in a certain way reducible to it, inasmuch as it gives to speculation its instruments, namely, syllogisms, definitions, and the like, which we need in speculative sciences. Wherefore, according to Boethius' Commentary on Porphyry, it is not so much a science as an instrument of science.

3. *Liberal arts.* It must be said: The seven liberal arts do not offer a satisfactory division of theoretical philosophy; but, as Hugh of St. Victor says in III *Didascalon,* certain things being omitted, these are to be enumerated, because it is by the former that those who wish to learn philosophy are first trained; hence these subjects are known as the *trivium* and *quadrivium* because by them, as if by certain roads, the eager mind enters into the secrets of philosophy. In this concurs the statement of the Philosopher, who says in II *Metaph.* that the means of science ought to be sought before the sciences themselves. And the Commentator says the same: that before all the other sciences one ought to learn logic, which teaches the method of the other sciences; and to logic the *trivium* pertains.

Moreover, he says in VI *Ethic.* that children can learn mathematics, but not physics, which requires experience. From this statement we are given to understand that, first of all, logic ought to be learned, and then mathematics, to which the *quadrivium* pertains; and so by these roads, as it were, the mind is prepared for the other physical sciences.

Hence also among the other sciences logic and mathematics are called arts because they have a value not only as regards theory, but by reason of relation to a certain work, which is immediately derived from their very nature, such as to regulate construction, to formulate the syllogism, and to direct speech; or to number, to measure, to compose melodies, and to compute the courses of the stars.

But other sciences have no concrete task to perform, but only value as knowledge (cognitive value), as divine science and the science of nature; hence they cannot claim the name of art, since art may be called "the reasonable way of doing something" [or "reason in action"], as is said in VI *Ethic*. Or, again, the arts are concerned with some corporeal work, as medicine, alchemy, and the like. Therefore these latter cannot be called liberal arts because activities of this kind are activities of a man directed toward that in which he is not free: namely, in regard to his body (as something corporeal).

As to the science of morality: although it is concerned with operation, this operation is not the act of science, but an act of virtue, as is evident in V *Ethic*. Hence it cannot be called an art; but rather, in these operations virtue assumes the place of an art; therefore the ancients defined virtue as "the art of noble and well-ordered living," as Augustine says in X *De civ. Dei*.

4. *"Practical" and "theoretical" as regards philosophy and medicine*. It must be said: As Avicenna declares in the beginning of his *Metaphysics*, "theoretical" and "practical" are distinguished in one way when philosophy is divided into theoretical and practical; and in another way when the arts are divided into theoretical and practical; and in still another way when medicine is so considered.

For, when philosophy or the arts are distinguished as theoretical or practical, this distinction ought to be made in view of the end of each; so what is ordained to operation

## QUESTION V

may be called practical; but what is ordained to the knowledge of truth only may be called theoretical. However, when philosophy as a whole and the arts are classified in this way, this is of interest, because the division of philosophy should be determined with regard to our last end, namely, beatitude, to which all human life is ordained.

For, as Augustine says in X *De civ. Dei*, in the words of Varro, "There is no other cause for man's philosophizing except that thereby he may be happy."

Whence it is that a double felicity is claimed by philosophers: one, contemplative; the other, active, as X *Ethic.* states. Accordingly they distinguish two parts of philosophy, calling moral philosophy "practical," but natural and rational philosophy, "theoretical."

But, when it is said, "Certain arts are speculative; others are practical," this is maintained with regard to some special ends of these arts; as when we say that agriculture is a practical art, but that dialectics is theoretical.

When, however, medicine is divided into theoretical and practical, the division is not established according to the end. For if so, all medical science would be contained under the heading of "practical," as ordained for operation; but the established division is determined according as those things which are treated of in the science of medicine are closely or remotely related to operation.

Therefore we call "practical" the part of medicine that teaches methods of healing patients; as, for example, in the case of what symptoms such and such remedies ought to be employed. But we call "theoretical" the part that teaches the principles by which the physician is guided in his operation, though not proximately; as, for example, that the temperaments are three, and how many different kinds of fever there are.

If some part of an essentially active science (a science essentially one of operation), such as this, is called theoretical, it does not follow that it should be listed under the speculative sciences.

5. *Subordination of the sciences.* It may be replied: One science may be contained under another in two ways.

a) In one way, one science may be part of another so that the same things may be the subject of one science, and some part of the subject of the other; as plants are a certain type of natural body; wherefore the study of plants is comprised under natural science as a part.

b) In another way, one science may be contained under another as subordinate to it, when, namely, in the higher science there is assigned the formal reason or cause of those things about which, in the lower science, we know only that they are (and not their formal reason), as, for example, the science of music is contained under the science of arithmetic.

Thus medicine is not classed under physics as a part; for the subject of medicine is not a part of the subject of natural science in the same way as it is a part of medical science. Although the curable body is a natural body, it is not, however, the subject of medicine inasmuch as it is curable by nature, but as it is curable by art. Since, however, in the healing which is effected by art, art is the minister of nature (because some natural power, aided by art, is the cause of healing), the principle or reason of the operation of art ought to derive from the properties of natural things. And thus medicine is subordinated to physics; and in the same way alchemy and the science of agriculture, and all other sciences of the same order.

Thus it remains that physics in itself and in all its parts is a speculative science; although some operative sciences are subordinated to it.

6. *Sciences differentiated by formal objects.* It can be said: Although the subjects of other sciences are parts of being, which is the subject of metaphysics, those other sciences ought not to be considered parts of metaphysics.

Each science considers one phase of being, or reality, according to a special mode, which is different from that according to which being is viewed by metaphysics. Therefore, properly speaking, the subject of such a science is not a part of the subject of metaphysics, but, according to its own manner of viewing reality, each special science is differentiated from others.

However, a science can be said to be a phase of the science of metaphysics in this way: if it be concerned with potency or act, or with unity, or with anything of a like nature, because these things require the same mode of consideration as that by which being is dealt with in metaphysics.

7. *Modes of being requiring metaphysical consideration.* It may be answered: Those modes of being require the same manner of treatment as being in general because they also do not depend upon matter; therefore science concerning these things is not distinguished from the science that is of being in general.

8. *Sciences differentiated according to the knowability of their objects.* It is answered: Those diversities of things which the objection sets forth are not differences *per se* of things inasmuch as they are knowable, and therefore the sciences are not differentiated by them.

9. *Relation of the first science, metaphysics, to mathematics and natural science.* It is answered: Although divine science is the first of all the sciences, naturally speaking, there are others which are prior in knowledge as far as we are concerned. Whence it is that Avicenna says in the beginning of his *Metaphysics:* "The order of this science is such that it is learned after the natural sciences, in which many things are determined which this divine science makes use of: as generation and corruption and motion and the like."

Likewise it ranks even after mathematics. For, indeed, to understand separated substances, this science requires a knowledge of number and of the order of the heavens, a knowledge which is not possible without astrology, a science in which all mathematics is needed. Other sciences, in truth, as music and ethics and the like also contribute to it.

Nor should it be said that the argument is a vicious circle since the same science which supposes or makes use of those things that are proved in others is the very science that proves or justifies the principles of these other sciences: for the principles which another science (for example, natural science) receives from first philosophy do not have as their proof those same things or facts that first philosophy takes from natural philosophy; but they are proved by principles that are immediately self-evident. And so first philosophy does not prove the principles which it hands down to natural philosophy by principles which it has received from that same natural science; but it proves them by certain self-evident principles; and thus there is no vicious circle in its definitions.

Furthermore, the sensible effects from which the demonstrations of the natural sciences proceed are more readily known, as far as we are concerned, at first. But when through them we have arrived at a knowledge of first causes, from these latter there is evident to us the reason of those effects from which, by *demonstratio quia,* the existence of the first causes had been proved.

And so, natural science contributes somewhat to divine science; yet through divine science the principles of natural science are justified (or more clearly revealed). Hence it is that Boethius places divine science last, because it is the ultimate science, as far as we are concerned.

10. *The knowledge of sensible things in relation to mathematics.* It is answered: Although natural philosophy is more readily learned after mathematics, inasmuch as general understanding of it requires experiment and time, nevertheless the things of nature, since they are sensible, are more naturally the objects of our knowledge than are mathematical entities, abstracted as they are from sensible matter.

QUESTION V 143

*Article 2*

WHETHER NATURAL PHILOSOPHY IS OF THOSE THINGS THAT ARE IN MOTION AND MATTER

**Objections.** 1. It seems that natural science is not about those things that are in motion and matter, for matter is the principle of individuation; no science, however, is of individuals, but of universals only, according to the opinion of Plato, which is set forth by Porphyry; therefore natural science is not about those things that are in matter.

2. Science pertains to the intellect; but the intellect knows things by means of abstraction from matter and the conditions of matter; therefore of those things which have not been abstracted from matter there can be no science.

3. In natural science there is considered a first mover, as VIII *Physic.* declares; but He Himself is exempt from all matter; therefore natural science is not alone about those things that are in matter.

4. All science is about necessary things; but that which is moved, as such, is contingent, as is affirmed by IX *Metaph.;* therefore no science can be of things in motion, and so neither can natural science.

5. Nothing universal is moved, for man, considered universally, is not healed, but this man, as is said in the beginning of the *Metaphysics;* but every science is of universals; therefore natural science is not of those things that are in motion.

6. Natural science treats of things that are not moved, such as the soul, as is proved in the beginning of the *De anima,* and as the earth, as is proved in II *De coelo et mundo;* for all natural forms do not become and are not corrupted; and for the same reason, they are not moved except *per accidens,* as is proved in VII *Metaph.;* therefore, not all that philosophy treats of is in motion.

7. Every creature is mutable, since immutability belongs

to God alone, as Augustine says. Therefore, if the consideration of natural science pertains to those things that are in motion, it will have to consider all creatures, which seems to be evidently false.

**Sed contra.** It pertains to natural philosophy to determine about the things of nature; but things of nature are those in which there is a principle of motion, and, moreover, where there is motion there must be matter, as is said in X *Metaph.;* therefore natural science is about those things that are in motion and in matter.

Again, there should be some speculative science of those things that are in motion and in matter, for otherwise there would not be a complete teaching of philosophy, which is knowledge of being; but these things are treated by no other speculative science, neither by mathematics nor by metaphysics; therefore natural science is concerned with these things.

Moreover, this is apparent from what the Philosopher says in VI *Metaph.* and II *Physic.*

**Response.** On account of the difficulty of this question, Plato was forced to propose his theory of ideas. For since, as the Philosopher says (I *Metaph.*), he believed that all sensible things are ever in flux, according to the opinion of Cratylus Heraclitus, and as he judged science could not pertain to such things, he supposed that there were certain substances separated from sensible things, concerning which there might be sciences and for which definitions might be given. But this defect occurred because he did not distinguish *per se* from what is *per accidens*. Indeed about the accidental, very often even the wise are deceived, as is said in *De sophisticis elenchis*. However, as is proved in VIII *Metaph.*, since in sensible nature are found both what is a whole (that is, a composite) and a reason (that is, its form) *per se* the composite is generated and decomposed, but not so the *ratio* or form except *per accidens*. For "house" does not come to be, but "this

## QUESTION V

house," as is there said. Moreover, any one thing can be considered without all those things that are not *per se* attributed to it; therefore the forms and reasons of things, although they exist in motion, are considered in themselves, without motion; and so there are sciences of these things, and definitions, as the Philosopher says in the same place. Sciences of sensible substances are not, however, founded upon a cognition of other substances separated from sensible things, as is proved in the same place.

Moreover, reasons of this kind which the sciences deal with in considering things abstracted from motion should also be considered in abstraction from those things that belong to being so far as it is mobile. Since, however, all motion is measured by time, and the first motion is local motion, and since, if this motion is removed, no other motion is present, it follows that a thing is mobile inasmuch as it is here and now. But this pertains to a mobile thing according as it is individuated by matter existing under designated dimensions. Wherefore reasons of this sort, according as there can be sciences of mobile things, ought to be considered apart from *materia signata* and apart from all things consequent upon it: not, however, apart from *materia non signata*, because on the notion of it depends the notion of the form which determines matter for itself. Therefore the *ratio* of man which the definition signifies, according to which science proceeds, is considered without this flesh and these bones, but not without flesh and bones, absolutely. And as the singulars include in their definition *materia signata*, so the universals include *materia communis*, as is said in VII *Metaph*. Therefore the aforesaid abstraction of the form is not said to be from matter absolutely, but of the universal from the particular.

Hence forms of this sort can be considered as abstracted in a twofold way: in the first way *secundum se*, in which they are considered without motion and *materia signata*, and this is not found in things themselves except as they are considered in the intellect.

In another way according as they are referred to things of which they are the forms; these things, indeed, are in matter and motion and so the reasons are principles of these things' being known, since everything is known by its form. Thus by means of the immobile forms of this sort, considered without particular matter, knowledge is obtained in natural science about things which, outside the mind, exist in motion and in matter.

**Answers to objections.** 1. It is answered: Matter is not the principle of individuation unless as existing under signate dimensions, and so, indeed, natural science abstracts from matter.

2. It may be said: The intelligible form is the quiddity of the thing: the object of the intellect is *quid,* as is said in III *De anima.* The quiddity, however, of a universal composite, as man or animal, includes *in se* matter in general, not in particular, as is said in VII *Metaph.* Whence the intellect ordinarily abstracts from *materia signata* and conditions relative to it: not however from *materia communis* in natural science, although even in natural science matter is not considered except as ordained to a form: whence, indeed, form has a place prior to matter in the consideration of natural things.

3. It is answered: Natural science does not treat of the prime mover as its subject or its partial subject, so much as it considers Him the end to which natural science leads. An end, however, is not of the nature of the thing of which it is the end, but has a certain reference to that thing, just as the end of a line is not the line, but has a certain relation to it. So the prime mover has a certain reference to natural things yet is of a nature other than that of these things. For He has a reference to them inasmuch as He imparts motion

## QUESTION V

to them, and so has a place in the consideration of nature, not in Himself, but inasmuch as He is the mover.

4. It is answered: "Science" is a term applied in a twofold manner to anything: in the first and principal manner, science is about universal aspects, which are its basis.

Science is of other things in a secondary sense, and, as it were, indirectly, and thus it is of those things [particular, contingent things] to which those reasons belong [i.e., from which the reasons are derived] inasmuch as it applies those reasons to the particulars to which they belong with the aid of the inferior powers [sense and imagination]. For science uses the universal aspect both as something known and as a means of knowing. For by the universal definition of a man, I am able to judge of this one or of that. Moreover, universal definitions of things are all immobile, and therefore, according as this is the case, every science is of the necessary: but inasmuch as these forms of things are in a certain way necessary and immobile and in another way contingent and mobile, to such a degree are sciences said to treat of contingent and mobile things.

5. It is answered: Although the universal is not subject to motion, it is the reason (form) of a mobile thing.

6. It may be said: The soul and other forms of natural things, although they are not moved *per se*, yet they are moved *per accidens;* and, over and above this, they are the perfections of mobile things, and according to this fall under the consideration of natural science.

Moreover, although the earth in its totality is unmoved, as happens inasmuch as it is in its natural place, in which it rests by the same nature by which it is moved to this place, yet its parts are moved from place to place, since they are outside their proper place. Thus the earth, by reason of its total state of rest, and by reason of the motion of its parts, falls under the consideration of natural science.

7. It is answered: The mutability which characterizes all creatures is not according to any natural motion but according to a dependence upon God; if they should fall away from Him they would lack that by reason of which they have any being. But this dependence is a consideration pertaining more to metaphysics than to natural science. Furthermore, spiritual creatures are not mutable except according to election. The mutation, however, is not attributed to the nature of things, but rather to Divinity.

## Article 3

### WHETHER MATHEMATICS CONSIDERS OBJECTS THAT ARE WITHOUT MOTION AND MATTER

**Objections.** 1. It seems that mathematics cannot consider, apart from matter, the things that are in matter; for, since truth consists in the adequation of a thing to the intellect, it must be that whatever is considered otherwise than it is, is falsely considered. If, therefore, all things that are in matter are considered without matter in mathematics, such a consideration will be false, and thus will be unscientific, since every science is of true things.

2. According to the Philosopher in I *Poster.*, it is the character of every science to consider a subject and the phases pertaining to that subject; but of all material things, according to their essence, matter is a part; therefore it is not possible that any science should treat of the things that are in matter without considering the matter.

3. All straight lines are of the same species; but the mathematician considers straight lines by numbering them; otherwise he would not consider triangles and quadrangles. Hence he treats of lines according as they differ in number and agree in species; but the principle of differentiating things that agree according to species is matter, as is plain from the pre-

## QUESTION V    149

ceding discussion; therefore matter is considered by the mathematician.

4. No science that altogether abstracts from matter demonstrates through a material cause: but in mathematics certain demonstrations occur which are not capable of being reduced except to a material cause, as when something is demonstrated about a whole by means of its parts. For the parts are the matter of the whole, as is said in II *Physic.*, whence also in II *Poster.* demonstration is reduced to a material cause when it is demonstrated that an angle which is in a semicircle is a right angle from the fact that each of the two parts of it is half a right angle; therefore mathematics does not abstract from matter.

5. Motion cannot be without matter: but the mathematician ought to treat of motion, because, since motion is measured according to space, it seems to belong to the same reason and science to consider both the measure of space and the measure of motion; but these alike pertain to mathematics; therefore mathematics does not altogther prescind from consideration of matter.

6. Astrology is a certain part of mathematics, and likewise the science of the motion of the sphere, and of weights, and of music, in all of which things there is consideration of motion and of things moved; therefore mathematics does not abstract entirely from matter and from motion.

7. The consideration of natural science is altogether concerned with matter and motion; but certain conclusions are demonstrated alike by mathematics and by natural science; for example, whether the earth is round and whether it is in the middle of the sky: therefore it is not possible that mathematics abstracts altogether from matter.

But if you say that it abstracts only from sensible matter: I reply that sensible matter is particular matter because the sense belongs to particulars, from which all sciences abstract; and so the consideration of mathematics ought not be said to be more abstract than that of the other sciences.

8. The Philosopher in II *Physic.* says there are three fields or realms of thought. The first is of things mobile and corruptible; the second of things mobile and incorruptible; the third, of things immobile and incorruptible. The first is the realm of natural science; the second, mathematics; the third, divine, as Ptolemy explains in the beginning of the *Almagestus;* therefore mathematics deals with things in motion.

**Sed contra.** On the contrary is what the Philosopher says in VI *Metaph.*

Again, certain things, although they are in matter, do not suppose matter in their very definition, and in this respect a curve differs from a curved nose. But it pertains to philosophy to consider all beings: therefore some part of it ought to consider this particular kind of being, and this belongs to mathematics, since it pertains to no other branch of philosophy. Moreover, those things that are prior according to the intellect can be considered without those things that are posterior; but the things of mathematics are prior to natural things, which are in motion and matter, for they are related to mathematics by addition, as is said in III *De coelo et mundo;* therefore the consideration of mathematics can be apart from motion and matter.

**Response.** For the clarification of this question, we must know in what manner the intellect by its own operation is able to abstract. Therefore, according to the Philosopher (III *De anima*), we should know that the operation of the intellect is twofold. By one, which is called the intelligence of indivisibles, it knows of anything what it is. By another operation, however, it composes and divides, as by formulating affirmative or negative enunciations, and these same two operations correspond to two aspects in regard to things. The first operation, indeed, regards the nature itself of the thing, according as a certain object of the intellect acquires a certain grade in being, whether it is a complete thing, as some whole, or incomplete, as a part or an accident. The second operation looks to the existence of the thing, which, indeed, results from an aggregation of principles in composites, or is concomitant with the simple nature of the thing in the case of simple substances. And because the truth of the intellect resides in this, that it is conformed to a thing, it is evident that according to this second operation the intellect is not able truly to abstract what, on the part of the thing, is joined to it, because in abstracting is signified that there is a separation according to the very essence of the thing, just as if I should abstract man from whiteness by saying: "Man is not white," and should signify separation in the thing. Whence if, in reality, man and whiteness are not separate, the intellect will be false. By this operation, therefore, the intellect cannot truly abstract except from things that are on the part of the object separate, as when it is said: "Man is not an ass." But, according to the first operation of the intellect, it is possible to separate things which on the part of the object are not separate, not indeed all, but some.

For since everything is intelligible inasmuch as it is in act, as is said in X *Metaph.*, it must necessarily be that a nature or quiddity of a thing is known either according as it is a certain act (as happens in the case of forms and simple substances); or according to that which is its act, as composite substances are intelligible through their forms; or according to what is in place of act, as prime matter is known through its relationship to form, and a vacuum through privation of any objects located with it, and this connection with act is that by which each nature determines its definition.

Therefore when that by which the essence of a thing is constituted, by which the very nature is understood, has an order and a dependence in regard to something else, then it is certain that such a nature cannot be understood apart from that other, whether it is joined to it in the same way as the part is joined to the whole, as a foot cannot be understood without comprehension of an animal, because that by reason of which foot has the meaning of a foot depends on that by which an animal is an animal; or whether it is united in the same way as form is joined to matter, as a part of a composite, or accident to subject, so that it is not possible to understand pug nose without understanding nose; or whether it is a separate thing, as "father" cannot be understood without an understanding of "son," although these relations are found in diverse things.

But if one thing does not depend upon another according as it constitutes the meaning of the nature, then the one cannot be abstracted from the other by the intellect so that it is understood without it, not only if they are separate in reality, as man and stone, but also if in reality they are joined, whether in the manner of part and whole, as a letter can be understood without the syllable, and the animal without a foot, but not conversely: or whether, indeed, this conjunction is after the manner of that by which form is joined to matter and accident to subject, as white can be understood without reference to man, and conversely.

So, therefore, the intellect distinguishes one from another differently according to either of these operations; because, according to the means by which it composes and divides, it distinguishes one from another by this fact, namely, that it understands that the one is not the other. But in the operation by which it understands what a thing is, it distinguishes one from another, while it understands what the thing is, not by understanding anything concerning the other, or what may be with it, or what may be separate from it. Whence this manner of distinction is not properly termed separation, but the first type only. This kind of distinction, however, is rightly called abstraction in so far as the things of which one is understood without the other are objectively one and the same thing.

## QUESTION V    153

For an animal is not said to be abstracted from a stone, if by the intellect an animal is understood apart from a stone. Hence, since abstraction cannot take place, properly speaking, unless there is conjunction of things objectively, according to two modes of conjunction referred to above, namely, according as part is joined to whole, or form to matter, abstraction is twofold: one sort by which form is abstracted from matter; the other, by which the whole is abstracted from its parts. Now a form can be abstracted from matter if the nature of its essence does not depend on matter. But a form cannot be abstracted by the intellect from that matter upon which the meaning of its essence depends. Therefore, since all accidents are compared to substances as forms to matter, and the meaning of any accident depends upon substance, it is impossible for such a form to be separated from substance, but accidents are associated with substance in a certain order. For quantity is primarily related to it, then qualities, then passion and motion.

Therefore quantity can be understood in a substance before there is understanding of the sensible qualities on account of which it is termed sensible matter. And so, according to the nature of its substance, quantity does not depend on sensible matter, but on intelligible matter only. For accidents having been removed, substances do not remain unless as comprehensible by the intellect, since sensible potencies do not attain to the comprehension of substances. And concerning such abstractions is mathematics, which considers quantity and those things that follow upon quantity, such as figure and the like.

The whole, indeed, cannot be abstracted altogether from the parts. For there are certain parts upon which the meaning of the whole depends, since it is its essence to be a whole of a certain kind because composed of such and such parts, as a syllable is related to letters, and a mixture to elements. Such parts are said to be specific or formal since without them the whole cannot be understood, but they are supposed in the very definition of it. There are certain parts which are associated with the whole as such, as, for instance, the semicircle is related to the circle. For, in the case of a circle, it happens that it can be divided into two equal parts, or even more: but in the case of a triangle it does not happen that three lines chance to be designated in respect to it, because by this very fact a triangle is a triangle. Similarly it pertains to a man *per se* that in him is found a rational soul and a body composed of the four elements; hence without these parts man cannot be understood; and thus whatever parts are specific and formal must be posited in the very definition of man. But fingers, feet, and hands, and other things of this sort add to that contained in the idea of man; wherefore the meaning of man does not essentially depend upon these since he can be understood without them. It matters not whether he has feet or not: as long as there is supposed the union of a rational soul and a body composed of the four elements properly commingled, which such a form requires, he is a man.

We call material parts those parts that are not contained in the definition of the whole, but conversely suppose it, and so all signate parts are related to man as this soul and this body, this mouth, and the like, for these are material parts which are, indeed, parts of Socrates and of Plato, but not of man inasmuch as he is man: and therefore man can be abstracted by the intellect from these parts, and such an abstraction is that of the universal from the particular.

Thus there are two abstractive operations of the intellect. One corresponds to the union of form with matter or accidents with subject, and this is abstraction of form from sensible matter. The other corresponds to the union of whole or parts, and to this corresponds the abstraction of the universal from the particular, which is total abstraction, in which some nature is considered absolutely, according to its

## QUESTION V

essential meaning separated from all those parts which are not specific, but accidental.

Moreover, there are not any other abstractions different from these, in which part is abstracted from the whole or matter from form, because the part cannot be abstracted from the whole by the intellect, if it is a material part in the definition of which the whole is posited: or, even if it can be understood without the total essence if the part is specific, such as lines without the triangle, or letters without the syllable, or elements without the mixture. For, in the case of things which according to their essence can exist, though divided, the process is one of separation rather than of abstraction. In like manner also, when we say that form has been abstracted from matter, we do not understand this of the substantial form, because the substantial form and the matter corresponding to it are mutually dependent, and one cannot be understood without the other, because the proper act must be in its own proper matter: but it is understood of accidental form, namely, quantity and quality, from which sensible matter cannot be abstracted by the intellect, since sensible qualities cannot be understood without first a comprehension of quantity, as is clear in the matter of surface quality and color: nor can a thing even be understood as a subject of motion unless it is so understood as possessing quantity.

A material substance can be intelligible without quantity; but to consider a substance apart from quantity pertains more to the nature of separation than to that of abstraction.

Thus, therefore, in the operation of the intellect, a threefold distinction is found. 1. According to the operation of the intellect as it composes and divides, which is properly called separation; and this mode relates to divine science or metaphysics. 2. According to the operation which formulates the quiddities of things; and this is abstraction from sensible matter, which pertains to metaphysics. 3. According to the differentiation of the universal from the particular; and this concerns even physics and is common to all the sciences, because in every science there is a disregarding of the accidental and a retaining of that which is *per se*.

Certain persons, not understanding the differences of the last two from the first, fell into error, so that they viewed mathematics and the universals as separated from sensible things, as did the Pythagoreans and the followers of Plato.

**Answers to objections.** 1. It may be said: A mathematician, when he makes an abstraction, does not consider a thing other than as it is. For he does not regard a line to be without sensible matter, but he considers the line and its attributes without consideration of sensible matter, and so there is no conflict between his intellect and the thing, because, even objectively, what is of the nature of a line does not depend on that by which a material essence is sensible, but conversely: and so it is evident that deceit is not to be attributed to those who abstract, as is said in II *Physic*.

2. It may be answered: Not only can that be called material which has matter as a part of itself, but also that which has its being in matter, and in this manner a sensible line can, in a certain way, be said to be material. Therefore nothing prevents a line without sensible matter being understood. For sensible matter is not compared to a line as a part, but as to a subject in which it can exist; and so it is also in the case of surface and color. For mathematics does not consider a body as in the genus of substance inasmuch as matter is a part of it, but inasmuch as it is in the genus of quantity, perfected in three dimensions, and thus it [the body under the aspect in which it interests the mathematician] is compared to a body that is in the genus of substance, and considered as having physical matter, as an accident is compared to a subject.

3. It is answered: Matter is not the principle of diversity according to number, except in so far as, being divided into many parts, and receiving in each part a form of the same kind, it constitutes many individuals of the same species.

## QUESTION V 157

Matter, however, cannot be divided except by reason of presupposed quantity; if this is removed, any substance remains indivisible, and so the first principle of diversifying things that are of one species belongs to quantity. And this belongs to quantity inasmuch as by its nature it has location as constitutive difference, which is none other than the order of parts. Wherefore, even after quantity has been abstracted from sensible matter by the intellect, we can still imagine things of the same species, diverse in number, as many equilateral triangles, and many equal straight lines.

4. It may be answered: Mathematics does not abstract from all matter whatever, but only from sensible matter. The parts, or phases, of quantity from which certain types of demonstration are taken, as seems to be the case in that drawn from a material cause, pertain not to sensible matter, but to intelligible matter, which is found even in mathematics, as VII *Metaph.* makes clear.

5. It is answered: Motion according to its own nature does not pertain to the genus of quantity, but it participates in the nature of quantity in another manner, according as the division of motion has its source in the division of space or in the division of a moving object. Hence, to consider motion does not pertain to a mathematician, but the principles of mathematics can be applied to motion; therefore, as the principles of quantity are applied to motion, natural science ought to treat of the division of both continuum and motion, as is stated in VI *Physic.* And in sciences midway between mathematics and natural science one studies the measure of motions, as in the science of spherical motion and in astrology.

6. It may be answered: In composite things simple elements and their properties are preserved, although according to another manner, as the proper qualities of elements and their proper activity are found in what is composite. But what is proper to composites [as composites] is not found in the elements. Hence it is that the more a science is concerned with

things more abstract and simple, the more are its principles applicable to other sciences: whence the principles of mathematics are applicable to natural sciences, but the converse is not true, since physics presupposes mathematics, but not conversely, as is clear in III *De coelo et mundo*.

And therefore it is that regarding the natural sciences and mathematics three orders of sciences are found.

For certain sciences are purely natural. These consider the properties of natural things as such, as physics and agriculture, and the like.

Certain sciences are purely mathematical. These determine questions about quantity absolutely, as geometry about magnitude, and arithmetic about number.

Certain others are sciences midway between the two. These apply the principles of mathematics to natural things, as music and astrology. However, they are more closely related to mathematics, since in their consideration what concerns the physicist is quasi-natural, but what concerns the mathematician is quasi-formal: as music considers sounds not inasmuch as they are sounds, but inasmuch as they are proportionable according to number, and so it is in the others: and on this account they demonstrate their conclusions regarding natural things, but through the medium of mathematics, and thus there is no obstacle to their being concerned with sensible matter, inasmuch as they have something in common with natural science. Inasmuch as they have something in common with mathematics, they are abstract.

7. It may be said: The intermediate sciences, concerning which we have spoken, share in the nature of natural science according to what is material in their consideration, and they differ according to what is formal in their consideration; and therefore there is no reason why they should not sometimes have the same conclusions as those of the natural sciences; nevertheless they do not demonstrate these conclusions by the same method, unless according as the sciences are mixed and

QUESTION V 159

one from time to time makes use of what pertains to another, as the rotundity of the earth is proved in natural science by the motion of weights (gravity), while astrology proves the same by consideration of the eclipses of the moon.

8. It may be answered: As says the Commentator in the same place, that the Philosopher did not there intend to distinguish the speculative sciences, because in whatever way a thing is mobile, whether it be corruptible or incorruptible it falls within the province of natural science. Mathematics, however, as such, does not consider anything mobile.

However, he intends to distinguish things which the speculative sciences treat of, things which must be treated of separately and according to an order; although these three kinds of things can be applied to three sciences.

For beings which are incorruptible and immobile pertain precisely to metaphysics. But beings which are mobile and incorruptible, on account of the uniformity and regularity of their motion can be determined in regard to the motion they possess by the principles of mathematics; but in regard to the immobile corruptibles this cannot be said: and therefore, the second class of beings is attributed to mathematics, by reason of [i.e., through the medium of] astrology: but the third remains altogether proper to natural science, and so says Ptolemy.

*Article 4*

WHETHER DIVINE SCIENCE TREATS OF THOSE THINGS THAT ARE WITHOUT MATTER AND MOTION

**Objections.** 1. It appears that divine science is not about things separated from motion and matter. For divine science seems especially to be about God; but we are not able to attain to a knowledge of God except through visible effects, which are constituted in matter and motion. Rom. 1:20: "The invisible things of Him, from the creation of the world, are clearly seen, being understood by the things that are made"; therefore divine science does not abstract from motion and matter.

2. That to which motion in some manner appertains is not altogether separated from motion and matter; but motion in some way appertains to God: wherefore it is said, concerning divine wisdom (Wisd. 7:24), that it is active and more active than all active things. And Augustine (VIII *super Genes.*) says that God moves Himself without time and place; and Plato supposes that the first mover moves himself: therefore divine science, which treats of God, is not altogether separated from motion.

3. Divine science has as its function the study not only of God, but also of the angels; but the angels are moved according to election, since from being good, they have become bad; and likewise according to place, as is clear in regard to those who have been sent as messengers; therefore the things that divine science considers are not altogether separated from motion.

4. As the Commentator seems to say in the beginning of the *Physics*, all that is, is either pure matter or pure form, or a composite of matter and form; but an angel is not form, because if so it would be pure act, which is true of God alone; nor is it pure matter; therefore it is composed of matter and form; and so divine science does not abstract from matter.

5. Divine science, which is considered the third part of speculative philosophy, is the same as metaphysics, which has being as its subject, and especially being which is substance, as metaphysics declares; but being and substance do not abstract from matter, for otherwise no being would be found which had matter; therefore divine science is not an abstraction from matter.

6. According to the Philosopher (I *Poster.*), it pertains to a science to consider not only a subject, but also the parts and possible attributes of that subject: but being is the sub-

## QUESTION V

ject of divine science, as has been said; therefore it pertains to divine science to consider all beings: but matter and motion are certain beings; therefore divine science does not abstract from them.

7. As the Commentator says (I *Physic.*), divine science demonstrates by means of three causes: efficient, formal, and final. But the efficient cause cannot be considered without considering motion; neither, in like manner, can the final cause, as is stated in III *Metaph.* Hence in mathematics, because its objects are immobile, no demonstration is given through causes of this kind; therefore divine science does not abstract from motion.

8. Theology treats of the creation of heaven and earth and of the acts of men and many things of this kind, which in themselves contain matter and motion; therefore theology does not seem to abstract from motion and matter.

**Sed contra.** On the contrary is what the Philosopher says in VI *Metaph.*, that first philosophy is concerned with beings separable from matter, and with things immobile; but first philosophy is divine science, as he says there also; therefore it is abstracted from motion and matter.

Moreover, the noblest science is about the noblest beings; but divine science is the noblest science. Since, therefore, immaterial and immobile things are the noblest of beings, it is of them that divine science treats.

Furthermore, the Philosopher says in the beginning of the *Metaphysics* that divine science is of first principles and causes; but immaterial and immobile things are of this order, and therefore divine science treats of them.

**Response.** In order to clarify this question, it is necessary to know which one of the sciences ought to be called "divine science." It is to be noted, therefore, that whatever science considers a particular class of things as its subjects must consider the principles of that class since science is not perfected except through knowledge of first principles, as is stated by the Philosopher in the beginning of the *Physics*. But there are two kinds of principles.

1. There are certain principles that are in themselves complete natures, yet principles of other things, just as the heavenly bodies are in a certain way principles of inferior bodies, and simple bodies of those that are mixed. Consequently these things are considered by the sciences which treat of them not only as principles, but as things in themselves, and on this account not only is there study of them in sciences that consider them as principiates, but they have also a distinct science of their own: just as a certain branch of natural science deals with heavenly bodies, apart from that branch in which inferior bodies are considered, and about the elements there is some science besides that which treats of the mixed bodies.

2. But there are certain other principles that are not complete natures in themselves, but are only principles of natures, as unity of number, and a point of a line, and form and matter of a physical body. Consequently principles of this kind are not dealt with except in a science that treats of the things of which they are the principles.

Now, as there are certain principles belonging to any determined class (or genus) and extending to all the principles of that class, so also all beings, according as they communicate in being, have certain principles that are the principles of all beings. These principles can be called common for two reasons, as Avicenna says in his *Sufficientia*.

1. In one way, by predication, as when I say that "form" is common to all forms because it is predicated of any form whatever.

2. In another way, because of a relation of causality, as we say that the sun, numerically one, is the principle of all generation.

Of all beings there are, then, common principles, not only according to this first mode, which the Philosopher (II

*Metaph.*) calls having the same principles "according to analogy," but also according to another mode, as there are certain things numerically the same, existing as principles of all things, for example, principles of accidents are reduced to substances, and principles of corruptible substances to substances that are incorruptible. Thus in each grade and order beings can be reduced to certain principles of all beings. And because what is the principle of being for all things ought to be in the strictest sense being, as is said in II *Metaph.*, principles of this kind should be most complete, and on this account they must be especially in act and have nothing, or the very least of potentiality, because act is prior to and more powerful than potentiality, as is said in X *Metaph*. Therefore these principles must be without matter, which is potential, and without motion, which is the act of that existing in potentiality. Of such an order are divine things; because, if the divine anywhere exists, it exists above all in such a nature: immaterial and immobile, as is said in VI *Metaph.*

Thus, therefore, can divine things be considered in a twofold manner, because they are the principles of all being, and yet they are natures complete in themselves; in one way, for as much as they are the principles common to all being, and according to another mode, inasmuch as they are certain things in themselves.

But first principles of this kind, although they are in themselves most knowable, yet in relation to our intellect they are as the light of the sun to the eyes of owls, as is said in II *Metaph*. Hence by the light of natural reason we are not able to attain to them except as we are led to them through their effects; and thus the philosophers arrived at a knowledge of them, as is said in Rom. 1:20: "The invisible things of Him, from the creation of the world, are clearly seen, being understood by the things that are made."

Therefore divine things are not dealt with by philosophers except in so far as they are the principles of all things; and hence they are considered in that science in which things common to all beings are studied, which has being as its subject, inasmuch as it is being; and this science is termed among the philosophers "divine science." However, there is another manner of knowing things of this sort, not as they are made manifest through their effects, but according as they manifest themselves. And this manner the Apostle alludes to in I Cor. 2:11 f.: "The things also that are of God no man knoweth, but the Spirit of God. Now we have received not the spirit of this world, but the Spirit that is of God"; and (2:10), "To us God hath revealed them, by His Spirit."

And in this way divine things are considered according as they subsist in themselves, and not only in so far as they are the principles of all things. Thus theology, or divine science, is twofold. According to one approach, divine things are studied, not so much as the subject of the science but as the principle of its subject matter, and of this kind is that theology which the philosophers sought to master, which, according to another name, is called metaphysics.

But of another sort is that theology which considers divine things on their own account as the very subject matter of its science, and this is called Sacred Scripture. Both types of theology are concerned with the things that are essentially separated from matter and from motion, but in different ways, according as a thing can be considered as separated from matter and motion essentially in either of two ways.

According to one mode, a thing is called separate if by reason of its very nature it can in no way exist in union with matter and motion: and in this manner God and the angels are said to be separate from matter and motion.

In another way that can be called separate which is not by its very nature associated with matter and motion but can exist apart from both matter and motion, though it may happen to be found in matter. Thus being and substance, potency and act, are separated from matter and motion because, according to their very essence, they do not depend upon matter and motion, as mathematics depends, which never can have existence apart from matter, although it can be understood without sensible matter.

Philosophical theology treats of separated things, therefore, in the second way, as the principles of its proper subject. But the theology of Sacred Scripture treats of separate things in the first mode, as its own proper subjects, although in this science some things that are in matter and in motion may be considered because the manifestation of divine things requires this.

**Answers to objections.** 1. It is answered: Things that are not taken under consideration in a science except for the purpose of clarifying other matters do not pertain to that science *per se*, but only accidentally. Thus in mathematics certain things from the field of natural science are dealt with; and likewise nothing inconsistent arises in the case of divine science that it should treat of certain things which are in matter and motion.

2. It is answered: "To be moved" may be attributed to God not properly, but metaphorically, and this in a twofold manner. In one way according as improperly the operation of the intellect or the movement of the will is spoken of, and according to this sense a person is said to move himself, since he knows and loves himself. And according to this mode of expression the saying of Plato can be verified, for he said that the First Mover moves Himself, since, indeed, He knows and loves Himself, as the Commentator says in VIII *Physic*. In a second manner, according as that outflowing of effects from first causes can be called a procession, or according as a certain motion of the cause is in that caused, inasmuch as in its effect there is left a likeness of the cause. Thus the cause that was at first in itself is afterward in its effect by its own similitude. And in this way God, who confers a likeness of Himself upon all creatures, is said to be moved after a certain fashion through

all things and to proceed to all things. This manner of speaking is frequent with Dionysius. According to this mode is to be understood what is said in Wisd. 7:24: "Wisdom is more active than all active things, and reacheth everywhere." But this is not properly to be moved, and therefore the conclusion (proposed in the objection) does not follow.

3. It is answered: Divine science which has been received through divine inspiration does not treat of the angels as of a proper subject, but only as of those things that are considered in order to make manifest what is the proper subject matter. Thus, therefore, in Sacred Scripture there is treatment of the angels, even as of other creatures. But in that divine science which the philosophers pursue there is consideration of the angels, whom they call intelligences, in the same way as there is consideration of the First Cause, who is God, inasmuch as the angels are second principles set over the motion of the universe, but to whom no physical motion can be attributed. Moreover, motion that is according to election is attributed to the same order as that by which the operation of the will or intellect may be termed motion—an improper use of the term, a sort of metaphorical use. Moreover, the motion by which the angels are said to be moved according to place is not in relation to circumscribed place, but according to that operation which is exercised in this or that place; or because of a certain relation which they have to a place, although this relation is quite different from that which a corporeal body has to a place. Hence it is evident that "motion" in reference to the angels has no agreement with that by which physical bodies are said to be in motion.

4. It is said: Act and potency are more common (principles) than matter and form. Therefore in the angels, although there is found no composition of matter and form, there can be potency and act. For matter and form are the principles of a being composed from matter and form; hence in such

things there is found only composition of matter and form, one of which principles stands to the other as potency to act.

But what is able to be is able also not to be; therefore one part can be found with the other and without the other, and hence a composition of matter and form is found, according to the Commentator (I *De coelo et mundo* and VII *Metaph.*), only in those things which are corporeal by nature.

Nor does it matter that a certain accident is always conserved in a certain subject, as figure in the sky, since indeed the celestial body would be impossible without such a figure; because figure and all such other accidents follow from a substance as from their cause, and thus the subject is related to its accidents not only as passive potency, but even as active potency and hence some accidents are naturally always found in their subjects.

However, matter is not in this same way the subject of form, and therefore any matter that is the substratum of any form can also not be its substratum unless it is retained as a substratum by an extrinsic cause, just as we hold that it is by divine power that some bodies composed of contrary elements are incorporeal, as are the bodies of those risen from the dead.

But since the essence of an angel is according to its very nature incorruptible, there is in it no composition of matter and form. However, because an angel has not being from itself it is in potency to existence, which it receives from God; and thus its existence received from God is related to its simple essence as act to potency. Consequently it is said that angels are composed of that *ex quo est* and that *quod est,* so that existence is understood by *quo est,* but the angelic nature by *quod est.*

Moreover, if the angels were composed of matter and form, this could not be sensible matter from which mathematical beings must be abstracted, and those of metaphysics separated.

5. It is answered: Being and substance are said to be separated from matter and from motion, not by reason of the fact that it is of their nature to be without matter and motion, as it is of the nature of an ass to be without reason, but because it is not required by their nature that they should be in matter and in motion, although sometimes they are in matter and motion, just as the term "animal" does not suppose rationality, though a certain animal may be rational.

6. It is answered: A metaphysician considers singular beings, but not according to their proper natures as such and such a being, but according as they participate in the common nature of being. Thus matter and motion are considered by him.

7. It is answered: To act and to be passive do not apply to beings according as they are regarded as abstract beings, but as they are in existence. Mathematics considers abstract things, in the realm of thought (*in consideratione*) only. Hence these things, in so far as they are the subject of mathematics, cannot be the principle or the end of motion; and therefore mathematics makes no demonstrations through efficient and final cause.

But the beings that divine science deals with are separate from things actually existing in the real world; such can be the principle and end of motion. Therefore nothing hinders metaphysics from demonstrating through efficient and final causes.

8. It is answered: Faith, which is a theological habit, has the First Truth as its object, yet certain other things pertaining to creatures are comprised in the articles of faith, inasmuch as they refer in some way to the First Truth. In the same way theology has God primarily as its subject; but it treats also of creatures as His effects, or in whatever way they have relation to Him.

## QUESTION VI

## CONCERNING THE MODES ATTRIBUTED TO SPECULATIVE SCIENCE

Next, inquiry is made concerning the modes which Boethius has attributed to speculative science. In regard to this matter, four things are to be considered:

1. Whether in regard to the things of nature one proceeds by way of reason (*rationabiliter*) and in regard to mathematics, by way of discipline (*disciplinabiliter*), and in regard to divine things, by way of intellect (*intelligibiliter*).

2. Whether in considering divine things imagination must be altogether relinquished.

3. Whether our intellect can contemplate the divine form or essence itself.

4. Whether this can be attained by way of any of the speculative sciences.

### Article 1

#### WHETHER WE OUGHT TO PROCEED BY REASON IN REGARD TO THE NATURAL SCIENCES, BY LEARNING IN REGARD TO MATHEMATICS, AND BY INTELLECT IN REGARD TO DIVINE SCIENCE

**Objections to the first part.** 1. It seems we ought not to proceed in regard to natural sciences by way of reason. For the philosophy of reason is different from the philosophy of nature. But to proceed by way of reason seems properly to pertain to rational philosophy; therefore such a method is unsuitably attributed to natural science.

2. The Philosopher, in the *Physics,* often distinguishes the method of approach to rational conclusions from that by which conclusions are attained about physical things; therefore it is not proper to proceed by way of reason in natural science.

3. What is common to all sciences ought not to be exclusively claimed by any one: but every science proceeds by means of ratiocination, discursively, either from effects to causes, causes to effects, or from some kind of signs; therefore this method ought not to be appropriated by natural science alone.

4. Ratiocination is distinguished as contrary to scientific knowledge in VI *Ethic.;* but natural science is concerned with scientific knowledge; therefore it is not suitable that rational procedure should be attributed to it.

**Sed contra.** On the contrary is what Boethius says in V *De consolatione:* "Reason, since it regards the universal, though using neither imagination nor sense, apprehends imaginable and sensible things"; but to comprehend imaginable and sensible things pertains to natural science alone; therefore rational procedure is aptly attributed to natural science.

Again, it is said in the book *De spiritu et anima* that reason is concerned with the forms of corporeal things; but to consider bodies especially pertains to natural science; therefore a method of rational procedure is suitable to natural science.

**Objections to the second part.** 1. It seems that mathematics is not rightly said to proceed by way of learning, for learning seems to be nothing other than the receiving of knowledge; but in any part of philosophy at all knowledge is received, because all branches proceed by way of demonstration; therefore progress by learning is common to all phases of philosophy and should not be called proper to mathematics.

2. So far as a thing is the more certain, it seems that it is

# QUESTION VI

the more easily learned; but natural things are evidently more certain than mathematics, because they are grasped by sense, from which all cognition originates; therefore this method applies to natural science rather than to mathematics.

3. As stated in V *Metaph.*, the beginning of science is from that which is the more easily learned: but the beginning of learning is received from logic, which ought to precede mathematics and all other sciences; therefore the method of disciplined procedure should rather be attributed to logic.

4. The method of natural science and of divine science is derived because of the powers of the soul, namely, reason and intellect; therefore the method of mathematics likewise should be related to some power of the soul, and so for its method to be called that of learning is not a proper determination.

**Sed contra.** To proceed by way of discipline or learning is to proceed by demonstration and through certitude: but, as Ptolemy says in the beginning of the *Almagest*, "Mathematics alone, if one gives diligent attention to it, grants to the search of the inquirer firm, stable, and necessary certitude, inasmuch as demonstration is made by ways that are unquestionable"; therefore to proceed by the method of discipline is proper to mathematics.

Again this is clear from many places in the books of the Philosopher, where he speaks of the mathematical sciences as disciplinary sciences.

**Objections to the third part.** 1. It seems that to proceed by way of intellect is not the method proper to divine science. For intellect, according to the Philosopher, is concerned with principles; knowledge, with conclusions: but not all the things treated of in divine science are principles, but certain conclusions are there considered; therefore to proceed by intellect is not proper to divine science.

2. In things transcending every intellect, we are not able

to proceed intellectually; but the subject matter of divine science exceeds every intellect, as Dionysius says in *De div. nom.* (chap. 1), and the Philosopher in his book *De causis;* therefore such things cannot be intellectually considered.

3. Dionysius in *De div. nom.* (chap. 7) says that the angels have intellectual power inasmuch as they do not derive their knowledge of divine things from sensible matter or from composite beings; but such a power is above that of the human soul, as is also said; therefore, since that divine science which is here discussed is a science of the human soul, it seems that to proceed intellectually is not the method proper to it.

4. Theology seems to be concerned principally with the things that are of faith; but to understand is the end of the things that are of faith, according to another version of Isa. 7:9: "Unless you believe, you shall not understand" [Douay: "If you will not believe, you shall not continue"]; therefore this intellectual process should not be considered the method of theology, but its end.

**Sed contra.** On the contrary, it is said in the book *De spiritu et anima* that intellect is the property of spiritual creatures, but intelligence belongs to God Himself; but of such things does divine science principally treat; therefore to proceed intellectually is proper to it.

Moreover, the method of a science ought to correspond to its matter; but divine things are things intelligible in themselves; therefore the method of intellectual procedure is proper to divine science.

**Response to the first part.** I answer that, in regard to the first part, it must be said that the process by which one advances in the sciences is called "rational" in a threefold manner.

1. In the first place, on the part of the principles by which we proceed, as when we advance to something that must be proved by making use of the apparatus of reason, that is,

## QUESTION VI

genus and species, and opposition, and concepts of this sort which logic considers. And so we are said to proceed rationally when in any science use is made of the propositions that logic provides as principles; namely, according as we make use of logic so far as it has a teaching function in relation to the other sciences. But this method of procedure cannot properly be said to be that of any particular science, for in them error will arise unless we proceed from certain principles belonging properly to each. However, this method is rightly applied in metaphysics and logic since it is common to each science, and they have, in a certain manner, the same subject matter.

2. In another sense we say that procedure is rational on account of the end or goal established for the process. The ultimate goal, toward which the investigation of reason should lead, is the understanding of principles; in grasping and penetrating them we are enabled to form judgments. But when this is the result, it is called, not a process or a natural proof, but a demonstration. When, however, rational investigation does not attain to the ultimate goal, but remains within the bounds of investigation itself, when, namely, two possible paths still lie open to the investigator (which happens when one makes use of probable arguments which are adapted to produce opinion and faith, but not science), then rational investigation is distinguished from demonstration. And by this method we can proceed rationally in any science at all, as from probabilities the road is prepared for necessary conclusions. And this is another mode of logic made use of in the demonstrative sciences, not indeed as docent, but as useful. According to these two ways the process employed by physical science is called "rational," for logic, which is a rational science, is used in these two ways in demonstrative sciences, as the Commentator says in I *Physic*.

3. In a third way a method of procedure may be called rational in relation to a rational potency, inasmuch as in the process there is conformity to the way in which the rational

soul properly comes to know; and under this aspect the process of the science of nature is very properly called "rational." For natural science in its methods of proceeding observes the method proper to the rational soul in two ways.

a) As the rational soul receives from sensible things, which are more knowable as far as we are concerned, its knowledge of intelligible things, which in their own nature are more knowable (as I *Physic.* declares), so natural science proceeds from those things that are more knowable on our part, but less knowable in their own nature: and the demonstration which is through sign or through effect is that commonly used in natural science.

b) In the second place, the method of natural science has this characteristic of reason: as it is proper to reason to advance from one thing to another, so the same discursive method is employed in the natural sciences where from the knowledge of one thing we arrive at knowledge of another as from knowledge of an effect to that of a cause. And this procedure is not from one thing to another according to reason (or definition) alone which would not be according to the thing itself, as if from "animal" we advanced to the concept of "man." In mathematical science, indeed, procedure is through those things only that are the essences of things, since these sciences demonstrate only through formal cause. So there is in them no demonstration of one thing by means of another thing, but through the proper definition of that thing. For, although there are certain demonstrations made concerning a circle by means of a triangle, or conversely, this is only in so far as in the circle there is the triangle potentially, or conversely. But in natural science in which demonstration is made through extrinsic causes, one thing is proved by means of another thing altogether extrinsic to it. So the natural mode of the reason is especially served by natural science and hence, among all others, natural science is more in conformity with the intellect of man. A rational mode of procedure, therefore, is attributed to natural science, not because it applies to it alone, but because it belongs to it in a very special manner.

**Answers to objections to the first part.** 1. It may be said: The reason offered is concerned with the process termed "rational" according to the first mode; for thus the "rational mode" is proper to rational and to divine science but not to natural science.

2. It is answered: The reason offered concerns the process called rational according to the second mode.

3. It is answered: In all sciences a rational method is observed in so far as all proceed from one thing to another, as regards reason; but procedure is not from one thing to another thing except in natural science, to which this method is proper, as has been said.

4. It is answered: The Philosopher there employs "according to reason" and "according to opinion" in the same way; evidently, therefore, this pertains to the second mode assigned. For these two expressions the Philosopher attributes in the same way to those things concerned with human action, among which is the science of morals by reason of its contingency. Therefore from his words we can draw the conclusion that "rationability" in the first mode is especially proper to rational science; in a second way, to moral science; and in a third, to natural science.

**Response to the second part.** To the second part it must be said that to proceed *disciplinabiliter* is attributed to mathematics, not because it alone proceeds "by way of learning," but because this mode applies to it particularly. Therefore, since "to learn" means nothing else than to receive scientific knowledge from another, we say that we proceed "by way of learning" when our advance leads us to certain knowledge, which is another name for science; and this indeed occurs in the mathematical sciences. For, although mathematics holds the middle place between natural science and divine science, it is more certain than either of these others. It is more certain than natural science because its objects of speculation are not limited by matter and motion, whereas the considerations of natural science are confined to matter and motion. From the fact that natural science is concerned with what is material, it is dependent upon many more things; it is restricted by the necessary consideration of matter and form, and of the material dispositions and properties consequent upon form as found in matter. Wherever it is necessary to consider many things in order to come to a knowledge of a thing, cognition is thereby the more difficult. Hence it is said in I *Poster.* that a science which is attained by way of additions is the less certain, as geometry in comparison with arithmetic. Indeed since the considerations of natural science are concerned with things in motion, and with those things that have no uniform relationships, knowledge of it is the less certain, because its demonstrations are for the greater part based upon a fact that, contingently, might have other relations (to other facts or circumstances).

Therefore, in proportion as any science approaches to a consideration of singulars, as do the sciences of operation, such as medicine, alchemy, and ethics, it is the less capable of possessing certitude, because of the multitude of things that must be considered in such sciences; for errors frequently arise if any single fact is omitted, and also because of the variability of the facts themselves.

Moreover, the procedure of mathematics is a more certain one than that of divine science, because those things that are the objects of divine science are farther removed from sensible things, from which our knowledge has its origin, both as regards separated substances (for what we know by way of our senses gives us only inadequate knowledge of these objects), and as regards those things that are common to all beings, and so are furthest removed from those particular things that belong to sense knowledge. But the objects of

## QUESTION VI

mathematics are such as come under the senses and they are the subjects of our imagination, such as lines, figures, number, and the like. Hence the human intellect, receiving its knowledge from phantasms, the more easily forms concepts, doing so in regard to these things more certainly than it grasps things purely intelligible, or even such things as the quiddity of a substance, potency, act, and the like. So it is evident that the subject matter of mathematics is both easier and more certain than that of natural science or theology, and much easier and more certain than any of the practical or operative sciences. Therefore it is said to proceed by way of learning. This is what Ptolemy says in the beginning of *Almagest:* "The other kinds of speculation one should call opinion rather than scientific knowledge: theology, on account of its hidden and incomprehensible character; and physics, on account of the instability and obscurity of its matter. Mathematics alone will grant to the inquirer firm and abiding certitude, since it offers demonstrations through indubitable reasons."

**Answers to objections to the second part.** 1. It may be answered: Although in every science some knowledge is received, this knowledge is attained more easily and certainly in mathematics, as has been said.

2. It is said: Although the objects of natural science fall under the senses, yet, on account of the changeableness of these same objects, they have not the great certitude of things outside the domain of sense knowledge. Such are the objects of mathematics, which, according to their essence, are outside the realm of motion and matter and yet are able to come under sense and imagination.

3. It is answered: In learning we begin from what is easier, unless necessity requires otherwise. This is so because in the learning process we must begin, not with what is easier in itself, but with that upon which the cognition of subsequent things depends. Hence, in the acquisition of science, we should begin with logic, not because it is itself easier than

other sciences, for indeed, being of an intellectual order, it has great difficulty, but because other sciences depend upon it since it teaches the method of procedure for all sciences. For one must first know the method of science, rather than science itself, as is said in II *Metaph.*

4. It is answered: The methods of the sciences have their origin in the potentialities of the soul, owing to the mode which the potency of the mind has in its operation. Therefore the methods of the sciences do not correspond to the potentialities of the soul as such, but to the modes by which the potentialities of the soul are able to proceed. These are diversified not only according to the potentialities in question, but also according to various objects, and so the mode of any special science should not be denominated by any potency of the soul at all. Nevertheless it can be said that the method in physics is termed "by way of reason" according as it receives its data from the senses, but the mode of divine science, "by way of intellect" according as it considers anything in relation to God. And so also the method of mathematics is determined according as it receives its objects presented by the imagination.

**Response to the third part.** It is answered that, just as to proceed by way of reason is attributed to natural philosophy because in it a reasonable mode is especially observed, so to proceed by way of intellect is attributed to divine science since in it an intellectual method is especially employed. Moreover, reason differs from intellect as multitude from unity. Therefore Boethius says in VI *De consolatione* that reason is related to intellect as time is to eternity, and as a circle is to its center. For it is the nature of reason to be concerned about many things and from them to establish some one, simple fact of cognition. Whence it is that Dionysius says (*De div. nom.*, chap. 7) that souls, according as they have reason, encompass the truth diffusively. In this respect they are inferior to the angels; but as they resolve

## QUESTION VI 179

many things into one concept, after a certain manner they become the equals of the angels.

Intellect, however, in a converse manner, as compared with reason, considers first unified and simple truth, and in it grasps its knowledge of a whole multitude of truths, as God, by comprehending His own essence, knows all things.

Therefore Dionysius says (*ibid.*) that the minds of the angels have intellectuality inasmuch as they understand uniformly the intelligible essences of divine truths.

Thus it is evident that the consideration of reason finds its termination in intellection (or understanding) by way of completion, since from many facts the reason assembles one, simple truth. And again, the consideration of the intellect is the principle of that of reason in its way of composing and of invention, since intellect grasps many things in one. Hence that consideration, which is the terminus, or goal, of all human ratiocination is chiefly intellectual consideration. Moreover, the entire consideration of reason in its endeavors so to reduce the truths found in all the sciences, has for its end the knowledge of divine science.

For sometimes, as has been said, the reason proceeds from one thing to another according to the matter, as when demonstration is made through causes or through extrinsic effects. This it does by a method of composing when the process is from causes to effects, as it were, resolving them. But when the process is from effects to causes, since causes are simpler than effects and more immovable and uniformly permanent, the process is a kind of resolving different from the first, the converse of it. The ultimate goal of this method of reduction is attained, therefore, when one has arrived at the supreme and simplest causes, which are separated substances.

But sometimes the process is from one thing to another, according to reason, as when the advance is made according to intrinsic causes. This is by a method of composing when from most universal forms we proceed to consider those more particular. But it is a process of resolving when the direction is the opposite one (particular to universal), since the more universal is the simpler. Now, the most universal things are those common to all beings. Hence the final goal in this process of reduction is the consideration of being and of the things that are attributes of being inasmuch as it is being.

However, these are the things that divine science treats of, as was said above, that is, separated substances and those things common to all beings. Hence it is apparent that its consideration is, above all, intellectual. And so it also follows that it confers principles upon the other sciences, since the consideration of the intellect is reasonably the principle of speculation, on which account it is called first philosophy. Yet it is studied after physics and other sciences, since intellectual speculation is the terminus of what is rational, and consequently is called metaphysics or, as it were, *transphysica*, because it is attained by further reduction, after (transcending) physics.

**Answers to objections to the third part.** 1. It is answered: To proceed by way of intellect is not attributed to divine science as if this science did not make use of ratiocination in proceeding from principles to conclusions, but because its method of reasoning is nearest to intellectual speculation, and its conclusions nearest to its principles.

2. It is answered: God is above every created intellect as to comprehension. But He is not above that Intellect which is uncreated, since He, by understanding Himself, comprehends Himself.

In fact, He is above every intellect of those who are wayfarers in this life, as regards that cognition by which "what God is" may be understood; but not as regards "whether God exists." By the blessed, moreover, what God is, is likewise known, for they behold His essence. Nevertheless, divine science is not merely about God, but also about other things, which do not exceed the power of the human intellect in its present state in this life, inasmuch as something can be known concerning them.

3. It is answered: As was said above, human knowledge, or speculation, as regards its terminus reaches up, in a certain way, so as to attain to angelic cognition, not by way of equality, but by a kind of likeness [as assimilation]. Therefore Dionysius says (*De div. nom.*, chap. 7) that by the resolving of many things to unity, souls are rightly considered equal to the angelic intelligences, in so far as this is proper and possible for souls.

4. It may be said: Knowledge that is of faith pertains especially to the intellect. We do not, indeed, receive it as a result of an investigation by our reason, but we assent to it by the simple submission of our intellect in accepting it. We are said not to understand these objects of faith, since the intellect has no full knowledge of them; but this is promised to us by way of reward.

## *Article 2*

### WHETHER IN SPECULATION ON DIVINE THINGS IMAGINATION MUST BE ALTOGETHER RELINQUISHED

**Objections.** 1. It seems that in treating of divine things we must use images. For divine science is nowhere more competently treated than in Sacred Scripture; but in Sacred Scripture we are led, in treating of divine things, to images, since divine things are presented to us under the figures of sensible things; therefore in divine science we rightly use the imagination.

2. Divine things are not comprehended except in the intellect, wherefore in regard to them speculation ought to be of an intellectual order, as has been said; but intellection is impossible without phantasms, as the Philosopher says (I and III *De anima*); therefore in divine science we rightly use imagination.

3. Divine science becomes known by us especially through the illumination of divine light: but as Dionysius says (*Coel. hier.*, chap. 1), "It is impossible for the divine light to illuminate us from above except as veiled round about by a variety of sacred coverings," and these sacred veils of which he speaks are the images of sensible things; therefore in divine science we should make use of imagery.

4. Concerning sensible things, we must proceed with the aid of imagination; but we receive our knowledge of divine things from these sensible effects, according to Rom. 1:20: "The invisible things of Him from the creation of the world are clearly seen, being understood by the things that are made"; therefore in divine science we should make use of imagination.

5. In things regarding cognition, we should be especially guided by that which is the principle of cognition, as in natural sciences we are guided by the senses, from which our knowledge begins; but the principle of intellectual cognition in us is imagination, since the phantasms are related to our intellect in the same manner as colors to sight, as is said in III *De anima;* therefore in divine science we should make use of imagination.

6. Since our intellect does not employ any corporeal organ, the action of the intellect is not impeded by an injury to a bodily organ unless perhaps this bodily injury affects the imagination; but through injury to a bodily organ, namely, the brain, the intellect is impeded in its consideration of divine truths; therefore, the intellect in its contemplation of divine science depends upon imagination.

**Sed contra.** On the contrary is what Dionysius says (*Theol. myst.*, chap. 1), speaking to Timotheus: "Do thou," he says, "O friend Timotheus, in mystic visions leave the senses behind"; but imagination is none other than a sense faculty, since as to its act it is set in motion by sensation, as is said in II *De anima;* therefore, since speculation of divine things is especially mystical, in these considerations there should be no dependence upon images.

Again, in the consideration of any science, what causes error in it should be avoided; but, as Augustine says in his book *De Trinitate*, the prime error in regard to divine truths is the error of those who attempt to transfer to divine science those things which they know about corporeal things; therefore, since imagination deals only with corporeal things, it seems that we should not be dependent upon images.

Moreover, a lower power does not extend its dominion over that which is proper to a higher power, as is evident through the words of Boethius, V *De consolatione;* but to know divine and spiritual truths pertains to the intellect and to intelligence, as is said in the book *De spiritu et anima;* therefore since, as there stated, the imagination is inferior to intelligence and intellect, it seems that in regard to divine, spiritual matters, we should not depend upon images.

**Response.** I reply that it must be said that in any kind of cognition two things are to be considered: a beginning and an end or goal. The beginning, indeed, pertains to apprehension, but the end pertains to judgment, for the cognition is there perfected. Hence the beginning of any of our cognitions is in sensation, because from apprehension of sensation arises apprehension of the phantasm, which is moved by sense, as the Philosopher says. From this then arises intellectual apprehension in us, since phantasms are to the intellective soul as objects, as is said in III *De anima*. But the terminus, or goal, of cognition is not uniformly the same; for it is sometimes in sensation, sometimes in imagination, and sometimes in the intellect alone. When it is a case of the properties and accidents of a thing which are demonstrated by sensation, these adequately disclose the nature of the thing, and then the judgment regarding the truth of the thing, which the intellect makes, ought to conform to the things that are known with certainty by the senses concerning it. Of this order are all things of the natural world which are determined to sensible matter. Hence, in natural science, cognition should be terminated at sense knowledge, since we judge of natural things in accordance with what sense experience demonstrates about them, as III *De coelo et mundo* declares. He who disregards the data of the senses in regard to natural things falls into error. And those things are "natural" which are associated with sensible matter and motion both in their existence and in consideration of them.

But in the case of certain other things the judgment of them does not depend upon the data perceived by means of the senses, because, although according to their existence they are in sensible matter, according to their definite nature they are abstracted from sensible matter. Moreover, the most powerful judgment about anything is that which is according to the definite nature of the thing: but because, according to this definite nature, certain things do not abstract from matter altogether, but only from sensible matter and from sensible conditions, there still remains something imaginable. Therefore, in regard to such objects, it is fitting that judgment should be made according to that which imagination demonstrates; and of this order are mathematical objects. In mathematics, indeed, cognition as regards judgment should be terminated by imagination, not by sensation, because mathematical judgment goes beyond the apprehension of the senses. Wherefore a judgment made concerning a mathematical line is not the same as that concerning a line that is sensible, as in the case where a straight line touches a sphere at a point only, which applies to an abstract (separate) straight line, but not to a straight line in matter, as is said in I *De anima*.

But there are certain other things surpassing what falls under the senses and what belongs to imagination, as do those altogether independent of matter, both as to their existence and as to their consideration. Hence cognition of them, as to

## QUESTION VI

judgment, ought to be terminated neither at imagination nor at sensation.

Nevertheless we arrive at cognition of these things from the things comprehended by the senses or by imagination, either by way of causality, as when from an effect we know a cause (though this cause is not commensurate to its effect, but excels it), or by way of transcendence or abstraction when we separate the object from all those things which senses or imagination apprehend. These modes of arriving at knowledge of divine things from those that are sensible, Dionysius sets forth in his book *De divinis nominibus*.

Therefore, in regard to divine things, we can use both sense and imagination inasmuch as they are principles or starting points of our speculation, but not as ends or goals; as indeed the things that we judge to be divine are the very things which sense and imagination gave us initial apprehension of. However, to depend upon something means to be terminated [or limited] by it. Hence in divine science we should not depend upon either sense or imagination; though in mathematics we are dependent upon imagination, but not on sensation; whereas in regard to natural things we are indeed dependent upon the senses. Thus they err who maintain that in the three divisions of speculation the procedure is uniform.

**Answers to objections.** 1. It may be answered: Sacred Scripture does not propose to us divine truths under the figure of sensible things in order that our intellect should remain there (on that same level of the sensible), but that from these things it should mount up to such as are invisible: wherefore use is made of things most common, that there may be even less occasion for remaining at their level, as says Dionysius (*Coel. hier.*, chap. 2).

2. It may be said: The operation of our intellect in its present state does not proceed without phantasms as the principle, or starting point of cognition; but this does not

imply that our cognition is necessarily terminated by phantasms, since, indeed, what we apprehend we judge to be such a particular thing according to the kind of phantasm by which we apprehend it.

3. It is answered: The authoritative passage from Dionysius has reference to the beginning of cognition, not to its termination, or to the goal at which we arrive from sensible effects, by means of the three modes previously mentioned, namely, to the knowledge of divine things. Moreover, judgment about divine truths ought not be formulated according to the mode which these sensible effects possess.

4. It may be said: Reason itself proceeds in accordance with whatever principle is sufficient for leading on to that which we are seeking knowledge of. So the senses are this principle in regard to natural things, but not in regard to such as are divine, as has been said.

5. It may be said: The phantasm is the principle of our cognition since from it the operation of intellect has its origin, not as from a thing of passing importance, but as permanent and, in a way, as the very foundation of intellectual operation. As principles of demonstration should abide in every process of science, so the phantasms are related to the intellect as its objects, in which it beholds all that it does behold either according to a perfect representation or by way of negation. Hence, when cognition of the phantasms is impeded, it follows necessarily that in its cognition of divine things the intellect is altogether impeded also. For evidently we are not able to understand God as the cause of bodies or as above all bodily things or as apart from corporeity itself, unless we are able to imagine bodies; nevertheless judgment of divine things is not formulated according to imagination. Therefore, although imagination is necessary for attaining to any cognition whatever of divine things in this life, yet in the contemplation of divine truths we are not limited to imagination.

## Article 3

### WHETHER OUR INTELLECT CAN BEHOLD THE DIVINE FORM ITSELF

**Objections.** 1. It seems that we are not able to behold the divine form, at least not in this life. For Dionysius says in his first epistle to Caius: "If anyone seeing God, thinks that he beholds Him, he does not see Him, but some one of those things which are His, which exist and are known"; but the divine form is God Himself; therefore we are not able to behold the divine form.

2. The divine form is the divine essence itself; but in this life no one can see God through His essence; therefore neither can we behold His form.

3. Whoever beholds the form of a thing, knows something of the thing itself: but, according to Dionysius (*Theol. myst.*, chap. 1), our intellect, according as it is better, can be united to God, while at the same time it knows absolutely nothing of Him; therefore, we cannot behold the divine form.

4. As has been said, the beginning of all our cognition is from the senses; but the things that we know by sense perception are not adequate for demonstrating the divine form, or even such as are separated substances; therefore we are not able to behold the divine form.

5. According to the Philosopher (II *Metaph.*), our intellect is related to the manifestations of things as the eye of an owl to the sun; but the eye of an owl cannot see the sun; therefore neither can our intellect behold the divine form or other separated forms, which are by their nature most manifest (or intelligible in themselves).

**Sed contra.** On the contrary is what is said in Rom. 1:20: "The invisible things of Him, from the creation of the world, are clearly seen, being understood by the things that are; His eternal power also, and divinity." The divine form, moreover, is nothing other than Deity itself; therefore, by our intellect we can, in some way, know the divine form.

Again, on Gen. 32:30, concerning the passage, "I have seen God, face to face," the gloss of Gregory says: "Unless a man, in some way did, indeed, behold (divine truth), he would not feel himself incapable of beholding it"; but we do feel that we cannot perfectly know the divine essence; therefore in some way we have intellectual vision of it.

Further, Dionysius (*Coel. hier.*, chap. 2) says that the human mind tends to be elevated through visible things to supermundane heights, which means nothing other than to a knowledge of separated forms; therefore in some way we are capable of knowing separated forms.

**Response.** I answer that it must be said that a thing is known in a twofold manner: in one way, when what we know about it is *"whether* it is"; in another way, when *"what* it is" is known.

That we may have knowledge of the essence of anything (what it is), it is required that our intellect penetrate to the quiddity or essence of the thing itself, either immediately or through the mediation of such things as sufficiently reveal its essential nature.

In this life, however, our intellect cannot immediately attain to the divine essence or to other separated essences, because immediately it reaches only to phantasms, to which it is related as the eye is to color, as is said in III *De anima*. And so, immediately, our intellect is able to conceive the quiddity of a sensible thing, but not, however, that of an intelligible thing. Wherefore Dionysius says (*Coel. hier.*, chap. 2) that our analogous knowledge is not strong enough to extend its dominion into the realms of invisible objects of contemplation immediately. But there are certain invisible things whose quiddity and nature is perfectly revealed by the essences of sensible things that are known to us, and of such intelligible objects we can know what they are, though mediately; just as from what is known concerning the essence of "man" and of "animal," we come to know the relation of one to the other, and from this come to a knowledge of the nature of "genus" and of "species."

However, sensible natures, even when understood, do not adequately reveal to our intellect the divine essence, or even other separated essences, since they are not, naturally speaking, of the one genus. And the word "quiddity" and all other terms of this sort are employed with a certain equivocation concerning sensible things and concerning these other substances. Hence the likenesses of sensible things, when transferred to immaterial substances, Dionysius (*Coel. hier.*, chap. 2) calls "dissimilar similitudes" ("likenesses that are unlike"). In another mode are those things which, while possessing intellectuality, are found in some way in sensible things and so, by way of similitude, such substances are not adequately known from those (in matter).

They are not, indeed, known by way of causality, because those things that are found to have been produced by those substances in inferior things are not effects that are adequate to the potentiality (of those substances) so that thus one could arrive at a knowledge of the quiddity of the cause. Therefore, concerning these immaterial substances, we cannot in this life know their essences. And this is so not only as regards our natural way of cognition, but we cannot know them even by way of revelation; for the illumination of divine revelation comes to us according to our nature (enlightening our mind according to its mode of knowing), as Dionysius says. For, although by revelation we are lifted up to a knowledge of what would otherwise be hidden from us, this elevation is not of such an order that we possess this knowledge otherwise than by means of sensible things. Wherefore Dionysius says (*Coel. hier.*, chap. 1) that it is impossible for the divine light otherwise to enlighten us than when veiled by a variety of sacred coverings. But the road to knowledge which is through sensible things cannot lead to a quidditative knowledge of supernatural substances. Hence it remains true that immaterial forms are not known by us essentially; we can know only that they are, whether this knowledge is attained by natural reason drawing conclusions from effects in created things, or given by revelation through likenesses derived from sensible things.

Nevertheless it is to be noted that we cannot know of the existence of anything without also knowing its essence in some way, either with perfect cognition or with a confused knowledge. Therefore the Philosopher says (I *Physic.*) that things defined are known before the parts of a definition.

For it is needful that one knowing that man exists and seeking to ascertain what man is, should know by definition what this word "man" signifies. This could not come about in any other way unless he conceived a certain thing which he knew to exist, although he did not know its definition. For such a person has a concept of man according to his knowledge of some genus, proximate or remote, and of certain accidents which are externally apparent. Indeed, definitive knowledge, just as demonstration, must have its beginning in some pre-existing knowledge.

So we are unable to know of the existence of God and of other immaterial substances unless we know, after a fashion, what they are, although this may be a confused knowledge. In this case, however, such knowledge cannot be through the concept of any genus, proximate or remote, since God is in no genus, for He has "that which He is," His quiddity, only from His own being; but in all genera quiddity must be derived from or referred to another, as Avicenna says. However, other immaterial substances, since they are created, are in a certain genus. Although, considered logically, they agree in the same remote genus with sensible things, that is, in the genus of substance, yet, naturally speaking, they do not fall in the same genus; in the same way the heavenly bodies are

## QUESTION VI

not classed with those of an inferior order. Indeed, what is corruptible and what is incorruptible are not in the same genus, as is said in X *Metaph.*

Now, the logician is concerned with intentions (concepts) absolutely, according to which nothing hinders him from associating material things with immaterial, and incorruptible with corruptible. But the natural scientist and the metaphysician consider the essences of things according as they have existence in things. Therefore, when they find diversity in mode of potency and act, and a consequent diversity in mode of existence, they say things are of different genera. Similarly also God has no accidents of any kind, as will be proved later. In the case of other immaterial substances, if they have certain accidents, the accidents are not known by us, and hence we are not able to comprehend them, because by a confused knowledge, immaterial substances are known to us by our knowledge of the genus and the apparent accidents. But, in the place of knowledge of the genus, in these substances we have knowledge by negation, as when we know that substances of this kind are immaterial and incorporeal, not having figures, and other things of the kind. And the more negations we know about them, the less confused is our cognition of them, so that through subsequent negations the first negation is contracted and determined, as a remote genus is contracted and determined by differences. Therefore even heavenly bodies, so far as they are of another genus from that comprising inferior bodies, are known as fully as possible by us through negations, as, for example, by saying that they are neither heavy nor light, neither hot nor cold.

Moreover, in place of accidents, we have, in the case of the aforementioned substances, their relationships to sensible substances, either according to the relation of cause to effect or a relation of eminence. Thus, therefore, concerning immaterial forms we have existential knowledge, and we have, in place of essential knowledge, knowledge of them by way of causality and eminence: these modes Dionysius treats of in his book *De divinis nominibus*. In this way, therefore, Boethius understood that the divine form could be known by our intellect through the disregarding of all imagery; but he did not hold that the quiddity or divine essence in itself could be known.

**Answers to objections.** By these explanations, the solution of difficulties proposed is evident, because the first objections are concerned with that cognition which is perfect, and the others with imperfect knowledge, both of which have been discussed.

*Article 4*

WHETHER BY WAY OF ANY SPECULATIVE SCIENCE IT IS POSSIBLE TO KNOW THE DIVINE ESSENCE OR THE FORMS OF OTHER SEPARATE SUBSTANCES

**Objections.** 1. It seems that it is possible to arrive at an intellectual vision of the form of God through speculative sciences. For theology is a part of speculative science, as Boethius says; but it pertains to theology to contemplate the divine form, as is also declared; therefore it is possible to attain to knowledge of the divine form through the speculative sciences.

2. Concerning immaterial substances there is determination in some one of the speculative sciences because they form the objects in divine science; but whatever science treats determinately of any substance studies the form of that substance, since [all cognition is through form, and] the beginning of all demonstration, according to the Philosopher, is the essence of a thing (*quod quid est*), therefore we are able to consider the forms of separate substances through the speculative sciences.

3. The ultimate felicity of man, according to the Philosopher, consists in the intellectual contemplation of separated substances. Now, since felicity is the most perfect of opera-

tions, it follows that it should pertain to the best of those operations that fall under the domain of intellect, as can be learned from the Philosopher in X *Ethic.* For that felicity of which the philosophers speak is the operation proceeding from wisdom, since wisdom is the most perfect virtue of the most perfect of potencies, namely, the intellect, and in this intellectual activity felicity consists, as is said in X *Ethic.* Hence through wisdom separated substances are understood; but wisdom is one of the speculative sciences, as is declared in the beginning of *Metaph.* and in VI *Ethic.;* therefore through the speculative sciences we are able to contemplate separated substances.

4. There is frustration if anything is unable to attain the end on account of which it exists; but the consideration of all the speculative sciences is ordained to a cognition of separated substances as to a final end or goal, since what is most perfect in any genus is its end; therefore, if by means of the speculative sciences substances of this immaterial order could not be known, all sciences would be in vain; but this is unacceptable.

5. Anything that is naturally ordained for some end possesses certain predisposing principles by which it is able to arrive at that end, for nature is the principle of all natural motion; but man is by nature ordained to a knowledge of immaterial substances as to an end, as is affirmed by the holy prophets and by the philosophers. Therefore he possesses within himself naturally implanted principles of this cognition; but everything to which we are able to attain by means of these principles of natural knowledge pertains to the consideration of some one of the speculative sciences; therefore the knowledge of immaterial substances pertains to the speculative sciences.

**Sed contra.** On the contrary is what the Commentator says, III *De anima:* that, according to this position, it follows: either that the speculative sciences are not yet perfected, since those sciences have not yet been discovered by which we are able to know separate substances, and this is the case if it chances that it is because of our ignorance of certain principles that we do not yet understand these immaterial substances: or, if it chances to result from a defect in our nature that we are not able to discover these sciences, then it follows that, if any have been born and so endowed as to find these sciences, we and they are not men in the same way, but only equivocally; but of these two alternatives, the first is improbable, and the second, impossible; therefore, that we should know substances of this order by means of any of the speculative sciences is not possible.

Again, in speculative sciences, definitions are analyzed by which the essences of things are understood by means of the division of genera into differences, and by investigating the causes of things, and by consideration of their accidents, all of which contribute a large part toward our knowing what a thing is. But this we cannot know concerning immaterial substances, because, as has been said, naturally speaking, they do not agree in genus with these sensible substances known to us. Moreover, they either have no cause, as is the case with God, or this cause is deeply hidden from our knowledge, as is the cause of the angels; and even their accidents are beyond our comprehension; therefore there can be no speculative sciences by which we may attain to a knowledge of immaterial substances.

Furthermore, in the speculative sciences the essences of things are known through their definition: a definition, however, is a composite term, derived from the genus and differences of substances, but the essences of these immaterial things are simple and in their quiddity there is no composition with matter, as is maintained by the Philosopher and by the Commentator in IX *Metaph.;* therefore by means of the speculative sciences we cannot have an intellectual understanding of the aforementioned immaterial substances.

**Response.** I answer that it must be said that in the speculative sciences the procedure is always from something previously known, both in demonstrating conclusions and in coming to a definition. For, just as from propositions known beforehand one arrives at knowledge of a conclusion, so from the concept of genus and difference and of other causes of a thing, one attains to knowledge of species. This procedure, however, cannot be carried on to infinity, because in this case every science would fail both with regard to demonstrations and in the formulation of definitions, since the infinite cannot be traversed. Hence all the consideration of the speculative sciences is reduced to certain principles that man does not necessarily have to learn or to find out, lest he be thereby bound to an infinite process. But of these principles he has a natural knowledge, and of this order are the indemonstrable principles of demonstration, such as: "Any whole is greater than its part" and other things of a like nature to which all the demonstrations of sciences are reduced, and also the first concepts of the intellect as those of "being" and of "one" and the like, to which all the definitions of the aforementioned sciences can be reduced.

From this it is evident that nothing can be known in the speculative sciences, either by way of definition or of demonstration, except what is referred to the previously mentioned principles known naturally to us. Moreover, objects of this natural order of cognition are made manifest to man by the light of the active intellect, which is natural to man, by which light things are manifested to us only inasmuch as through phantasms they are made intelligible in act. For this is the act or function of the active intellect, as is said in III *De anima.* The phantasms, moreover, are received from the senses, wherefore the source of our knowledge of the aforesaid first principles is from sense and memory, as is stated by the Philosopher at the end of his *Posterior Analytics.* Thus principles of this sort do not lead us farther than to those things of which we are able to acquire knowledge from things apprehended by the senses.

The essence of separated substances, however, cannot be known through the things we perceive by means of sense, as is clear from the foregoing, although by means of sensible things we can know that substances of this order exist and we can know some of the conditions of their existence. Therefore through none of the speculative sciences is it possible to know the quiddity of any separated substance, although we can know the existence of such substances and certain of their conditions, as, for example, that they must be intellectual and incorporeal, and the like. And this is the opinion of the Commentator regarding III *De anima,* although Avempace had expressed a contrary view, for he thought that the essences of sensible things gave adequate representation of the essences of immaterial substances. But this view is evidently false, as the Commentator there says, since "quiddity" as applied to one or the other is employed with a certain equivocation.

**Answers to objections.** 1. It is answered: Boethius did not intend to say that through the science of theology we are able to contemplate what the divine form is in its very essence, but only that we know it is above and beyond all imaginable things.

2. It is answered: Certain things are, as far as we are concerned, knowable in themselves, and in the manifestation of such things the speculative sciences make use of their definitions in order to demonstrate their properties, as happens in the sciences that make demonstration through causes (*propter quid*).

But there are certain other things that are not knowable of themselves, to us, but must be known through their effects. If, then, the effect is adequate to its cause, the quiddity of the effect is taken as the starting point for demonstrating the existence of the cause and for investigating its essence in so far as its properties are discernible. If, however, the effect is not adequate to its cause, then the effect gives us a starting point for demonstrating the existence of the cause and certain of the conditions of its existence, although the essence or quiddity of the cause must be unknown. And this is what occurs in respect to separated substances.

3. It must be said: The felicity of man is twofold. The one is an imperfect felicity, which man may possess in this life, a felicity that the Philosopher speaks of, consisting in the knowledge of separated substances which man has by the virtue of wisdom. Yet this is imperfect, being only such knowledge or felicity as is possible on our journey as wayfarers, since the very essence of things, being itself, is unknown.

Of another sort is that felicity by which, in heaven, God Himself will be made visible to us through His essence, and other separated substances will be known; but this will be a felicity attained, not through any of the sciences of speculation, but through the light of glory.

4. It may be answered: The speculative sciences are ordained to an imperfect knowledge of separated substances, as has been said.

5. It can be said: There are inscribed upon our minds certain inherent principles by means of which we can prepare ourselves for perfect cognition of separate substances even if (in this life) we cannot attain to it by means of them. For although man naturally tends toward his ultimate end, he cannot gain possession of it by purely natural means or powers, but only by grace. And this is so because of the (supernatural) eminence of that end.

ON THE UNICITY OF THE INTELLECT,
AGAINST THE AVERROISTS OF PARIS

BY

ST. THOMAS AQUINAS

TRANSLATED BY

SISTER ROSE EMMANUELLA BRENNAN, S.H.N.

## TRANSLATOR'S PREFACE

If St. Thomas ever had time to grow reminiscent over his University days, either as student or as teacher, it is not probable that he recalled Paris as a calm abode of ivy-clad tranquillity. Leisure and peace may remain the ideal conditions for philosophical development; but it was in the midst of strife that St. Thomas studied, wrote, and taught. The conflicts of the hour were his *Deus vult,* as they must be for philosophers today. The peace which was his could have been only that assured companion of "much patience"; and for St. Thomas, patience meant endurance in activity.

Two major battles he fought at Paris: that in defense of the religious orders and that against Latin Averroism. His refutation of the leaders of the Averroist movement at the University, particularly of Siger of Brabant, formed the chief controversy of his life.

The problem created by the Latin Averroists was concerned with the interpretation of Aristotelian texts and commentaries, introduced into the West by Arabian scholars. Certain difficulties had arisen because of obscurities on the part of Aristotle himself. Notably there was the problem of explaining the dualism which Greek philosophy had established between the world of matter and that of spirit. Offering no clear or final solution of this question, the text of Aristotle lay open to various interpretations.

At the time of St. Thomas, two lines of commentators had produced opposing groups of Aristotelians. On the one side, were those who followed Averroes and Alexander of Aphrodisias, having as their leaders at the University, Siger of Brabant, Boethius of Dacia, and Bernier of Nivelles. On the other side, were those who accepted Aristotle in the main, but who did not hesitate to abandon theories that seemed to be opposed to truth, or to interpret questionable passages in the sense most conformable to the teachings of faith. This line had included John Philopon, Simplicius, Avicenna, and St. Albert. St. Thomas, though regarding Averroes as "The Commentator" of Aristotle, became the champion of the orthodox Aristotelians against Averroes' errors.

Of all the Averroist "heresies," that which was of greatest importance was the doctrine of the unicity of the active intellect. Averroes had interpreted Aristotle to mean that the human intellect is actually twofold: composed of an individual, material intellect, fundamentally the same in all men; and of an active, spiritual intellect, numerically one, in which the material, passive intellects of men commonly participate. Regarded as physically and topically separate from the body and material soul, the active intellect was deemed the source of universal ideas, the power by which the potentially intelligible was made actually so. The individual soul, containing nothing superior to matter, was, of course, considered corruptible. The active, universal intellect was thought to be eternal; but there could be no personal immortality. Nevertheless, Averroes had professed belief in individual immortality, saying that, by reason, he had necessarily concluded that the active intellect is one; but that, by faith, he held firmly to the contrary. This distinction was adopted by his followers who claimed that what was true in philosophy might be false in theology, and vice versa.

Obviously this doctrine of the unicity of the intellect had direct bearing on fundamental tenets of Catholic faith and philosophy. Besides its connection with the doctrines of immortality and of the nature of truth, such a teaching conditioned theories about the origin of ideas, the union of soul and body, essence and existence, the principle of individuation, freedom of will, and the question of personal, moral responsibility. More than any other doctrine of Averroism, it promoted pantheistic thought, fostered a new paganism in ethics and the destruction of social order.

It is not surprising that scholastic philosophers directed their writing and teaching against it, and that it incurred the official condemnation of the Church on three different occasions. The principal Averroists against whom St. Thomas wrote were Bernier of Nivelles, Boethius of Dacia, and Siger of Brabant.

a) *Bernier of Nivelles* was involved with the other two in the condemnation of Averroism by the Bishop of Paris in 1270. On October 23, 1277, he was again cited to appear before the council of Simon Duval, Inquisitor of France. Since at this time he is mentioned as "Canon of St. Martin of Liège," Mandonnet concludes that he had probably left the University after his earlier difficulty.[1]

This same author states also that Bernier and Siger were clerics, and that, following the trial of 1277, both may have gone to Rome, since Siger of Brabant had petitioned for a rehearing of his case. If this is true, probably Bernier also decided to remain in Italy, as did Siger, and that his death took place there.

Twenty-five volumes in the library of the College of the Sorbonne are ascribed to him.

b) *Boethius of Dacia* shares with Bernier of Nivelles only the faint renown of being listed with Siger of Brabant as one of those whose Averroist doctrines were officially condemned by Church councils at Paris in 1270 and 1277. Mandonnet says that Boethius was the chief one condemned along with Siger of Brabant.[2]

Tilly remarks that, in view of the importance and extent of their erroneous influence, all three were treated with great

---

[1] Pierre Mandonnet, *Siger de Brabant et l'Averroisme latin au XIIIe siècle* (Collectanea Friburgensia, apud Bibliopolam Universitatis, 1899), p. 267.
[2] *Ibid.*, p. 269.

mildness. "It was fortunate for them that the University exercised its own theological censorship and was able to keep in check the Inquisition." [3]

The last years of Boethius of Dacia are, like those of his associates, veiled in obscurity. Mandonnet, however, seems to accept the tradition that Boethius may have spent them as a member of the Dominican Order, though the commonness of the name "Boethius" makes this view doubtful. "We have a second possibility: That Boethius of Dacia, confronted by the disastrous consequences threatening to overtake him after the episcopal decision of March 7, entered the Order of St. Dominic. This was a means of evading the ordinary jurisdictions and of finding safety and repose in an atmosphere where the life of study at that time was most intense. A move of this sort would not be unprecedented. In that event all the difficulties, except one, in the matter of identifying Boethius would be solved." [4]

Recently Dr. Martin Grabmann has added to previous knowledge of the works of Boethius of Dacia by publishing two newly discovered opuscula: *De Summo Bono, sive de vita philosophi,* and *De sompniis.* [5]

The only other works composed by Boethius of Dacia known to be extant are said by Grabmann to be a set of *Quaestiones* about the Prior and Posterior Analytics, a *Tractatus modis significandi,* and fragments of a *Commentary on Meteorology.*

Previous to Dr. Grabmann's discoveries of *De Summo Bono* and *De sompniis,* Boethius had been thought of principally as a logician.

A study of the newly published treatises, however, reveals two features of importance for a consideration of the forces of opposition arrayed against St. Thomas.

---

[3] Arthur Tilly, *Medieval France* (Cambridge University Press, 1922), p. 233.
[4] Mandonnet, *op. cit.*, p. 246.
[5] Martin Grabmann, *Mittelalterliches Geistesleben* (1936), II, 200–24.

1. The *De Summo Bono* unmistakably shows the trend toward an exaggerated naturalism which the Averroist doctrine contained. St. Thomas later pointed out that the acceptance of the Averroists' teachings about the nature of the human intellect implied a complete overthrow of the Christian order. The result, in one way, is shown by this short work of Boethius. That Bishop Tempier's condemnation of the rationalist influence of Averroism was not unwarranted, a few excerpts from this treatise indicate.

"The highest good possible to man should be for him according to the intellect . . . which is the good of the intellect itself. . . . The highest good possible to man according to the speculative intellect is the knowledge of the true in individual things and delight in that knowledge. . . . Philosophers are those men who devote their lives to the study of wisdom. . . . For in the highest goods there cannot be excess and sin. . . . This is a philosopher's life, and whoever has it not, does not have a right life. The name 'philosopher' I give to every man who lives in accordance to the right order of nature and who has sought the best and highest end of human life." [6]

2. The second treatise, analyzing the cause of dreams, tends to minimize the genuineness of any supernatural "vision," though Boethius says they could happen by the will of God.[7]

More than anything else, this work shows the current influence of the medical studies being made, particularly by Arabian physicians. A minimizing of "magic" and an investigation of natural causes was beginning to prevail.

c) *Siger of Brabant* was undoubtedly the head of Latin Averroism at the University of Paris from about 1260 to 1277. For ten years he led the forces of a violent and dangerous revolt. Though refuted by St. Thomas and condemned

[6] *Ibid.*, pp. 209 f., 213 f., 216.
[7] *Ibid.*, p. 222.

by Stephen Tempier, Bishop of Paris,[8] he continued his opposition to the scholastic masters and to the Church itself.

In 1277, after he was brought before the Grand Inquisitor of France, and after Latin Averroism was officially condemned (March 7, 1277),[9] his career as a teacher was brought to a close. It is said that he appealed his case unsuccessfully at Rome, and the general opinion is that he died at Orvieto sometime between 1281 and 1284.

In 1300, Dante speaks of him in the *Paradiso* (canto X, 133-38), where he represents St. Thomas pointing him out as Siger of Fiore, renowned in dialectics.

Mandonnet finds no conclusive evidence to confirm the tradition that Siger was put to death as a heretic or that he was assassinated by his secretary.

The published works of Siger of Brabant include the following:

1. *Impossibilia*, a work on logic, edited by Baeumker, 1898.

2. A group of five works published by Pierre Mandonnet, O.P., in his *Siger de Brabant et l'Averroisme latin au XIIIe siècle*, 1899: *De anima intellectiva, Quaestiones naturales, Quaestiones logicales, De aeternitate mundi, Quaestio utrum haec sit vera: Homo est animal nullo homine existente.*

3. A newly found collection of *Quaestiones,* discovered by Dr. Martin Grabmann, and published in Ehrle's *Miscellanea* (I, 103-47): "Neuaufgefundene Quaestionen Sigers von Brabant zu den Werken des Aristotles," 1924.

In these works are to be found abundant evidences of those teachings of the Averroists which were especially in conflict with Scholasticism: monopsychism, psychological determinism, denial of moral responsibility, the eternal and necessary

---

[8] *Chartularium Universitatis Parisiensis,* ed. by Deniflé and Chatelain (1889), I, 481.
[9] *Ibid.,* p. 556.

production of the world by a series of intermediary beings, denial of Providence, and a doctrine of "double truth."

It is no wonder that, besides St. Thomas, practically every great Scholastic of the thirteenth century fought these teachings.

In the two summas, in the *Commentary on the De anima*, and in the *Quaestiones disputatae de anima*, St. Thomas repeatedly dealt with the psychological errors of Averroism; but in his opusculum, he employs all the resources of his dialectic. Continual and insistent as other refutations had been, this exceeds them all in gravity and sternness.

He begins by indignantly upbraiding those whose errors had continued despite correction.

That his attitude will not be any adherence to a principle of "double truth," he next indicates, saying that, although this false doctrine may be refuted simply on the basis of its departure from the truth as known by faith, he will deal with it on the plane of philosophy. Proceeding by rational arguments from Aristotle's definition of the soul, and an exposition of Aristotle's true doctrine, he confronts Siger with evidence of his intrinsic fallacies, and points out the difficulties that would be created by an acceptance of his false doctrines. Furthermore, besides showing that the theory of the unicity of the intellect is philosophically untenable, he proves by passages, first from the Greek, then from the Arabian philosophers themselves, that neither Aristotle nor the Peripatetic School had been accountable for it.

We should note that St. Thomas is more denunciatory of Siger of Brabant than he is of Averroes. The great Arabian he looks upon as an infidel worthy of pity; but the Christian Siger he reproves severely for assuming that, in withdrawing from the truth of faith, he could by reason find another truth.

In conclusion, his words dart to a fiery climax. The evidence brought forward, he says, has been gathered, not from the testimony of faith, but from the arguments and words of the philosophers themselves. But if anyone wishes to champion a pseudo-science and has anything to say in reply, let him not do his speaking in out-of-the-way corners or before youths incapable of judging in difficult matters. "Let him write an answer—if he dare—and he will find, not me alone, who am the least, but many others who know and foster the truth, by whom his errors may be refuted or his ignorance enlightened." [10]

Despite the fact that a tone of challenge may be noted in connection with other of the polemics, this triumphant and fighting finish shows St. Thomas in a different character from that which he maintains in his other writings. The ring of his *"Si audet!"* makes us think that Siger could not have been greatly encouraged to renew the conflict with his great adversary or with the "others," whom the words of their leader seem to conjure up in mass formation. What Siger thought or what we may think about their being men who "foster the truth," among whom St. Thomas was "the least," needs no comment.

It was of particular importance that in treating this problem, St. Thomas went for evidence to the very sources upon which the Averroists had drawn for support of their principles.

Because, in this controversy, St. Thomas made Aristotle himself the spokesman for orthodox opinion, the truth of Aristotle was saved. It was in a special manner owing to St. Thomas' victory over the Averroists in the battle waged over the nature of the human intellect that new translations of the works of Aristotle, from the Greek, were undertaken, and his philosophy became the permanent foundation upon which the Christian, scholastic system was built.

[10] *De unitate intellectus,* closing paragraph.

## CHAPTER I

## THE PURPOSE OF THE AUTHOR

As all men naturally desire to know the truth, so there is in men, by nature, the desire to shun errors and to refute them when possessed of ability to do so. Among all errors, moreover, the one that seems to be especially unbecoming is the error about the intellect; for we have been born to know the truth by the power of this intellect through the avoidance of errors.

Of late there has sprung up an erroneous doctrine about the intellect on the part of many men who take their starting point from certain works of Averroes. They assert that the intellect, which Aristotle called the possible intellect (he also inaptly called it "immaterial"), is evidently a kind of substance separate, by its very nature, from the body, yet in some way united to the body as its form; and further, that this possible intellect is one for all men.

Against this doctrine we have already written much. But since the boldness of those in error has not ceased to assail the truth, it is our intention once more to direct an answer to this false teaching in order that its error may be manifestly confounded.

At this time it will not be our method to show that the aforesaid position is erroneous as being repugnant to the truth of Christian faith: this is at once sufficiently evident to anyone. For if there is no diversity of intellect among all men, and the intellect appears to be the only incorruptible and immortal part of the soul, then it follows that after death nothing of the souls of men survives except the one common intellect. Thus would be destroyed any possibility of retribution, of rewards and punishments, or any diversity in recompenses.

However, we intend to show that their position is not less in conflict with the principles of philosophy than it is with the certain testimony of faith.

Since for certain men concerned in this matter the words of the Latin philosophers have no savor, and since they claim to be followers of the Peripatetics (though of their books on this subject they have seen none, except those of Aristotle, who was the founder of the Peripatetic school), we shall point out that their position is altogether at variance with his words and express opinion.

## CHAPTER II

## THAT THE INTELLECTUAL SOUL IS THE ACT AND FORM OF THE BODY, AND THAT THE INTELLECT IS SOMETHING BELONGING TO THE SOUL

First of all, there must be acceptance of the definition of the soul which Aristotle proposes in II *De anima*, saying: "The first act of a physical, organic body."

And lest, perhaps, someone may say this definition is not altogether applicable to all souls because of what Aristotle previously had conditionally stated; namely, "that it is necessary to predicate something that is common to all souls" (which they would understand to mean that such a thing cannot be), the following words of his must be noted. He says: "We have now given an answer to the question, What is soul—an answer which applies to it in its full extent. It is substance in the sense which corresponds to the definitive formula of a thing's essence. That means that it is the essential whatness of a body" (i.e., of a naturally organized body).

Lest it be thought that from this universal definition the intellectual faculty is excluded, this presumption is dispelled by what he afterward says: "The soul is inseparable from its body, or at any rate certain parts of it are—for the actuality of them is nothing but the actualities of their bodily parts. But, in truth, as regards other of its faculties, nothing prevents separation; since there are acts which belong to no body whatever." But this cannot be understood except of those acts that pertain to the intellectual faculty, namely, intellect and will. Wherefore it is clear that of the soul, which Aristotle had previously defined universally and called "the act of the body," certain faculties are the act of certain parts of the body; but other faculties are the act of no body. For it is one thing that the soul should be the act of the body, and another thing that a part of it should be the act of the body, as will be explained later. Hence also, in the same chapter, he shows clearly that the soul is the act of the body, since certain of its faculties are the act of the body, when he says: "One must consider in regard to the parts what has been said of the whole."

Moreover, in subsequent passages it appears even more clearly that the intellect is included under this general definition, as is shown by statements that follow. For, although he had previously given sufficient proof for the fact that the soul is the act of the body (since, if the soul is separated from it, the body no longer is in act as a living thing), he reiterates his position, because a thing may be called "actual" by the presence of a thing other than its form, if that thing were only an efficient cause; just as a combustible thing catching fire by proximity to something burning is "in act," and as a movable thing is "in act" when by the power of a mover it is set in motion. Hence doubt might arise in some one's mind as to whether the body is alive, or in act, by the effect of the soul's presence as any movable thing is moved by the power of an extrinsic agent, or whether it is in act as matter is, by its union with its form. There was special need for Aristotle to clarify his position, since Plato had held that the soul was not united to the body as its form, but rather as a "mover" and "governor," as is evident from Plotinus and Gregory of Nyssa. I may certainly cite these men, since they were not Latins, but Greeks.

The uncertainty of this problem, therefore, the Philosopher implies by what he afterward adds to earlier statements, saying: "We have no clear light on the problem whether the soul is the actuality of its body in the sense in which the sailor is the actuality of the ship." Therefore since, even after previous explanation had been given, some doubt remained, he added a supplement, saying: "Thus figuratively a definition and description of the soul is given," because no one has yet demonstrated the truth to the point of certainty.

In order, therefore, to remove this doubt, he proceeds to reveal the things that are, of themselves and according to their nature, the more certain by means of the things that are less certain in themselves, but more certain as far as we are concerned; that is, he undertakes his demonstration through considering the effects of the soul, effects that are its acts.

Hence he immediately makes distinctions in the operations of the soul, saying that an animate thing is distinguished from an inanimate by the fact of living, and that there are many things that pertain to life: namely, understanding, sensation, and change, both change of place and alteration connected with nutrition and growth; so that anything in which any of these characteristics is found may be said to "live."

Furthermore, having shown how these powers are related one to another—how a being possessing one without the others is said to live, and how one can exist without the other—he concludes in this manner: The soul is the source of these phenomena and is characterized by them, namely, by the powers of self-nutrition, sensation, thinking, and motivity; and all these can be united in one and the same subject, as in man.

Moreover, since Plato had supposed that there were diverse souls in man according as different operations of life were found in him, he had inspired doubt whether each one of these were a soul, *per se,* or only a part of the soul; and if they were parts or faculties of the one soul, whether they differed only according to reason, **or** whether they were distinct according to place, that is, in organic location. And Aristotle added: "Regarding certain of these questions, there seems to be no difficulty, but others possess uncertainty." For, he pointed out, one thing is made clear about the things that pertain to the vegetative soul and the things that pertain to the sensitive soul by this fact: that plants and certain animals from which a part has been severed continue to live, and in each part all the operations of the soul which had gone on in the whole organism appear to endure. But of those questions that are doubtful he makes note when he says: "Concerning the intellect and power of foresight, nothing is yet distinctly evident."

This statement he does not make because he wishes to show that the intellect is not a faculty of the soul, as the Commentator and his followers have perversely implied. For evidently this does not follow upon what he had previously said, that "some things, indeed, are uncertain."

Therefore he must be understood to have meant that it is not as yet evident whether the intellect is the soul or part of the soul; and, if a part of the soul, whether it is distinct as to place, or only according to reason. And although he says the matter is not yet clear, he subsequently adds what seems at first sight to be true: "But it seems that the soul is of another genus."

Now, this ought not be interpreted as the Commentator and his school have perversely explained: namely, that he said this because the intellect is equivocally spoken of in regard to the soul, or because he could not harmonize his conclusion with the previous definition; but how it ought to be interpreted is evident from what follows: "In this respect it pertains to the intellect to be 'separate': namely, as the eternal is distinct or separate from the corruptible."

In this, therefore, consists the fact that the intellect is another genus, because our intellect in this respect appears to be in a certain way eternal, but the other parts of the soul, corruptible. And because the corruptible and the eternal do

## THE INTELLECTUAL SOUL

not seem capable of union in the one substance, it seems that this one of the soul's faculties, namely, the intellect, should be separate, not indeed from the body (as the Commentator falsely maintained), but from the other faculties of the soul, and thus not communicate in the same way in the one substance of the soul. That this should, in truth, be the interpretation is clear from what follows: "The other parts of the soul, it is evident, are not separable according either to substance, to reason, or as to place."

Concerning this, inquiry had previously been made, and this, from the above cited passages, has been proved. Moreover, that the separability of the intellect should be regarded as meaning separability, not from the body, but that of the potentialities of the soul from one another, is evident from what follows: "It is certainly evident from reason that these powers are mutually distinct. Clearly, sensation is one thing, and opinion another."

Hence he points out plainly by this determination his answer to the question proposed above. For the previous inquiry had been as to whether one part of the soul were distinct from the others according to reason only, or by actual location. Having dismissed this question as regards the intellect, concerning which he makes no definite answer, he says that, in regard to the other parts of the soul, it is clear that they are not separable as to location, but are distinct according to reason.

In maintaining that the soul is determined by its vegetative, sensitive, intellective, and motive powers, he wishes to show that in regard to all these faculties the soul is united to the body, not accidentally as a pilot in a ship, but as form is united to matter, that is, substantially. Thus it will be made manifest what the soul is in general, this manifestation having been made only in figurative language heretofore.

Moreover, he further proves what the soul is by considering its operations as follows: Evidently that by which anything is first enabled to operate is the form of that operator just as we say we know by means of the soul and by means of science; although that we know by means of science is prior [in consciousness or reflection] to the fact that we know by means of the soul, because we do not know through the soul except in so far as it possesses science. Likewise we are said to be healed in body and in health, but in health primarily. Thus also it is evident that science is a form of the soul, and health a form of the body. And in this way he proceeds.

"It is the soul by or with which we live." This he says because the soul is vegetative; "and that principle by which we experience sensation," because it is sensitive; "and that by which we are moved," because it is capable of motion; "and that by which we think," because it is intellective. And he concludes: "Because it will ever be a certain nature and species, but not as matter and a subject."

Evidently, therefore, as he said above, the soul is the act of the physical body, so here he concludes that it is not only the act of the vegetative, sensitive, and motive powers, but also the act of the intellect.

Hence this was the opinion of Aristotle: that by which we understand is the form of the physical body. But, lest some one should think Aristotle did not say that that by which we understand is the possible intellect, but something else, then, plainly this is refuted by what he states in III *De anima* concerning the possible intellect. There he says: "By mind I mean that whereby the soul thinks and judges."

But, before we reach these words of Aristotle, which are in Book III of *De anima*, we should pause somewhat longer upon those remarks of his which are in Book II of *De anima*, so that from various statements assembled for comparison there may be clearly deduced what his opinion was about the soul.

# THE INTELLECTUAL SOUL 217

Now, after he had defined the soul in general, he began to distinguish its faculties; and he says: "The powers of the soul are vegetative, sensitive, motive, and intellective." That the intellective faculty is the intellect, he states clearly in what he adds later in explaining this division of powers: "One of them is, indeed, intellective, and is the intellect, as in men." He wishes, therefore, to make clear that the intellect is a power of the same soul which is the act of the body. And that he had called the intellect a faculty of this soul; and, furthermore, that the definition of the soul is commonly inclusive of all its parts, is evident from his conclusion: "It is now evident that a single definition can be given of soul only in the same sense as one can be given of figure. For, as in that case there is no figure distinguishable and apart from the triangle, etc., so here there is no soul apart from the forms of soul just enumerated."

Hence no other soul is to be sought for in addition to the ones already discussed, to which the definition of the soul given above is commonly applied.

In the Second Book, Aristotle reveals nothing further of his theory about the intellect except that he adds, farther on, that ratiocination and understanding are the highest powers, and that they are also the least because, indeed, they are in very few creatures, as hereafter will be made clear.

But because there is a great difference in operation between the intellect and the imagination, he speaks in regard to the speculative intellect of "another nature"; yet he postpones discussion of this question to the Third Book.

No one, however, should say (as Averroes falsely states) that Aristotle declares that there is "another reason" or "nature" in the speculative intellect because the intellect is not in the soul, or any part of the soul. This is immediately excluded as a possible interpretation in the beginning of the Third Book, where he resumes his discussion of the intellect; for he speaks here as follows: "Concerning that part of the soul, by which the soul possesses knowledge and wisdom."

Neither should anyone say, as some have dreamed of doing, that Aristotle says this only according as the possible intellect is distinguished from the active. For this passage occurs before Aristotle proves that there is a possible as well as an active intellect; wherefore he speaks here of the intellective part of the soul in common, according as it comprises both the active and the possible intellects (even as in the Second Book he clearly distinguishes the intellective from the other parts or faculties of the soul, as has been said).

Moreover, the admirable precision and order of Aristotle's method of procedure must be observed. Now, in the Third Book, he begins his treatise concerning the intellect, which, in Book II, he had left undecided. There he had previously allowed two things to remain uncertain.

First, the question whether the intellect is distinct from the other faculties of the soul only according to reason, or whether it is also distinct as to location. This he had dismissed indefinitely when he said: "We have no evidence as yet about mind or the power to think."

This position he at first resumes when he asks: "Whether in existence it is separable (from other parts of the soul), or is inseparable from the quantity of the body but distinct or separable according to reason."

In this passage he employs the phrase, "secundum magnitudinem" to indicate what he had previously spoken of as "separabile loco."

Secondly, he had left in uncertainty the difference of the intellect as compared to the other faculties of the soul, when in conclusion he said: "In regard to the speculative intellect, however, there is another nature."

This he straightway questions when he says: "What kind

## THE INTELLECTUAL SOUL 219

of difference the intellect possesses must be considered." He undertakes to assign it such a difference as could stand according to both of the premises already proposed: namely, whether the soul is separable spacially in respect to certain parts of the body, or not; and this intention he himself plainly enough indicates by his manner of speaking: "Turning now to the part of the soul with which the soul knows and thinks (whether this is separable from the others in definition only, or spacially as well) we have to inquire what differentiates this part and how thinking can take place."

From this it is evident that he did not intend to show that the difference was one of substantial separation from the body; for this position could not be maintained in view of both the alternatives proposed, but he intended to assign to the intellect a difference in mode of operation. Hence he continues: "And according to what manner it comes to understand."

Consequently, by means of those statements which we are able to gather from the words of Aristotle himself, it is evident, thus far, that he wished the intellect to be regarded as a faculty of the soul, which is the act of the physical body.

But since, from certain other words, Averroes has tried to make it appear that Aristotle meant that the intellect was not the soul, which is the act of the body, nor any part of such a soul, further statements must also be attentively considered.

Immediately after raising the question as to the difference between the intellect and sensation, Aristotle inquires in what way the intellect is like the senses and in what way it differs from them.

Now, previously he had concluded two things about sensation: namely, that a sense is in potency to sensible objects, and that a sense is impaired or even destroyed by the excellence of sensible objects. On this point, therefore, Aristotle makes inquiry, saying: "If to understand is the same as to experience sensation, or to be passive to something, then in the same way the intellect will be passively impressed by its intelligible object, and will be overpowered by the excellence of that object, just as the senses are by the too-great excellence of sensible things, and in like manner of other things."

Thus the question is this: Is the act of understanding something quite similar to that of experiencing sensation, or is it, on the contrary, different in this respect, that it is not possible?

To this question, he immediately answers (deriving his conclusion not from previous statements but from those which he makes subsequently, which later statements are, however, clearly evident from an analysis of the former) that this part of the soul ought to be impassible and not subject to the same alteration or corruption as the senses. Yet it has a certain passivity, but this is of another sort, according as the term, "to understand," commonly means "to be passive." In this respect, therefore, it differs from sensation.

But at the same time he shows how it agrees with sensation: for, indeed, this part must be capable of impression by intelligible species and be in potency to species of this kind, and not, by its own nature, in act—even as he had previously stated that a sense is in potency to sensible objects and not, of itself, in act. From this he concludes that the intellect must be related to intelligible objects just as a sense is to sensible things.

Now, he stated this in order to reject the opinion of Empedocles and other ancient philosophers who taught that the knower is of the same nature as the thing known, so that, being composed of earth, we know earth, and being also of water, we know water.

Aristotle, however, had shown previously that this is not true in regard to the senses, because a sense faculty is not in act, but only in potency to that which it experiences as a sensation; and the same, he says, obtains in regard to the

## THE INTELLECTUAL SOUL 221

intellect. There is, nevertheless, this difference between the senses and the intellect: that each sense is not capable of experiencing all sensations, but sight is in potency only to color, hearing to sound, and so of the others; whereas the intellect is, absolutely, empowered to know all things.

The ancient philosophers, thinking that the knower had to possess the same nature as the object known, had said furthermore that this fact, that the soul was capable of knowing all beings, must be on account of its being composed of the principles of all things. But, because Aristotle had now proved by comparison with sensation that the intellect is not in act as regards what it comes to know, but in potency only, he concludes, on the contrary, that since the intellect knows all things, it must be without any mixture; that is, not composed of all the elements, as Empedocles had stated.

To support this theory, he also calls upon the testimony of Anaxagoras, even though he had spoken not of this same human intellect, but of that mind (*Nous*) which moves all things. But just as Anaxagoras had declared that that intellect, in order to govern all things by setting them in motion and keeping each in its proper course, must be simple, or unmixed, so we can say of the human intellect that it must be simple in order to know all; and this Aristotle consequently proves, and the Greek text says:

"Now, that which is within, evidently hinders and prevents the extraneous from entering, as can be understood by a comparison with vision." For if there should be any color intrinsic to the pupil of the eye, that interior color would prevent the seeing of the color outside, and in some manner hinder the eye from seeing other things. Likewise, if any nature of those things which the intellect knows—for example, earth or water, warmth or cold, or anything else of the sort—were intrinsic to the intellect, that intrinsic nature would be an obstacle to the intellect, and in some way prevent its knowing other things. Since, therefore, the intellect does know all things, Aristotle concluded that it could not possess any determinate nature derived from the natures of sensible things which it knew, but that its nature was constituted by this alone, that it must be possible of determination; that is, that as regards its nature it must be in potency to those things which are intelligible, but become active by understanding them in act; just as the senses are made to be in act by the sensible in act, as he had previously said in the Second Book.

He concludes, therefore, that the intellect, before understanding renders it "in act," is not actively any of the things which exist—a conclusion which is contrary to what the ancients claimed: namely, that it was actually all things.

Moreover, because he had mentioned the statement of Anaxagoras in which he speaks of that intellect which governs all things, Aristotle, lest anyone believe that he had drawn his conclusion about that same intellect, employs this manner of explanation: "Anaxagoras called this the soul's intellect. I speak, however, of that intellect by which the soul thinks and understands, which is actively none of those things which exist before they are understood."

From this, two facts are evident.

First, that he certainly is not speaking here of an intellect which is some kind of separate substance, but of the intellect which, as he said above, is that power and faculty of the soul by which the soul understands. Secondly, the fact that he had previously proved; namely, that the intellect has no nature which is determinate in act.

He has not yet proved that it is not a power existing in a body (as Averroes says), but this he immediately concludes from the foregoing, when he says: "Therefore the rational faculty has no admixture of that which is corporeal."

This second statement he proves by means of the first, which he previously explained: namely, that the intellect posesses actively none of the natures of sensible things. From this it is evident that there is in it no union with anything corporeal; for if it were intermingled with some bodily substance, it would possess some kind of corporeal nature. And he adds: "For indeed, a thing would become some kind of thing, either warm or cold, if it were united to a bodily organ, just as in the case of the sensitive faculties."

Now, each sense is proportioned to its own organ and is bound, as it were, or restricted to its own nature. Hence, according to the immutability of the organ, the operation of each sense is immutable.

Thus, therefore, he understood that the intellect was not blended with the body; namely, that it has no organ as have the senses. Moreover, that the soul's intellect has no organ is clear from the statement of those who say that the soul is the *locus* of the intelligible species (accepting the term "locus" broadly in the sense of Plato, as meaning that which is all-receptive); unless to be the locus of the species is not proper to the whole soul, but to the intellect alone. For the sensitive part of the soul does not receive species into itself, but in an organ. The intellective faculty, however, receives them in no organ, but in itself. Moreover, the *locus* of the species is not such that it possesses these in act by its nature, but that it is in potency to possess them.

Since, therefore, he has shown what befits the intellect, by means of comparison with the senses, he now returns to what he had first said: that the intellective faculty must be capable of receiving species; and so, with admirable subtlety, by means of a likeness, he concludes to dissimilarity. Hence he subsequently shows that the passibility of the senses and that of the intellect are not similar by the fact that a sense faculty is disturbed by the excellence of a sensible object, but the intellect is not overpowered by the excellence of its intelligible object. The reason of this he assigns as derived from the preceding discussion: namely, that the sensitive faculty is not incorporeal, but the intellectual is, being "separate."

fThis last word, "separate," some have especially seized

upon as a prop for their error, for they would interpret him to mean by it that the intellect is neither the soul nor a faculty of the soul, but a separate substance; but they too quickly forget what Aristotle said but a little before. Now, just as here he says that the sense faculties are not incorporeal, but the intellect is separate, so previously he had said that the intellect would be of a certain quality, either warm or cold, if it possessed any organ, as the sense faculties do.

By this method of reasoning here, he is stating that the senses are not incorporeal, but the intellect is "separate," since a sense faculty has an organ, but the intellect has not.

Most evidently, therefore, it appears from the words of Aristotle that, without any doubt, this was his opinion about the possible intellect: namely, that the intellect is some part of the soul, which is the act of the body; but that, nevertheless, the soul's intellect has no corporeal organ, as have the other powers of the soul.

Moreover, how this can be—that the soul is the form of the body, and yet that some power of the soul should not be a power of the body—is not difficult to understand if we consider that same situation in regard to other things. For we see, in many cases, that a certain form is the act of a body composed of a mixture of elements, and yet it has a certain power which is not that of any of those elements, but which belongs to such a form from some other principle: namely, from a heavenly body, just as a magnet has the power of attracting iron, and jasper has the power of checking the flow of blood. And we see that, by degrees, those forms which are the nobler possess powers which more and more exceed those of matter. Wherefore the highest of forms, which is the human soul, possesses one power which altogether transcends the material body: namely, the intellect.

In this way, therefore, is the intellect "separate," since it is not a corporeal power, but a power in the soul; though this same soul is the act of the body. Neither do we say that the soul, in which the intellect resides, so excels its material body that it does not require to be in a body, but only that the intellect, which Aristotle calls a power of the soul, is not the act of the body.

Nor is the soul the act of the body through the mediation of its faculties, but it is itself, *per se*, the act of the body, giving to it its specific nature; whereas some of its faculties are the acts of certain parts of the body, perfecting them as regards certain operations.

Thus that faculty which is the intellect is the act of no part of the body, since it requires no corporeal organ.

And lest it seem to anyone that I say these things according to personal interpretation, departing from the intention of Aristotle, the words of Aristotle himself can be cited which expressly state the same opinion. For, in II *Physic.* he asks just how far one ought to know a species and what a thing is: For it does not pertain to physics to study every form. He subsequently gives as his answer: "In the same way as a physician must know a nerve, or as the smith must know bronze: that is, in view of a certain end."

And to what "end" he has reference, he later shows: "In view of whatever the purpose of each is."

This is as if he would say: The physician studies the nerve only inasmuch as it pertains to the health, on account of which the physician considers the nerve; and likewise, the smith considers the bronze only in view of his craft; and since the physician considers the form so far as it is in matter—for thus it is the form of a body subject to change—in like manner, it must be understood that natural science considers a form only inasmuch as it is in matter. The terminus of the physicist's consideration of forms is in those forms which are in matter after a certain fashion, but which, in another way, are not in matter. For these forms are on the boundary line of separate and immaterial forms; wherefore, he adds: "Regarding this, the consideration of the physicist is, indeed, of forms which are separate, but as they are specific forms in matter."

What these forms are, he indicates, saying: "Man generates man from matter,—man, that is, and the sun."

The form of man, therefore, is in matter and yet separate. It is in matter inasmuch as it gives existence to the body, and thus it is, indeed, the cause of generation; but it is separate as regards that faculty which is properly that of man: namely, the intellect.

It is not impossible, therefore, that a form should be in matter and that a faculty of it should be separate, as has been shown in respect to the intellect.

CHAPTER III

REASONS OFFERED BY THOSE HOLDING THAT
THE INTELLECT IS NOT A FACULTY OF
THE SOUL, AND REFUTATION OF THE
SAME

There are still some, however, who undertake to show in another way that the opinion of Aristotle was that the intellect is not in the soul, that it is not a faculty of the soul which is united to the body as its form.

In many places, Aristotle says that the intellect is eternal and incorruptible, as, for example, he declares in II *De anima:* "This befits a separate form alone, as eternal is distinguished from corruptible."

And in Book I, where he says: "The mind seems to be an independent substance, and to be incapable of being destroyed." He has also stated in Book III: "The separated form alone is that which truly is, and this only is immortal and eternal."

This last quotation, however, some do not apply to the possible, but to the active intellect.

From all these passages it is clear that Aristotle wished it understood that the intellect is something incorruptible. Yet it seems that nothing incorruptible could be the form of a corruptible body. For, indeed, it is not accidental to this form, but pertains to it essentially to be in matter; otherwise from the union of matter and form there would result only an accidental whole. But nothing can exist without that which belongs to it essentially; consequently the form of the body cannot exist without the body. If, therefore, the body is corruptible, it follows necessarily that the form of the body also is corruptible.

Furthermore, forms separated from matter, and forms existing in matter, are not of the same species, as is proved in VII *Metaph*. Much less, therefore, can one and the same form, numerically, be now incorporeal, and now in a body. Hence, if the body is destroyed, the form of the body either will be destroyed or will pass into another body. If, therefore, the intellect is the form of the body, it seems to follow of necessity that the intellect is corruptible.

Now, it must be noted that this manner of reasoning influenced many philosophers: Gregory of Nyssa, for example, interpreted Aristotle in a contrary way by supposing that, because he had said that the soul is the form of the body, he judged it to be corruptible. Certain others, moreover, because of this same statement, have supposed that the soul migrates from one body to another. Still others have held that the soul possesses some kind of incorruptible body from which it is never separated. Hence it must be shown from Aristotle's words how it was that he judged that the soul was the form of the body, and yet judged also that it was incorruptible.

In XI *Metaph.*, after he had explained that forms are not antecedent to their matter—because, just as at the time when a man is healed, simultaneously there is health; and as the figure of a bronze sphere is simultaneous with the bronze figure—he next inquires whether any form remains after the corruption of the matter, and he answers in the affirmative, according to the opinion of Boethius: "But it must be considered whether, in truth, anything does remain afterward apart from the matter. In certain cases nothing would hinder this being so, if the soul were of this order: that not all of it would remain—for, perhaps, that would be impossible—but that the intellect, of all its powers, would remain."

Hence, it is evident, he says, that nothing would prevent the intellectual faculty of the soul, which is the form, from

## INTELLECT A FACULTY OF THE SOUL

remaining after the body, even though it did not exist before the body. For, although he had said, absolutely, that efficient causes are antecedent, but not formal causes, he does not question whether any form might exist prior to matter, but whether any form could remain after matter; and he says that nothing would hinder this on the part of that form which is the soul as regards its intellectual faculty.

Since, therefore, according to the foregoing words of Aristotle, this form which is the soul could continue to exist after the body—not in its entirety, but the intellect—it remains to consider why the intellectual part of the soul should survive the body rather than the other faculties, and rather than other forms which do not survive their matter. The reason of this, indeed, can be gathered from the words of Aristotle himself. For he says in III *De anima:* "The separate [form] is that alone which truly exists, and that alone which is immortal and eternal."

He seems, therefore, to assign this as a reason: that since the intellect alone seems to be immortal and eternal, it alone is separate. But concerning what intellect it is that he here speaks of, there can be doubt. According to some, he is speaking of the possible intellect; according to others, of the active. But, that both these groups of interpreters are mistaken is evident if the words of Aristotle are considered attentively. For both the possible and the active intellect Aristotle had called "separate." It is certain, therefore, that anything he may say of either the active or the possible intellect individually can be understood as applying to the whole intellectual faculty, since it possesses no corporeal organ of operation, as is evident from Aristotle's own words

Moreover, Aristotle had said in I *De anima:* If there is any way of acting or being acted upon proper to soul, soul will be capable of separate existence; if there is none, its separate existence is impossible. Rather [its existence] is that with which it shares a common nature.

Since everything operates inasmuch as it exists as a being, so the mode of the action of each thing is conformed to its mode of existence. Therefore forms that have no operation except in conjunction with their matter do not themselves act; but it is the composite that acts through its form. Wherefore forms of this kind, properly speaking, are not; but something is possessed by them. In the same way as heat does not warm, but something hot warms; so also heat itself does not exist by means of that which *has* heat, properly speaking; but that which possesses heat does exist through that which is heat-in-itself.

On this account, Aristotle says in X *Metaph.* that it is not truly said of accidents that they are "beings," but more truly that they are "of a being"; and the same reasoning is employed about substantial forms that have no operation when not united with matter, except that the principle of substantial existence belongs to this form. Therefore a form that possesses an operation of its own, according to any of its faculties, or a power independent of matter, is subsistent; nor does it exist by means of the existence of the composite, as do other forms, but rather the composite exists through it. Hence, if a composite is destroyed, that form which possesses existence from the composite is likewise destroyed. On the other hand, it would not follow that the destruction of a composite would bring about the destruction also of a form by whose existence the composite exists, and which does not owe its existence to that of the composite.

If, however, some one objects that Aristotle (I *De anima*) says: "To understand and to love and to hate are not its activities, not phenomena of the soul, but activities of him possessing the capacity to know and to love and to hate. Wherefore in case of corruption the soul neither remembers nor loves, for these things do not belong to it properly, but were common attributes, as the saying is"—then an answer is provided by the statement of Themistius who, commenting on

## INTELLECT A FACULTY OF THE SOUL

this says: "Aristotle here assumes more the attitude of one in doubt than of one teaching authoritatively."

Now, at this point, he had not yet refuted the opinion of those who said that the intellect and the senses are not different; wherefore in this entire chapter he speaks of the intellect as of a sense faculty. This is particularly apparent where he proves the incorruptibility of the intellect by the example of a sense faculty that is not impaired by old age. Hence throughout he speaks conditionally and in a way to imply doubt as if seeking an answer, always linking things that pertain to the intellect with mention of the senses—a fact made especially evident by what he says in the beginning of this discussion: "We may admit to the full that being pained or pleased, or thinking, are movements (each of them a 'being moved')."

If, however, anyone holds that Aristotle is speaking precisely, there remains this reply: that to understand is said to be an act of the intellect united to the body, not *per se*, but *per accidens*, inasmuch as the object of the intellect (the phantasm) is in a corporeal organ; but the act of the intellect is not exercised through a corporeal organ.

However, someone may inquire further and ask: "If the intellect is incapable of understanding without the phantasm, how will the soul have any operation after it has been separated from the body?" We reply that whoever raises this objection ought to know that the solution of this problem does not pertain to natural philosophy. Hence, in II *Physic.*, when speaking of the soul, Aristotle says: "How the separable form will be related to other things, and what kind of being it is, is the task of first philosophy to determine. Now, the separated soul must be judged to possess a mode of knowledge other than that which the soul has while conjoined with matter"—a knowledge like that of other separate substances.

Therefore, not without reason, Aristotle inquires, in III *De anima,* whether an intellect not separated from spacial magnitude can know anything that is separate. By this question he gives us to understand that the separated intellect is able to understand something which the intellect which is not separate is incapable of knowing. In these same words, moreover, it is to be noted that, whereas he had formerly called both the possible and the active intellect "separate," so here he speaks of both as "not separate." For they are "separate" to the extent that their acts are not the acts of any corporeal organ; yet they are "not separate" in that each is a faculty or power of the soul, which is the act of the body, as has previously been said.

Furthermore, it is most certainly possible to show that Aristotle solved questions of this kind in those books which, from what he says in the beginning of XII *Metaph.*, we are sure that he wrote concerning separated substances; and of these books I have seen fourteen, though they have not yet been translated into our language.

Accordingly, it is clear that his reasoning involves no necessary contradiction: It is essential to the soul that it should be united to a body, but by this it is restricted only accidentally, not on its own part, but on the part of the body, which is corruptible; just as, *per se*, bodies that are light or subtle have their place above the heavier, and it is essentially characteristic of these light bodies so to exist on high. But, as Aristotle says in VIII *Physic.*, it may happen that on account of something weighing it down, such a body would, nevertheless, not be in its proper, higher place.

In this way, he offers the solution of the other difficulty. For, just as that which has a nature to be above other bodies differs specifically from that which does not have the nature to be so; and as that which essentially is thus subtle has its own same nature, numerically and specifically, whether it is in its proper place above others, or whether, on account of some impediment, it is not, so also two forms differ specifically if one of them has the nature to be united to a body

# INTELLECT A FACULTY OF THE SOUL

and the other has not. Nevertheless, that having the nature to be united to a body will be, numerically and specifically, one and the same form both when it is actually united to a body and when, on account of some interference, it is not actually so united.

## FURTHER OBJECTIONS: THE INTERPRETATION OF ARISTOTLE'S STATEMENT THAT THE SOUL COMES FROM WITHOUT

However, some still bring up, as a prop for their error, what Aristotle says in his book, *De generatione animalium:* "The intellect alone comes from without and it alone is divine."

Now [those proposing the objection say that] no form which is the act of matter comes to that matter from without, but it is educed from the potency of matter. The intellect, therefore, is not the form of the material body.

They also say by way of objection that any form of a mixed body is caused by the elements; therefore, if the intellect were the form of the human body, it would not come from outside, but would be produced by its elements.

Some object further that it would follow that the vegetative and the sensitive souls would also be of extrinsic origin —a statement contrary to the opinion of Aristotle—especially if it is maintained that there is but one substantial soul whose powers are vegetative, sensitive, and intellective; since, according to Aristotle, the intellect is from an extrinsic source.

The solution of this difficulty, however, is at once evident from what has previously been said. For, although he said that any form is educed from the potentiality of matter, the phrase, "educed from the potentiality of matter," may be taken in two ways.

In the first place, a form may depend on matter both for existence and for its operation; but, in another way, it may mean that matter must exist prior to form.

Now, if the meaning is only that matter shall precede the form, it seems that the form could be considered to be "educed from the potentiality of matter." For if this is to say nothing else than that matter pre-exists in potentiality to a form, nothing hinders one from saying that corporeal matter pre-exists in potentiality to an intellectual soul, whence Aristotle in *De generatione animalium* says: "The vegetative soul must be considered to be potentially possessed in semination and conception, before separation from the parent; but such souls are not in act until, having been conceived, they become separated, procure food, and carry on the functions of such a soul. For, in the beginning, these appear to have all their life as the life of the parent."

The same must be said also of the sensitive soul, and even of the intellectual. For, necessarily, all these souls must be considered to be in potency before they are in act, so that it may not have the same meaning for them to be "in potency" and "in act." Now, it has been shown, in regard to those forms that have no operation apart from their union with matter, that they ought to be such in the act by which they exist as that with which they are combined or mingled, and with which they co-exist, since they possess the selfsame existence; wherefore, as their total existence is dircted toward concretion in matter, so they are said to be totally educed from the potentiality of matter.

The intellectual soul, on the other hand, since it has an operation apart from the body, has not an existence directed solely toward concretion in matter. Wherefore it cannot be said to be educed from matter; rather, it exists by reason of an extrinsic principle. This is apparent from these words of Aristotle: "It must be concluded, however, that the intellect alone comes from without, and it alone is divine."

And the reason for this conclusion he assigns when he says: "For no bodily operation shares in its operation."

However, I wonder at the source from which a second ob-

## INTELLECT A FACULTY OF THE SOUL

jection proceeds, namely, "If the intellectual soul is the form of a mixed body, it must be caused by a mixture of the elements, whereas no soul is caused by a commingling of elements."

Now, Aristotle says, immediately after the foregoing words: "But every power or potency of the soul seems to participate another kind of body than those called the elements—one of a more divine nature. Truly, inasmuch as souls differ among themselves as noble from ignoble, so also the natures of bodies differ. For there is in the generating principle of all things that which makes them to become fecund principles of generation: for example, that which is called heat is not fire, nor any property of it, but a 'spirit' which is contained in the generating principle and in the seminal vapor; and the nature which is in this spirit corresponds proportionately to the elements composing the stars." Therefore, from a mingling of elements not the intellect only, but not even the vegetative soul is produced.

The difficulty which the third objection proposes, namely, that it would follow that the sensitive and vegetative souls would also have existence from without, by an extrinsic principle, if the intellective soul has, is not relative to the discussion. For it is clear from Aristotle's words that he left it uncertain, whether the intellect differs from the other faculties of the soul both as to subject and as to location, as Plato held, or whether they are only logically distinct [i.e., according to reason].

But if it is granted that they are the same as regards their subject, as is the more probable, then there is no difficulty. For Aristotle says in II *De anima:* "The cases of figure and soul are exactly parallel." For always, in that which exists with greater complication (*consequenter*)—whether in geometric figures or in living things—there exists potentially that which is simpler, or prior; just as in a square, a triangle exists in a certain way, and in a sensitive being, that which is vegetative. That the intellect, in a similar way, exists in the same subject, he leaves in doubt. But it can be said that the vegetative and sensitive soul are in the intellective, just as a triangle and square are in a pentagon. Now, the square is indeed, absolutely speaking, an altogether different figure in species from a triangle, but not from a triangle which is contained potentially within it; just as four sides of a square are not specifically different from the three sides of a triangle which are a part of the same figure, though it is distinct from the triangle, existing independently. And if it would happen that diverse figures would be produced by different agents, a triangle existing independently of a square could have the same producing cause as the square and still have a different species of its own; but the triangle which is in the square would have the same producing cause.

Thus, therefore, a vegetative soul existing apart from a sensitive soul is specifically of another kind and has another producing cause. Nevertheless, in the case of a vegetative soul existing in a sensitive soul there is the same producing cause for both sensitive and vegetative. If, therefore, it is said that the vegetative and sensitive souls which are in the intellective have consequently an extrinsic cause, no difficulty ensues. For it is not inconsistent that the effect of a superior agent should have the same power as the effect of a lesser agent, yet, at the same time, possess additional powers of its own.

Therefore also the intellective soul, although it has its origin from an extrinsic agent, has the same powers that a vegetative soul and a sensitive soul possess, even though these souls may be caused by interior agents.

Thus, therefore, after a most careful examination of almost every word that Aristotle spoke about the human intellect, it seems that his judgment was this: The human soul is the act of the body, and one of its faculties or powers is the possible intellect.

## CHAPTER IV

## THE OPINIONS OF OTHER PERIPATETICS

### THEMISTIUS [1]

Now we should consider what opinion the other Peripatetics held on this same subject. Let us, then, first note the words of Themistius in his Commentary on *De anima* (ed. Barbari, Bk. III, chap. 23):

The intellect which we say is *in potentia* (the possible intellect) is more connatural to the soul, indeed, than is the active. I do not say to the soul in general, but to the human soul alone. Now, just as light makes things potential to vision, and at its coming, endowing these potential objects with colors, causes both sight and colors to be in act, so also this intellect which is active not only makes the possible intellect to be in act, but the same intellect also makes objects that are potentially intelligible to be actually intelligible.

And a little later he explains:

The operative intellect holds the same relation to that intellect which is in potency as does art to matter. On this account also, understanding is immediate with us whenever we wish. For art is not the possession of the inferior matter, but it exists within the total intellect, which is factive. Thus, if a builder in wood did not exist extrinsic to the wood, his power would penetrate it throughout. So, in fact, it is with the active intellect: supervening the intellect which is potential, it makes one intellect with it.

Shortly afterward he continues:

We, therefore, are like that which is in potency; but intellect, like that which is in act. So indeed, as in all things composed of

[1] Because of interesting doctrinal divergencies regarding the function of the active intellect, a translation of the *Periphrastica Hermolai Barbari translatio Themistii* is given below (pp. 278 ff.).

potency and act, this thing will be one thing and that which belongs to it will be another; so I will be one thing, and the existence which is mine will be another. Consequently the intellect is likewise a composite of what is potential and what is active. My existence is from what is in act: since those things which I think of and which I write, the intellect, composed of potency and act, writes. It writes, however, not inasmuch as it is in potency, but as it is active: for thus is operation derived from it.

And a little later he says more clearly:

An animal, therefore, is one thing, and the existence of an animal is another. The existence of the animal is from the soul of the animal. So also what I am is one thing, and my existence is another. However, my existence is from the soul; yet it is maintained, not from all the soul. For it is not from the sensitive soul, since that was matter for the imagination; nor again, from the imaginative soul, for that was matter for the potential intellect; nor from the possible intellect, for that was matter for the active intellect. Therefore, from the active intellect alone do I possess my existence.

Again, shortly afterward, he adds:

When, indeed, Aristotle replied that in every nature there is that which is as matter, and that which moves or perfects the matter, he necessarily says that in the soul also these differences exist: what is made to *exist* as this particular kind of intellect in the soul, and what makes it such in the soul. And nature, having progressed to this point of perfection ceases. . . . And so we are active intellect. Afterward also, rejecting the opinion of certain philosophers, he says that in the soul there is such an active intellect, and that of the human soul this is the worthiest, most exalted part. . . . From these same words it is proper to confirm that Aristotle thought the active intellect was something which belonged to us, or even was our very selves.

From the foregoing words of Themistius it is therefore evident that he says not only the possible intellect, but also the active intellect are parts of the human soul, and that Aristotle thought this; and moreover, that man is what he is, not by reason of the sensitive soul, as some have falsely said, but by reason of the intellective and more principal part of his soul.

# OPINIONS OF OTHER PERIPATETICS

### THEOPHRASTUS

I myself have not seen the books of Theophrastus. But Themistius introduces his words in the Commentary on *De anima*, quoting him as follows:

> It is better, however, to set forth the statements of Theophrastus regarding the possible intellect, and that which is active. In regard to the possible intellect, he says: "In what way is the intellect something 'from without' and in what way superimposed, yet connatural? And because nature of itself maintains a certain natural kind of existence, namely, that of act and potency in all things, it well completes this same order in higher beings. But it must not be understood that the possible intellect is nothing of itself—for this opinion must be disputed—but that it is a kind of potency, just as in material things. And the active intellect, that from without, must be considered not as an object, but as comprising generation itself."

Theophrastus asked two questions: first, how the active intellect is extrinsic to us and yet connatural; secondly, what is the nature of the possible intellect. He answers the second question by saying that the possible intellect is in potency to all things, not as though it were not existent, but as the senses are in potency to sensible objects. From this he infers the answer to the first question, by saying that the active intellect should not be thought of as extrinsic to the soul, as something added to it accidentally, or as preceding it in time, but as existing from the beginning of generation and as embracing and comprising human nature.

### ALEXANDER OF APHRODISIAS

That Alexander also held that the possible intellect is the form of the body, even Averroes admits, although I think he wrongly interprets the words of Alexander, just as he assumed too much from what Themistius said. For Averroes says that Alexander taught that the possible intellect is nothing else than a capacity or readiness which is in human nature for the active intellect and for intelligible objects. This readiness or aptitude he regarded as nothing other than the possible intellect which is in the soul, as related to intelligible objects. Hence he said it was not a power in the body, since this power had no corporeal organ and not as Averroes falsely claimed, because he thought no readiness or apt potency was a bodily power.

### ARABIAN AUTHORS

Furthermore, that we may pass from the Greeks to the Arabian philosophers, we note, in the first place, that Avicenna evidently considered the intellect a power of the soul, which is the form of the body; for thus he speaks in his book, *De anima:* "The active intellect, that is, the practical intellect, requires the body and the corporeal powers for all its actions. The contemplative intellect also needs the body and its faculties, but not at all times and in every way; for it is sufficient for itself, through itself.

"Moreover, the soul is none of these powers, but it is that which possesses them and, as we will show later, is a solitary substance, *per se,* which has an aptitude for various actions, some of which are not accomplished or in any way possible except through instruments and through use of them; but others of them have no need of such instruments."

Further, in the First Part, he says: "The human soul is the first perfection of the natural, instrumental body, since to it is attributed the power of deliberate, elective action and, by means of reflection, of arriving at an apprehension of universal ideas." But what he afterward states and proves to be true is: "The human soul also, according as it is proper to it in itself—namely, according to its power of intellect alone—is not related to the body as a form (which is limited to the body) and does not require any organ to be prepared for itself."

## OPINIONS OF OTHER PERIPATETICS

In addition, the statement of Algazel may be cited, for he says: "When the mingling of elements has been so well and so perfectly equalized that none fairer or more perfect can be found, then it is apt to receive from the Creator the form of forms, more beautiful than all others, that is, the human soul."

But in this soul are two powers: the one is operative, the other is knowing; and this latter he calls the intellect, as is evident in succeeding passages.

And afterward by many arguments he proves that the operation of the intellect does not take place through any bodily organ. This, however, we may omit, not wishing, as it were, merely by the authority of these philosophers to combat the error previously stated, but desiring only to show that not only the Latin philosophers—whose words certain of our opponents do not relish—but both the Greeks and the Arabs held this opinion: namely, that the intellect is a part or power or virtue of the soul, which is the form of the body.

Therefore, I wonder from which of the Peripatetics any may boastfully claim to have derived this error; unless, perhaps, it is because those holding it prefer less to be true in their thinking in company with the other Peripatetics, than to err in company with Averroes, who was not so much a Peripatetic as a corrupter of Peripatetic philosophy.

## CHAPTER V

## WHAT OUGHT TO BE HELD

### THE NATURE OF THE POSSIBLE INTELLECT AND THE MODE OF UNION WITH THE BODY

Having shown from the statements of Aristotle and of those following him, that the intellect is a power of the soul, which is the form of the body,—though this power which is called the intellect is not the act of any corporeal organ, because its operation does not involve any bodily operation, as Aristotle says—it is now our purpose to inquire into the reasons why this opinion must be held to be true. And since, according to the teaching of Aristotle, one ought to consider the principle of acts through its acts, it seems that our consideration should begin with that act which is properly the intellect's own—which is, to understand. In regard to this we can have no more assured definition than that which Aristotle proposes: The soul is the principle by which we live and understand. Therefore it is also the specific form of a certain body.

And to this reason he attributes such force that he speaks of it as a demonstration. In the beginning of the chapter he says: "To show what a thing is, one ought to give not only a comprehensive definition, as many do in defining terms, but one ought to show what the inner cause of a thing is, and demonstrate it." Then he gives an example: "Just as demonstration is given of what a tetragon or a square is, through the finding of a median proportional line."

The force of this kind of demonstration seems incontestible, because whoever would wish to turn aside from the road it points out must necessarily fall into inconsistency. Now it is evident that this individual man understands. Never, indeed, would we be inquiring about the intellect unless we possessed intelligence; and when we are carrying on our inquiries about the intellect we do not inquire about any other principle than that one by means of which we understand. Therefore Aristotle says: "I speak, moreover, of the intellect, by which the soul understands." And thus Aristotle concludes: "But if something is the first principle by which we understand, this must be the form of the body."

This he says because he had previously made evident that that by which a thing first operates is the form. And this is clear through consideration of action, since each thing operates inasmuch as it is in act. Moreover, each thing is in act through its form; whence it follows that that by which it first acts must be the form.

### AVERROES

If, however, one should say that the principle of this act of understanding, a principle that we have called the intellect, is not the form, then it is necessary to explain the way in which the action of this principle is the act of this man.

To this problem certain philosophers have offered various explanations. One of these philosophers, Averroes, proposes that the principle of understanding, which he calls the possible intellect, is not the soul or a faculty of the soul, except equivocally; but rather, that it is a certain separated substance, as he has said: The understanding, which belongs to the separated substance, is my understanding or that of another, inasmuch as that possible intellect is united to me or to you through the phantasms which are in me or in you.

Thus, he says, the process of understanding comes about. For the intelligible species, which becomes one with the possible intellect since it is its form and its act, has two subjects: one is the phantasm, the other is the possible intellect. Therefore, he says, the possible intellect establishes a continuity with us through its form, the phantasms acting as intermediaries; and thus, while the possible intellect understands, this man understands.

### THE REFUTATION OF AVERROES' THEORY

Three reasons, however, show clearly that this doctrine is not true.

First because, if this were the case, the union of the intellect with man would not be from the first moment of his generation, as Theophrastus says it is, and as Aristotle implies in II *Physic.*, where he says: The natural term of consideration about forms is for the form, according as man is generated by man and the sun.

It is clear, moreover, that the natural term of consideration is the intellect; but, according to the doctrine of Averroes, the intellect is not united to man by reason of his generation, but according to the operation of his senses, inasmuch as he is in act as a sentient being: "For the phantasm is activated by the senses according to their act," as is said in the Third Book of the *De anima*.

Secondly because this union would not be in relation to any one thing, but according to different things. Now, it is evident that the intelligible species, according as it resides in phantasms, is intelligible potentially. In the possible intellect, however, it is intelligible in act, inasmuch as it has been abstracted from the phantasms. If, therefore, the intelligible species is not the form of the possible intellect, except as abstracted from phantasms, it follows that through the intelligible species there is no conjunction of the intellect with the phantasms, but rather it is separate from these images; unless, perhaps, we should say that the possible intellect is continuous with the phantasms, just as a mirror is united to a man whose reflection happens to be in the mirror. But such a kind of union clearly does not suffice to explain united ac-

## WHAT OUGHT TO BE HELD

tion. For evidently what is the act of the mirror, namely, to reflect, cannot on this account be attributed to the man reflected; wherefore neither can the action of the possible intellect, according to the type of union proposed, be attributed to this man—for example, to Socrates—in such a way that this man should understand.

Thirdly because, granting that one and the same species, numerically, would be the form of the possible intellect and yet be simultaneously in the phantasm, still, it would not suffice to explain how this man would understand.

Evidently, through the intelligible species there is something to be understood, but through the possible intellect man understands that thing; just as also through the sensible species something is perceived, but it is through the sense faculty that one experiences sensation. In like manner a wall on which there is color—the sensible species of which is in act in vision—is seen but does not itself see; but an animal having a visual faculty in which this sensible species is possessed, does see.

Now, the proposed conjunction of the possible intellect with a man possessing in his imagination phantasms whose intelligible species reside in the possible intellect, would be like the union of the wall, on which there is color, with the eye, in which the species of its color would reside. Just as the wall, therefore, does not see—but its color is seen—so it would follow that man would not understand, but the phantasms that are his would be understood by the possible intellect.

It is impossible, therefore, to explain, according to the position of Averroes, how any man would understand.

### THE UNION OF SOUL AND BODY

But some philosophers, indeed, seeing that the conclusions reached by Averroes' road could not show how this individual man thinks, have turned aside into another road. They say that the intellect is united to man as a mover; and so, inasmuch as unity is produced by the conjunction of body and intellect, as by the union of a mover and the thing moved, so the intellect is a part of this man. Hence the operation of the intellect is attributed to the man, just as the operation of the eye, which is to see, is attributed to him.

### THE NATURE OF THE INDIVIDUAL PERSON

It must be asked, however, of one holding this theory, first of all, what kind of individual this is whom we call Socrates. Is Socrates the intellect alone—that is, the mover (*motor*)? Or is he moved by that which is the body, and yet animated by a vegetative and sensitive soul? Or is he a composite of both?

It seems from their position that the third opinion should be held: namely, that Socrates is a being composed of both. Let us, therefore, proceed against them through the statement of Aristotle in VIII *Metaph.*, where he says: "Now, when anything has parts, not as an aggregation but as a unified whole, there is in the totality besides the parts something that is distinguished as the cause of unity; as in some bodies the cause of the unity of the being is vitality; in others, the humors, or some other modification of being.

"But such a being (as Socrates) is a substance of a unique nature, not after the manner of Ilias, a city composed of parts, but a being of one existence. What is it, therefore, that makes a man one, in virtue of which he is unified and not multiple—for example, so that one part of him might be 'animal' and the other 'biped' (although there are some who say that this is the case: that he is truly an animal and truly a biped in such a way that the two are really distinct)?

"According to this view, man is not both these things, but they will be, by participation, men not the attributes of one man, but of two: the one, animal; the other, biped. And the ensemble will not constitute a man who is one and yet multiple—animal and biped. Hence undoubtedly (because some have been accustomed so to define man and so to teach their hearers) this doctrine does not solve the difficulty. But if, as

## WHAT OUGHT TO BE HELD

we have said, this one thing is matter, and that other, form —the one in potency, and the other in act—then the problem no longer seems to exist."

But if you say that Socrates is not an absolutely unified being, but a unity of a sort resulting from the aggregation of mover and moved, many difficulties would result.

First of all, because if anything is one in so far as and in the same way as it is being, it would follow that Socrates would not be anything, that he would not be in any species or genus, and that further he would not have any action, since there is no action except that of a being. Consequently we do not say that the sailor's ability to understand is attributable to the totality comprised by the sailor and his ship, but that understanding belongs to the sailor alone; and in like manner (according to the foregoing supposition) to understand will not be the act of Socrates, but of the intellect alone which makes use of the body of Socrates. For only in that totality which is a unity is the action of a part the action of the whole; and if anyone says otherwise, he speaks inaccurately.

And if you say that it is in this manner that the heaven understands, namely, through a mover, such an assumption only provides the matter of further difficulty; for what we know of the human intellect ought to be our means of attaining to knowledge about superior intellects, and not contrariwise.

But if it is said that this individual, that is, Socrates, is a body animated by a vegetative and sensitive soul, as seems to follow according to those who hold that this man is not specifically constituted by his intellect but by a sensitive soul which is in some way ennobled by the influence of the possible intellect, then the intellect will not be related to Socrates except as a mover is related to that which is moved. According to this theory, however, the act of the intellect, which is to understand, can in no way be attributed to Socrates, as is apparent for various reasons:

First because of what the Philosopher says in II *Metaph.*:

"In those things in which there is diversity between some work and the action producing it, the action is in that which is produced, as the act of building is in that which is built, and the act of weaving is in the cloth; and similarly in other things of the same order, the mover is wholly in the thing moved. But in the case of those things in which there is no product apart from the action, the action is in the beings producing the action, as light is in the one who sees, and a reflection is in the mirror which reflects."

Thus, therefore, even if it is granted that an intellect is united to Socrates as moving him, this does not prove that understanding is in Socrates, or that he understands; because understanding is an act which is in the intellect alone. Therefore it is also false to say, as they do, that the intellect is not the act of the body, but that man himself understands. For it is not possible that understanding should be attributed to a being that has not an act [form] which is intellectual; because intellection can only be in an intellect, as vision in an eye; wherefore there can be no vision except in one whose act is visual [whose substantial form makes vision possible].

Secondly because the action of a mover is not properly attributed to an instrument or to the being moved; on the contrary, the action of the instrument is attributed to the principal efficient cause. For it is not possible to say that a saw uses or controls the artisan; whereas it is possible to say that the artisan saws, although the work is that of the saw.

Now, the proper operation of the intellect is to understand. Therefore, even if it is granted that the act of understanding may be transient, passing over into another so as to move it to understand, it still would not follow that understanding would belong to Socrates, if the intellect were united to him only as a mover.

Thirdly because, in the case of those things whose actions are transient, passing over into another, these actions are attributed in contrary ways to the causes of motion and to the things moved. Accordingly a builder is said to erect a building, but the building is said to be erected. Therefore, if understanding, just as motion, should be transient action, passing over into another, still it could not be said that Socrates understands, inasmuch as intellect is united to him as a mover; but rather, it must be said that intellect understands, and that Socrates is understood; or that intellect, by means of Socrates who has been rendered intelligent, moves Socrates, and thus again, Socrates is moved.

Nevertheless it sometimes happens that the action of an efficient cause passes over into the thing moved: for example, when that which is moved, in virtue of that by which it is moved, initiates movement in another—just as something in which heat has been engendered, engenders heat. Therefore some one might be able to say that, though moved by intellect, man in the act of understanding initiates motion, so that from the very fact that he is moved, he understands.

This opinion, however, Aristotle opposes in II *De anima*, from which we have gleaned the principle of his argument. For, after saying that it is primarily by means of a form that we know and that we possess health, namely, the form of science and the form of health, he adds: "Acts, indeed, appear to be in the patient and in the subject of modification," as Themistius in explaining this says. "For, although science and health are, in a certain way, from others—for example, from a teacher and from a physician—nevertheless, in the patient and in his disposition for modification there reside acts which we have shown to be prior, since they are in them by nature."

It is, therefore, the intention of Aristotle—and, moreover, it is evidently true—that when one thing moves another and possesses the action of a mover, there must be in it some act from the mover, who has this sort of act; and this is the principle by which it operates, and it is both its act and form; just as, if anything is heated, it engenders heat through that which is in it from its own enkindling agent.

Granted, therefore, that the intellect may move the soul of Socrates either by illuminating it or in any other way, what results in Socrates from the influence of the intellect is that by which he first understands. Moreover, that by which, primarily, Socrates understands (just as by his senses he experiences sensation), Aristotle proves to be in potency to all things and accordingly to have no natural determination except this: that it is "possible" and therefore with no admixture of anything corporeal, but separate.

If it is conceded that some separate intellect moves Socrates, nevertheless it still must be maintained that this possible intellect of which Aristotle speaks is in the soul of Socrates, just as the sense faculties are, which are in potency to all the sensible things that Socrates perceives.

### PLATONIC THEORY

If, however, it is said that this individual man, Socrates, is not a being composed of intellect and animate body, and that he is not merely an animate body, but that he is intellect alone, then this will be to state the opinion of Plato who, as Gregory of Nyssa tells us, on account of this difficulty did not wish to consider man as consisting of soul and body, but of a soul using a body, and wearing the body, as it were, as one would a garment.

Plotinus also, as Macrobius indicates, held that man was a being of this kind, when he said: "The true man is not he who appears to the eyes, but he by whom the one seen is ruled. Thus, when at death animal life departs from the body, the latter, widowed of its ruler, undergoes dissolution; and this body is what appears mortal in man. The soul, however, which is the true man, is an alien to all conditions of mortality."

Now, this same Plotinus, one of the great commentators,

# WHAT OUGHT TO BE HELD

is listed among those of Aristotle, as Simplicius states in his commentary, *Praedicamentorum*.

Moreover, this opinion does not seem to be in conflict with the words of Aristotle. For he says in IX *Ethic.*, "It is the part of a good man to be zealous for the good, even by the grace which is his own. For intellect appears to be a grace possessed by every man." But he does not, indeed, on this account say that man is intellect alone, but that what holds the chief place in man is his intellect. Wherefore he subsequently says: "Just as a city-state, or any other organized society, appears to be the principal one, so does man." And to this he adds: "Every man either is this, intellect, or he is especially this." And in this latter sense, I think, the previously cited words of Themistius and those of Plotinus, just now quoted, were spoken when they said: Man is a soul, or intellect.

### REFUTATION OF FALSE THEORIES

That man is not intellect alone, or soul alone, may be proved in many ways:

1. [*On the basis of unity.*] First, by Gregory of Nyssa himself who, after citing the opinion of Plato, adds: "This statement contains a problem which is difficult, or even without solution. For what kind of unity can a soul 'clothed in a body' be? It cannot be altogether simple while wearing this garment of flesh."

2. [*Effects on the body.*] Secondly, because Aristotle in VII *Metaph.* shows that "man" and "a horse" and similar things are not forms alone, but a kind of whole composed of form and matter: a unified, individual being is constituted of prime matter and form, as Socrates.

Now, man also is similar to other things that are corporeal, and this Aristotle has proved by the fact that no part of the body can be said to be complete without some part or faculty of the soul; and, after the departure of the soul, one es not speak of an eye or of flesh except equivocally. But ...s would not be the case if man, or Socrates, were intellect alone, or only a soul.

3. [*Relation to the will.*] In the third place, it would follow that, since the intellect does not operate except by an act of the will (as is proved in III *De anima*), this would also be in the power of the will: namely, that a man should retain his body when he wished and abandon it when he wished, which very evidently is false.

Thus therefore it is clear that the intellect is not united to Socrates as a mover only, and that even if this should be so, it could not explain the fact that Socrates understands. Consequently those who wish to defend this position must either confess that they themselves understand nothing and so are disqualified from disputing about anything, or they must admit the truth of what Aristotle concludes: That by which we first understand is the species and the form.

This same conclusion can also be derived from the fact that this individual man is assigned to a certain species; but no species is determined except on the basis of form; therefore that through which this man's species is determined is his form.

4. [*Distinction of species.*] Any species, moreover, is distinguished by that which is the principal operation proper to that species. But the proper act of man, inasmuch as he is man, is to understand. Through this he differs from other animals; hence Aristotle says that in this operation man's ultimate felicity consists. The principle by which we understand is the intellect, as Aristotle says. Therefore it must be united to the body as its form; not indeed in such a way that the possible intellect itself is the act of any bodily organ, but because it is a power of the soul, which is the act of the physically organized body.

5. [*Moral effects.*] Furthermore, in view of this false position, the principles of moral philosophy are destroyed. In-

deed, whatever is in us [as attributable to us] is withdrawn. Now, nothing is in us as that for which we are accountable except through our willing it; wherefore that which is in our power is called "voluntary." The will, however, is in the intellect, as is clear from the statement of Aristotle in III *De anima*. It is evident also from the fact that in separate substances there is intellect and will; and likewise because it is in the power of the will to love or hate something in general, just as we hate all thieves as a class, as Aristotle says in his *Rhetorica*.

If, therefore, the intellect is not anything belonging to this man, or truly one with him, but united to him only through phantasms or as a mover (*motor*), there will be in man no will of his own, but it will reside in the separate intellect. Consequently this man will not be master of his own acts, nor will any act of his be laudable or blameworthy. But to accept such a view is to destroy the principles of moral philosophy. Since, however, such a thing would be absurd and contrary to human life (for in that case there would be no need to hold councils or to enact laws), it follows that the intellect is united to us in such a way that from it and from us a true unity is constituted. But this cannot come about except in the way that has been stated: namely, that the intellect also is one of the powers of the soul, which is united to us as our form.

The conclusion is, therefore, that without any doubt this opinion should be held not only because of the revelation of faith, as they say, but also because to oppose it is to go against philosophical evidence which is clearly apparent.

### REPLIES TO VARIOUS OBJECTIONS

It is not difficult to refute the reasons that some bring forward in opposition to this doctrine. There are those who maintain that, according to this position, it would follow that the intellect would be a material form and so not stripped of all the character of sensible things, and that consequently whatever is received in the intellect is received individually, as in matter, and not universally. They allege further that, if it is a material form, it is not actually intelligible and so the intellect cannot understand itself, though this is evidently false; for no material form is actually intelligible.

The solution of this difficulty is clear from what has previously been said. We do not say that the human soul is the form of the body according to the possible intellect, which, in the teaching of Aristotle, is not the act of any bodily organ. Therefore it remains true that the soul, as regards the possible intellect, is immaterial, is receptive of immaterial objects, and knows itself. Therefore also, Aristotle uttered these remarkable words about the soul: It is the locus of species—not the entire soul, but the intellect.

If, however, it should be objected that a faculty of the soul cannot be more immaterial than the essence, or more simple, then it may be said that the objection would be very well proposed if the essence of the human soul were a material form, which has no existence of its own, but only the existence of the composite—as is the case with other forms (below the human) which have of themselves neither existence nor operation apart from their communication with matter; and for this reason they are said to be immersed in matter. However, because the human soul by its essence is a form united with matter in such a way that matter does not entirely encompass [or absorb] it,—since the dignity of the form exceeds the capacity of matter—the soul is not hindered from having an operation or a power in which matter is not involved.

Anyone saying this should also consider that, if the intellective principle by which we understand should be essentially separate and distinct from the soul, which is the form of our body, it would be, by its very essence, intelligent and intelligible, and there would be no question of a time when it would understand and of another time when it would not. Nor would it require that it should know through intelligible objects or through acts, but it would have knowledge through its own essence, even as other separated substances. Neither would it be fitting that, to understand, it should have any need of our phantasms. For it is not found in the natural order of things that higher substances, to attain their principal perfection, depend upon inferior substances: so, for example, the heavenly bodies are not formed or fitted for their operations by inferior bodies. Therefore grave error is contained in the opinion of anyone who says that the intellect is a kind of principle which is separate substantially, and yet that, through species received from phantasms, it is perfected and made intelligent in act.

## CHAPTER VI

## THE POSSIBLE INTELLECT NOT ONE FOR ALL MEN

Thus far we have considered what some maintain: namely, that the intellect is not the soul, which is the form of the body, or a faculty of it, but that it is a separate substance. It remains now to discuss their contention that the possible intellect is one for all men.

Now, perhaps, to say this in regard to the active intellect might possess a certain amount of reason, and many philosophers have held this position. For no difficulty would seem to result if many beings were perfected by the one agent: just as by the one sun all the visual potentialities of animals are perfected so that they may actually see; but even this comparison with the active intellect is not in accord with the intention of Aristotle, who thinks that the active intellect is a certain power in the soul; wherefore he compares it to a light.

But Plato, judging that there is one separate intellect, compares it to the sun, as Themistius says. For there is one sun, but many rays of light diffused by that sun in order that there may be vision.

But, whatever be said in regard to the active intellect, to say that there is one possible intellect for all men cannot be true, for many reasons.

1. If the possible intellect is that by which we understand, then one must say either that this individual intelligent man is intellect, or that intellect formally inheres in him; not, indeed, in such a way as to be the form of the body, but

## THE POSSIBLE INTELLECT

because it is a power of the soul, which is the form of the body.

Moreover, if anyone says that this individual man is himself intellect, it follows that this individual man is not distinct from that other individual man, and that all men are one man, not merely by participation in the same species, but after the manner of one individual. But if an intellect is in us formally, as has been said, it follows that for different bodies there are souls that are different. For as man in general is constituted of body and soul, so this man—Callias, for example, or Socrates—is composed of this body and this soul.

But if souls are individually distinct, and the possible intellect is that power of the soul by which the soul understands, then it must follow that it is numerically different in every man; for it is impossible to conceive of there being numerically but one such power for things that are diverse.

2. Furthermore, if anyone says that man understands through the possible intellect, as through something that belongs to him as his own, but that it is not a part of him as form, but as mover, then, as has been previously shown, it is not possible according to this position to claim that Socrates himself understands. But should we grant that Socrates understands because his intellect understands—even though the *intellectus* be only the mover—then he understands just as a man sees because his eye sees. And, to carry out the comparison, let it be supposed that there is numerically but one eye for all men. It must then be asked whether all men will see as one man, or whether they will see as many.

To discover the true answer to this question, we must consider what the relation, on both sides, is between a principal agent and an instrument. Now, if many men make use of numerically one and the same instrument, there will be said to be many operations: as, for example, when many use the one machine to hurl or lift a stone.

But if one principal agent employs many instruments, notwithstanding that he who acts is one, the operations may chance to be diverse because of the different instruments used. Sometimes, however, there is but one operation even though many instruments are required for it. Thus, therefore, the unity produced by a worker is determined, not by the instruments, but by the principal agent who uses the instruments.

According to the previously stated position, therefore, if the eye should be the principal thing in man, in such a way that it would use all the powers of the soul and the parts of the body as its instruments, then many, having the one eye, would see as one.

But if, on the other hand, the eye is not principal in man, but there is in him something superior that uses the eye as an instrument and that is diversified in different subjects, then there would be many seeing, but only one eye.

However, it is clear that the intellect is that which is principal in man, and that which uses all the powers of the soul as well as all the members of the body; wherefore Aristotle has accurately said: "Man is principally intellect."

If, therefore, there should be but one intellect for all men, it would follow necessarily that there would be but one intelligent being and consequently one will and one agent using, according to the dictates of his own will, all those attributes by which men are differentiated from one another. Furthermore, from this fact it would likewise follow that there would be no difference among men as regards free election of the will; but the same things would be done by all if the intellect (in which alone resides the sovereignty and command over all the other powers) is one and the same in different men—a supposition evidently false and impossible. For such a doctrine is in opposition to facts that are clearly apparent. And it likewise would destroy the whole science of morality and all that pertains to the conservation of organized society which, as Aristotle says, is natural to all men.

3. Furthermore, if all men understood by means of one intellect, no matter in what way it were united to them (whether as form or as mover), it would necessarily follow that there would be numerically but one act of understanding for all men: that is, at one and the same time and in respect to the same intelligible object. For example: if I know a stone and you likewise know it, it must be that one and the same intellectual act is both mine and yours. For there can be numerically, on the part of the same principal active agent (whether that agent is form or mover), only one operation of the same species in respect to the same object at the same time. This fact is clear from what the Philosopher determines in V *Physic.*

Hence, if many men should possess one eye in common, the vision of all could be but one in regard to the same object at the same time. And similarly, if there be but one intellect for all men, it follows that for all men understanding the same thing at the same time, there is only one intellectual act; and, more remarkable still, none of those qualities by reason of which men are considered to differ from one another will be changed in the intellectual act. Now, the phantasms are the prerequisites [or predecessors] for the act of intellect, just as colors are for seeing. But, according to this theory, by their diversity the act of intellect is not diversified, especially the act of understanding a single intelligible object. It is by reason of these phantasms, nevertheless, that we judge the knowledge of one man to differ from that of another, inasmuch as the one understands those things that he possesses certain images of, while the other man understands those that he possesses phantasms of. But [according to this theory], in two men who know and understand the same thing, the operation of the intellect cannot be said to be diversified in any way because of different phantasms.

4. Moreover, it can also be shown that this position is evi-

dently at variance with the doctrine of Aristotle. For, after stating that the possible intellect is separate and that it is in potency to all things, he adds: "When it comes to know anything at all, it is in act; just as the one knowing is called the knower, according to the act, this title being derived from the act itself." In this way, science is an act, and the knower is said to be in act inasmuch as he possesses the habit of science. Thereupon Aristotle continues: "This, without doubt, is the case when a thing is able to act through itself. It is then still potential, in a certain way, but not in the same way as before learning or discovering something."

And, later, when he had inquired, "If the intellect were simple and impassible, having nothing in common with matter, as Anaxagoras said, how, then, could it understand if to understand is said to mean to be passive to something?"

To solve this difficulty, he replies: "The intellect is, in a certain way, in potency to intelligible objects, but it is not in act before it actually understands something. It must be, therefore, like a tablet upon which nothing has been written, and this is, indeed, the case in regard to the intellect."

Therefore it is Aristotle's opinion that the possible intellect, before it learns or discovers anything, is in potency, as a tablet is upon which nothing has actually been written. But after it has learned and discovered something, by virtue of its aptitude for knowledge—an aptitude or power by which it operates through itself—it is in act, although even then it is in potency to reflect further.

5. Here three things must be noted.

First, this aptitude for knowledge is the first act of the possible intellect itself which, because of it, comes to be in act and is enabled to operate through itself. For knowledge is not only because of the phantasms' being illuminated, as some say, nor is it a certain faculty acquired in us by frequent meditation and exercise so that we may be united with the possible intellect through our phantasms.

# THE POSSIBLE INTELLECT 261

Secondly, before our learning or discovering anything, the possible intellect itself is in potency, as a tablet is on which nothing has been written.

Thirdly, by our learning or discovering something the possible intellect is rendered active.

These statements, however, cannot be established as true if there is but one possible intellect for all men who are, who will be, and who have been.

Now, evidently the species are preserved or stored, as it were, in the intellect; for it is the locus of the species, as the Philosopher has said above, and as is also evident from the fact that science is a permanent habit. If, then, the intellect of any man has been activated as regards an intelligible species, through the enlightenment given him by a predecessor, and perfected by the habit of science, this acquired habit and the species remain in him. But, since any recipient must be [previously] without that which it receives, I cannot learn and discover what is received in the possible intellect.

If, nevertheless, some one says that, by reason of our power of discovery, the possible intellect is rendered active in regard to something for the first time—for example, if I come upon something intelligible, that it is found by reason of no predecessors—still it is not possible to establish this in the matter of learning; for I cannot understand a thing by learning it from another unless he who teaches me knows it. In vain, therefore, has he said that before learning anything the intellect is in potency.

But if any one adds that, according to Aristotle's opinion, men have always existed, it follows that there would have been no first man to understand anything, and so the intelligible species are not acquired by the possible intellect through the phantasms of any man, but are the intelligible species of an eternal possible intellect.

In vain, therefore, has Aristotle stated that there is an active intellect which renders those species that are potentially intelligible actually so. In vain has he declared that the phantasms are related to the possible intellect as colors are to vision, if the possible intellect receives nothing from the phantasms.

However, it seems to be unreasonable that substances separated from phantasms should receive ours, and that they should be unable to know themselves except after our learning, discovery, or understanding, since Aristotle has added to the foregoing words: "It is also, then, able to know itself either by learning or discovery."

For a separated substance has intellection through itself. Therefore the possible intellect, if it were a separate substance, would know itself through its own essence, and would have no need of those intelligible species that might supervene to it as a result of our intellection or discovery.

6. If, however, our opponents try to avoid this difficulty by saying that Aristotle makes all the foregoing statements in regard to the possible intellect as it exists in a restricted way in us, and not as it is in itself, we may reply that they do not understand the words of Aristotle; for, indeed, what is said is about the possible intellect and what is proper to it, as it is differentiated from the active intellect.

But if there is insistence as to Aristotle's words, let us suppose, as our opponents say, that the possible intellect possesses, from all eternity, intelligible species, through which a union is established with us, according as there are phantasms in us. Then it will be necessary to agree that the intelligible species in the possible intellect and the phantasms in us are related in one of three ways, of which one is: that the intelligible species in the possible intellect are received by the phantasm in us, as the words of Aristotle signify. But this cannot be the situation according to the former position, as has been shown.

The second possible mode is that these species are not received by the phantasms, but that they cast a radiance over the phantasms, illuminating them; just as, for example, certain images (*species*) in the eye might cast a light upon the colors that are on a wall.

And the third possible mode is that the intelligible species in the possible intellect neither are received by the phantasms nor make any impression upon them.

Now, if the second mode is accepted as true,—namely, that the intelligible species illuminate the phantasms, and that as a result they come to be understood—then the following must be true.

First, that the phantasms are rendered intelligible in act, not by the active intellect, but by the possible intellect and through its own species.

Secondly, that this illuminating of the phantasms could not bring about the rendering of the phantasms actually intelligible, for they become intelligible only through abstraction; but this process would be one of reception rather than of abstraction. And furthermore, since every act of reception is according to the nature of the thing received, the illumination by the intelligible species in the possible intellect of phantasms existing in us will not be in an intelligible mode, but only in a sensible and material way. Consequently, as a result of such illumination, we would not be able to understand anything universally.

But if the intelligible species of the possible intellect are neither received by the phantasms nor considered to illuminate them, they will be altogether unrelated and will possess no proportionality at all; and the phantasms will contribute nothing to the act of intellection. But this evidently runs counter to truth.

Thus, in view of every conceivable mode of relationship, the possible intellect cannot be one for all men.

## CHAPTER VII

## REASONS FOR PROPOSING THE UNICITY OF THE INTELLECT

It remains now to deal with those objections by which our opponents seek to exclude a plurality of possible intellects.

Of these objections, the first is that any form which is multiplied according to division of matter is a material form; wherefore there cannot be a plurality of separated substances in the one species. Hence, if there should be many intellects in many men numerically distinguished by division of matter, it would follow necessarily that the intellect would be a material form; but this is contrary to the statement of Aristotle and to his argument proving that the intellect is separate. If, therefore, it is separate and is not a material form, it can in no way be multiplied according to multiplication of bodies.

To strengthen this reason, some bring forward still another in saying that God could not create many intellects of the same species in diverse men. They say, indeed, that this implies a contradiction, because to have matter and to be numerically multiplied is opposed to the nature of a separate form. They even proceed beyond this, trying to conclude that a separate form is not numerically one, or an individual thing.

However, their error seems to be owing to a matter of vocabulary: for they say a thing is not numerically (*numero*) one unless it is one of many (*de numero*).

A form that is independent, or free of matter, is not one of many, since it has in itself no cause of plurality; for the cause of number is in matter.

**Reply.** On the contrary, in order that we may make a beginning from the latter part of their argument, we point out that our opponents seem to be ignorant of the proper sense in which the last statement was made. For Aristotle said, in IV *Metaph.*: The unity of the being of any substance is not accidental, and nothing is a unity except being.

A separated substance, therefore, if it is a being, is one according to its substance; especially since Aristotle says in VIII *Metaph.*: Those things that have no matter, have no cause that they should be one and being. The term "unity," however, is used in V *Metaph.* to indicate four kinds of unity: namely, numerical, specific, and generic unity, and the unity of proportion.

Now, it cannot be said that any separated substance is one only specifically or generically; for this is not to be one *simpliciter*. It remains, therefore, that every separate substance is numerically one. But "one" does not mean that a thing is numerically one because it is one of a number; for number is not the cause of the unity of a being. On the contrary, a being, since it is not divided, ranks among things that are numbered. For "one" is that which is not divided.

Nor again, is this true: that any number is caused by matter. If this were so, Aristotle would have inquired vainly in regard to the number of separate substances. Moreover, Aristotle also states in V *Metaph.*: Multitude is divided not only by number, but also by species and genus.

Neither is it true that a separate substance is not anything singular or individual; for in that case, it would have no operation, since "act is only of singulars," as the Philosopher says. Wherefore, opposing Plato, he says in VII *Metaph.*: If the ideas were separate, one idea would not be predicated of many, nor could any of them be defined; just as no other being which is the only one of a species can be defined: for example, the sun and the moon.

Matter, indeed, is not the principle of individuation in

material things except in so far as it cannot be participated by many individuals, since it is a "first subject," not existing in another; wherefore also, speaking of the ideas, Aristotle says: If the ideas were separate, each would be an individual substance that could not be predicated of many.

Separate substances, therefore, are individual and singular. However, they are not individualized by matter, because they are not so produced as to require to be in another, and consequently do not have to be participated in by many. Hence, if any form is produced to be participated in by another, in such a way that it is the act of certain matter, that form can be individualized and multiplied by reason of its relation to matter.

We have shown previously, however, that the intellect is united to the soul, which is the act of the body. In many animate beings there are many souls, and in many souls there are many intellectual powers, which are called "intellects." But it does not follow on this account that an intellect is a material power, as has already been proved.

Someone may object that, if numbers of souls are multiplied according to the numbers of bodies, then, when the bodies have been destroyed, a plurality of souls will no longer exist. The answer to such a difficulty is evident from what has already been stated. For everything is one inasmuch as it is being, as is said in IV *Metaph*. Thus, although the existence of the soul is in the body, inasmuch as it is the form of the body (nor does it exist before the body), nevertheless, when the body has been destroyed, the soul still remains in possession of its own existence, in such a way that each soul perseveres in its own unity; consequently many souls remain, constituting their own multitude.

Certainly, however, those others who try to prove that God could not create many intellects of the same species, present a clumsy argument, believing that this would involve a contradiction.

Now, though we should grant that it is not of the nature of an intellect to be multiplied, we cannot presume that for such an intellect to be multiplied would imply a contradiction. For even though the cause of some quality would not be in the nature of a being, still nothing would prevent its possessing this perfection from some other cause; just as a heavy body has the tendency by its own nature not to be above lighter bodies; nevertheless, for such a heavy body to be thus above does not involve a contradiction; though to be thus above would be, according to its own nature, contradictory. Thus, even if the intellect, by nature, were one for all men because of not having any natural cause for multiplication, still this multiplication could be alloted to it by a supernatural cause: nor would this imply any contradiction.

This fact we emphasize, not only in view of the immediate problem, but more in order that the same argument may not be extended to other discussions. For, in the same way, one might be able to conclude that God could not cause the dead to rise, and that sight could not be restored to the blind.

Still another reason is adduced by some in support of their error. For they inquire whether the intellection in me and that in you are altogether and perfectly one, or whether they are two in number and one in species. If one, then there is but one intellect; if numerically two, though one in species, then it will follow that the things intellected will possess the intelligible object. For whatever things are two in number and one in species are understood as one, because there is but one essence by which they are understood; and so one arrives at progression to infinity, which is impossible. Therefore [they say] there cannot be two things numerically intellected—one in me and the other in you. Hence there is but one thing understood, and only one intellect, numerically the same, in all men.

But the question must be asked of those who think that

they argue so subtly, whether for two intellects to be numerically distinct, yet one in species, is contrary to the nature of intellect, as intellect, or inasmuch as it is the intellect of man. According to the reason which they advance, it is evident that they mean it is contrary to the intellect as an intellect. For it is according to the nature of the intellect as such, that it should lack nothing that constitutes it as an intellect. Therefore, according to their reasoning, we can conclude absolutely that there is only one intellect—and not merely one intellect for all men.

For if there is only one intellect, then, according to their argument, it follows that there is only one in the whole world, and not simply one for all men. Therefore our intellect is not only a separate substance, but also it is God Himself, and any plurality of separate substances is rendered impossible.

Moreover, if someone should reply that the intellect of one separate substance is not the same in species as the intellect of another separate substance, since the intellects differ specifically, he would merely involve himself in further error: for what is understood is related to the act of understanding and to intellect, as an object is related to act and potency. Now, the object does not receive any species from the act or from the potency, but rather the contrary is true.

It must, therefore, be granted absolutely that the intellection of one thing—for example, of a stone—is but one, not only in all men, but even in all intellects.

It now remains to inquire what intellection is.

If they say that what is understood is an immaterial species existing in the possible intellect, they unwittingly are going over to the doctrine of Plato, who taught that we cannot have any science of sensible things, but that true science is concerned only with separate form. Nor does it affect the matter whether we say that the science about a stone is possessed in regard to the separate form of a stone, or concerning a form of the stone in the intellect. In each case it follows that science is not concerned with things that are here, but with separate beings only. But because Plato held that immaterial forms of this sort were *per se* subsistent, he was able also to suppose that many intellects participated in the knowledge of one truth from one separate form.

Those, however, who maintain that there are immaterial forms of this sort, which they say are understood, must hold that there is only one intellect, not only for all men, but one absolutely.

Therefore it must be said, according to the opinion of Aristotle, that what is understood, which is one, is the nature itself or the quiddity of the thing. For natural science and the other sciences are of things, not of intelligible species.

Now, if what is understood were not the very nature of the stone (which nature is in things), but were the species in the intellect, it would follow that I would not know the thing—that is, the stone—but only the idea abstracted from the stone. But it is also true that the nature of the stone, in so far as it is singular, is potentially intelligible, but becomes actually intelligible by this, that, through the mediation of the senses, the species from sensible things come eventually to the phantasm, and that by the power of the active intellect the intelligible species are abstracted, which are then possessed in the possible intellect.

These species, however, are not related to the possible intellect as the objects of its understanding, but as the species by which the intellect knows its object: just as also the species that are in the eye are not the things seen, but those things by which the eye sees—unless so far as the mind reflects upon itself: a thing that cannot occur in a sense faculty.

Furthermore, if understanding were an action passing over into exterior matter, as in the case of burning or moving it, it would follow that intellection would be according to the mode by which a nature really has its existence in singular things (as the action of fire is according to the mode of what is combustible). But because intellection is an action remaining in the person who understands, as Aristotle says in IX *Metaph.*, it follows that understanding is according to the manner of the one knowing, that is, according to the exigency of the species by means of which the intellect understands.

These intelligible species, however, since they are abstracted from their individuating principles, do not represent the thing according to any individual conditions, but only according to the universal nature of the thing. Now, if two qualities coexist in an object, nothing hinders one from being capable of representation, even in the senses, without the other; wherefore, the color of honey or of an apple may be seen by the eye without there being any experience of its taste. Thus the intellect understands the universal nature of things by abstracting from individuating principles.

One object, therefore, is understood by me and by you. But it is by means of one thing that it is so understood by me, and by means of another, by you; that is, by a different intelligible species. Thus my intellection is one thing, and yours is another. My intellect is one, and yours is another. Therefore Aristotle says in the *Praedicamenta:* Every science is individual in relation to its subject. Hence the grammar that a person possesses is said to be in his soul, but is not said to concern the whole person.

From this fact, it results also that when my intellect knows that it understands, it knows a certain singular act; but when it understands intellection, absolutely, it knows something universal; for singularity is not repugnant to intelligibility, but materiality is.

Therefore, since some singular things are immaterial, such as the separate substances previously discussed, nothing hinders such singulars from being intellected.

Hence it is also apparent how the same science can be in the pupil and in the teacher. The object known is the same,

## ANSWERS TO OBJECTIONS

but not the intelligible species by which each understands. Accordingly knowledge in me and in another is individuated; nor is it necessary that the knowledge of a pupil should be caused by the knowledge of the teacher, as is the heat of water by the heat of fire; but as health, which is in matter, by the health which is in the mind of the physician. For just as in the sick man there is a natural principle of health, to which the physician ministers by his skill in order to establish perfect health, so in the pupil there is a natural principle of science, namely, the active intellect, and the first principles, which are intuitively known, *per se nota*.

Moreover, the teacher furnishes certain aids by deducing conclusions from principles known in themselves; and, as the physician strives to produce health according to the manner in which nature heals (by making use of heat and cold), so the teacher develops science in that way by which the pupil may, through his own efforts, come to acquire knowledge: that is, by proceeding from the known to the unknown. And as health is restored to the infirm man, not because of the power of the physician, but because of a faculty of nature, so also knowledge is caused in a pupil, not as something owing to the power of the master, but according to a natural facility for learning.

But there are others who object further that, if many intellectual substances were to remain after the destruction of bodies, it would follow that they would be without any work to perform. So Aristotle in II *Metaph.* argued that, if there were separate substances that did not animate a body, they would have nothing to do. But if they had well considered this statement of Aristotle, they would have been able easily to solve this difficulty. For before introducing this idea, Aristotle had said previously: "Wherefore it is altogether reasonable to suppose that both these substances and immovable principles exist; but it is left to greater philosophers to declare that they necessarily do so." From this statement it is evident that he himself adhered to the idea that they were probable, and did not declare their necessary existence.

In the second place, since "to be without function or duty" occurs when a being does not tend toward the end to which it is ordained, we could not say, even with probability, that the separated substances would be without function if they did not give motion to bodies, unless perhaps we might declare that the moving of bodies is the end for which separate substances exist. But this is quite impossible, since the end must be greater than the beings that are ordained to it.

Therefore Aristotle does not say that separate substances would be useless if they did not move bodies, but he says that in his opinion "Every impassible substance, by reason of its very nature, should be assigned to an end supremely good."

It is an indication of the greater perfection of anything that it is good not only in itself, but that it causes goodness in others. Consequently, since the way separate substances cause good in lesser beings had not been revealed except through the motion of certain bodies, Aristotle derived from this a probable reason to show that there are no other separate substances than those made known to us by the movement of the heavenly bodies. However, that he did not hold this theory to be necessarily true, he himself declares.

Moreover, we concede that the human soul, after being separated from the body, has not the ultimate perfection of its human nature, since it is a part of human nature. Now, no part is an altogether perfect thing if it has been separated from the whole. Not on this account, however, is the soul without any action; for the end of the human soul is not to animate a body, but to understand; and in this its felicity consists, as Aristotle shows in X *Ethic.*

Still others add a further objection to their assertion of error, saying that if there were as many intellects as there are men, it would follow that there would actually be an infinite number, according to the position of Aristotle, who held that the world was eternal and that men had always existed. To this objection, however, Algazel makes answer in his *Metaphysics*. For he says: "In the case of whatever one of things shall have existed without the other, such as quantity or multitude without order, infinity will not be rendered impossible; even as it is not impossible in the motion of heaven." And later he adds: "Likewise the souls of men, which are separable from bodies at death, we concede to be infinite in number even though they have their existence simultaneously, inasmuch as there is among them no ordination of nature by reason of which some souls should cease to be, since none of them is the cause of the others, but they are altogether equal in nature and in rank, with no priority or posteriority. Now this priority and posteriority are not to be understood as referring to their creation according to time. However, in regard to their essential character, inasmuch as they are essences, there is no order of priority, but they are equal in existence; though they are not as regards time and bodies, and cause and effect."

How Aristotle would have solved this problem, we cannot tell because we do not possess that part of his *Metaphysics* in which he discussed separate substances. But the Philosopher does say in II *Physic*. The consideration of forms which are separate or of those which, although they are in matter, are separable from it, is the task of first philosophy.

However, no matter what he may have said, evidently on this point Catholics suffer no perplexity; for they hold it [on faith] that the world did have a beginning.

### CONCLUDING SUMMARY

The statement of our opponents, therefore, is evidently false: that it was a principle of all the philosophers, both Arabs and Peripatetics, that the intellect was not numerically multiplied, and that only among the Latin writers was this not held as true.

Now, Algazel was not a Latin, but an Arabian. Avicenna also, who likewise was an Arabian, says in his book *De anima:* "Prudence and stupidity and opinion and other like things do not exist except in the essence of the soul." Hence there is not one soul, but there are numerically many souls; and their species is one.

Furthermore, in order not to omit mention of the Greeks, the words of Themistius regarding this problem are to be noted. In his commentary on the *De anima*, after he had inquired whether the active intellect were one or many, he proceeds to give his answer: "Can it be truly said that there is but one first intellect illuminating all others, but that there are many which, having received this illumination, subsequently enlighten many others? In the same way, although the sun is only one, the light which goes forth from the sun and is given out by it is, as it were, separated from it and scattered and thus is diffused and distributed in many diverse rays. On this account, Aristotle did not compare the intellect to the sun, but to light; whereas, Plato compared it to the sun."

Hence it is evident from the words of Themistius that neither the active intellect of which Aristotle speaks is a single one enlightening all others, nor is that which is illuminated, the possible intellect, only one. But it is true that the principle of all illumination is one: namely, some separate substance: either God, according to Catholic philosophers, or the Ultimate Intellect, according to Avicenna.

The unicity of this separate principle, moreover, Themistius proves by the fact that he who teaches and he who learns understand the same thing. This could not be unless there were the same principle of intellectual light for both.

But it is true that Themistius afterward relates that certain philosophers had been in doubt whether the possible intellect were one. He says no more about it, however, because it had not been his purpose to investigate the various opinions of philosophers, but to present the judgments of Aristotle, Plato, and Theophrastus. Therefore at the end he concludes: "But I have stated that to pronounce judgment on what the Philosopher says is a task requiring singular zeal and care. However, this work has had for its purpose to indicate what one can gather from the statements we have collected as to the opinion of Aristotle, of Theophrastus, and more especially, of Plato himself. For the rest, it must be the place and task of another to determine what ought to be believed about the soul. But what the opinion of Aristotle was, and what that of Theophrastus and of Plato, I think can easily be discovered from the quotations from their own books which we have presented and analyzed."

Hence it is clear that Aristotle and Theophrastus and Plato himself did not hold it as a principle that the possible intellect is one for all men.

It is also evident that Averroes incorrectly presented the opinion of Themistius and of Theophrastus concerning both the possible and the active intellect. Therefore we have rightly called him the perverter of Peripatetic philosophy. Hence it is amazing that certain men, after seeing only the Commentary of Averroes, presume to declare, on his authority, that all the philosophers—Greeks and Arabians, excepting only the Latins—hold this opinion as certain.

However, it is a matter of much greater amazement, or rather even of indignation, that one who professes to be a Christian dares to speak so irreverently in regard to Christian faith. This he does when he says that the Latins do not accept this doctrine among their principles (namely, that there is but one intellect) because perhaps the law of their faith is in contradiction to it.

Now, in this there are two evils: first, because he doubts whether this teaching is against faith; secondly, because he implies that he himself is estranged from or outside this law, and because he afterward says: "This is the reason why Catholics seem to hold this opinion."

Here he calls an article of faith only an "opinion." Nor is it the less presumptuous that later he dares to assert that God could not create many intellects because this implies a contradiction.

However, what he subsequently declares is even more reprehensible: "By reason I conclude of necessity that the intellect is numerically one; nevertheless I firmly hold to the opposite by faith."

Therefore he judges that faith is concerned with doctrines the contrary of which can be concluded "of necessity." Since, however, what I conclude of necessity can be only what is necessarily true,—the opposite of which is false and impossible—it follows that faith must be demanded in what is false and impossible: a thing that not even God could do. But the ears of men who have faith cannot endure such words.

In his great temerity, moreover, he has not hesitated to dispute about questions that not only do not pertain to philosophy, but that are matters of pure faith: for example, that the soul suffers from the fire of hell, and that the judgment of the doctors on this point should be put aside.

With equal reason one might enter into philosophical disputation about the Trinity or the Incarnation and other like questions, concerning which none but a babbler would speak.

These, therefore, are the assembled arguments that we have written in refutation of the aforesaid error, not arguments amassed by reference to the doctrines of faith, but collected from the reasons and words of the philosophers themselves.

If any one, however, boastfully claiming a pseudo-science, wishes to say anything in contradiction to what we have written, let him not do his talking in out-of-the-way corners, or before mere boys who know not how to judge of difficult problems. But, if he dares, let him write an answer to what has been here written. He will find not me alone, who am the least, but many others who know and foster the truth, by whom his error may be refuted or his ignorance enlightened.

# APPENDIX

## PERIPHRASTICA HERMOLAI BARBARI TRANSLATIO THEMISTII

It is necessary to assign to the human soul two different intellects: the possible and the active intellects. This latter intellect, joined with and embracing the first, leads it, as it were, from darkness into light, and establishes it in act. Then it also forms in it a kind of abode in which the universal notions of things and those things known are gathered together. For, in the same way that neither the rough rock nor the unpolished bronze, in which there is potentially in one case a house and in the other a statue, can receive either the form of a house or that of a statue unless an artisan gives shape to those materials that have been assembled for the house and the statue,—but he creates and imposes an artificial form, and thus finally a house and a statue emerge—so the possible intellect must be perfected by the other intellect. This latter, since it is itself perfect and always in act, being neither associated with nor identified with any other power, activates and arouses the potentiality and facility of the other intellect to understand, as the skill of the artist raises and gives order to the house; and it sets free the intelligible element in things. This intellect, moreover, is separate and impassible, being simple and without any admixture. Now, the possible intellect, although truly the same as the active intellect in dignity and authority, since it is more conjoined and united to the human soul, seems by its association to suffer some loss or detriment of its nobility.

Just as when light falls upon both eyes and colors, it brings "act" not only to vision, but also to the colors, so the active intellect, when it activates the potential intellect, not only ministers to the action of the intellect, but also makes actually intelligible those things which are the objects of the possible intellect; now, these are the material forms and the general notions derived from individual, sensible things.

And a little later, Themistius adds the following: The comparison of the artist to the material may be applied to the active intellect in its relation to the possible intellect. In the same way, the one makes all things, while the other becomes all things; from which it follows that it is in our power to understand and to speculate when we will to do so, for the active intellect is not, after the manner of the artist, outside or independent of its matter, but altogether interwoven with, or immersed in the possible intellect.

Suppose an escutcheon to be made from bronze or iron: is it not intrinsic? Does it not pervade and penetrate the whole mass of the metal? In the same way, the active intellect, while assisting the possible intellect, remains one with it, since it is one and the same being which is constituted of matter and form; yet this result of their fusion has two aspects.

And after a few more words, he continues as follows: We, therefore, are a union of both intellects. Now, if all things composed of act and potency were so related that in them the thing would be one thing and the essence another, it would follow that I would be one thing and my essence another, so that I would be that being constituted of act and potency, while my essence would be that alone; so that what I consider, that also I write and inscribe. But the intellect writes: the intellect which is composed from potentiality writes, I say, not inasmuch as it has its origin from potentiality, but inasmuch as the intellect is active, since this is the source, as it were, from which all action springs and is produced.

Then, a little further along, he continues more clearly: In order that we may return, therefore, to the point from which we departed: since an animal is one thing, and to be an animal is another, and since an animal depends for its existence on an animal soul, so I am one thing, and my existence is another, and my essence is still another thing. But this essence does not come from the sensitive soul, since it certainly is related only as matter to the possible intellect, which in turn is related as matter to the active intellect. It remains, therefore, that from the active intellect alone my essence can be said to have its source—on this alone can it be said to depend. Only the active intellect can be said to be the form, properly speaking, and in the full extent of the term; it may, in truth be called even "the form of forms"; while other inferior forms are sometimes considered subjects and at other times forms. Without doubt, this order and procession occur in nature: that, in respect to inferiors, superiors should hold the place of forms; and in respect to superiors, inferiors should hold the place of matter.

He has established, however, that the highest and the supreme form is the active intellect, which at one and the same time goes forth and is perfected, and in it he places the limit —the "final hand," as it were—as that to which no form could be considered superior or nobler, in relation to which this active intellect could hold the place of "matter." Thus it is that we are, properly, mind and intellect.

Then, after refuting the opinions of certain others he continues: For since Aristotle held that in all nature one thing held the place of matter in relation to another, which as its form moves and perfects it, it necessarily follows that these difference (he says) be found in the soul, and that the power of intellection be present as the most excellent faculty of the soul.

And he adds a little later: From the words of the same authority, I wish it to be established and confirmed in conclusion that Aristotle's opinion was that the active intellect is either something belonging to us, or even our very selves.

# APPENDIX 281

Here, I think it will be valuable if I make note of the words of Theophrastus concerning the active intellect.

[It is clear, therefore, from the foregoing words of Themistius, that not only the possible intellect, but also the active intellect is a faculty of the human soul, and that Aristotle thought this to be true; and further, that man is a being constituted not by the sensitive soul, as certain philosophers have falsely asserted, but by the intellectual and more principal soul.

The books of Theophrastus I have not seen, but Themistius introduces into his Commentary on the soul the words of this philosopher, saying:][1] "Since the intellect comes as something extrinsic to man, and yet is united and incorporated with him, the question arises as to the way in which it may be said to be congenital to man, and also what its character or nature is."

Certainly, the saying that the intellect is not in act, but capable of becoming all things, is rightly said only in a restricted sense, not indeed in such a way as to reject the proposition entirely or utterly to deny any activity to it; for this is not the case, and such a statement would be untrue and the occasion of contention and dispute; but the saying must be understood in this wise: that in the soul there is a potency which, *sui generis*, holds the place of subject and preserver of forms—such a potency as that faculty in material things which serves as foundation for their constitution and concrete reality.

Further, when it is said that the mind comes as something extrinsic, it must not be regarded as something really superimposed or fastened to a man, but as that which is simultaneous with our coming into being and which claims comprehensively and determines our whole nature.

[1] The preceding lines within brackets are given in other editions of this work, but not in the Parma edition.

# INDEX
## De Trinitate

Abstraction, 154 f.: degrees of, 135 f.; process of, 151 f.
Accidents, variety of, 104-13: numerical difference and, 72
Angels in theology, 166
Arianism, 93: errors of, 70
Arts, liberal, 137
Astrology, 142
Augustine, St.: *De Trinitate*, 5 ff.

Beatitude: full cognition of divine truths, 77; joy in knowing the truth, 75
Bodies: relation to place, 116; two in same place, 113-21
Boethius
 condemnation of, 2
 *De consolatione philosophiae*, 2
 *De Trinitate:* contents of, 5 ff.; difficulty of writing the, 176; four causes of 14 f.; matter of, 9; mode of, 11; purpose of, 11
 Lectio I, 67: St. Thomas' Commentary, 68 ff.
 Lectio II, 125: St. Thomas' Commentary, 125-30
 Preface of, 12
Brain, intellect in relation to, 182

"Catholic": applied to Christian religion, 86-90; use of the term, 69
Christian religion, "Catholic" applied to, 86-90
Cognition: beginning of, 183; supernatural, 8 f.
Composite beings, 103: generation and decomposition of, 144 f.
Compound, elements in a, 120
*Corpulentia*, 118 ff.

*De consolatione philosophiae* by Boethius, 2
*De Trinitate:* importance of, 2 f.; influence of, 1 f.
Difference, variety of location and numerical, 121-24
Dimensions, 110 f.
Diversity: of location, 123; matter as principle of, 111; according to number, 104-13, 123; principle of, 72; according to species, 124
Divine form, possibility of beholding the, 187-92
Divine light, illumination of, 20-27
Divine science; *see* Theology
Divine things, knowledge of, 20-44: manifestation of, 45-66
Divine truths: concealment of, 62-66; need of faith for knowledge of, 77 f.; science of, 50-55
Division, cause of, 101

Earth, unmoved, 147
Eccentrics, 121
Elements in a compound, 120
Epicycles, 114, 121
Essence, 152 f.: and existence, 190
Essence, the divine: knowing it by speculative science, 192-97
Ethics, science of, 138
Existence, essence and, 190

Faith
 acts of, 86
 distinction between religion and, 82 f.
 divine truths and matters of, 50-55
 doctrine of Trinity an article of, 90 ff.

Faith (continued)
  gift of God, 79
  the habit of, 81
  knowledge possessed by, 74-98
  the matter of, 87
  necessary for society, 76
  necessity of, 74-81
  needed for knowledge of divine truths, 77 f.
  object of, 168
  opinion and, 76
  and philosophical reasoning, 56-62
  philosophy in service of, 60
  principle of science, 55
  reason and, 56-62
  and religion compared, 82-86
  science and, 50-55, 76
  Trinity a matter of, 41, 90-98
Felicity: imperfect, 197; man's ultimate, 192
Fire, species of, 120
Form: intelligible, 146; matter and, 110

"Genus," the term, 109
God
  faith needed for our knowledge of, 77 f.
  how He is known, 29 f.
  motion in, 165
  not the first knowledge known, 35
  possibility of knowledge of, 27
  whether first object known, 33-38

Happiness, man's ultimate, 192
Heavenly bodies, substance of, 121
Heraclitus, 144

Idea of God, our, 27
Ideas, Plato's theory of, 144
Imagination: intellect and, 185; in speculations of divine science, 181-87
Inquiry, method of: applied to divine truths, 45-50
Intellect
  abstraction by, 151 f.
  the active, 24
  brain in relation to, 182
  divine science by way of, 169-81

Intellect (continued)
  imagination and, 185
  object of, 135
  operations of, 150, 154
  possibility of beholding the divine form, 187-92
  the possible, 24
  the practical, 134
  the speculative, 134

Judgment, 184

Knowability of things, 141, 197
Knowing, twofold way of, 29
Knowledge
  of divine things, 20-44: manifestation of, 45-66
  of essence and existence, 190
  about God, 27
  kinds of, 188
  need of illumination for, 20-27
  possessed by faith, 74-98
  process of, 183

Latria, 84
Learning: mathematics by way of, 169-81; process of, 177
Liberal arts, 137
Location: diversity of, 123; numerical difference and variety of, 121-24
Logic, 137

Man: perfection of, 47; ultimate felicity of, 192
Materia communis, 145 f.
Materia signata, 145 f.
Mathematics, 117, 171, 175 f.
  objects of, 148-59
  as part of speculative science, 131 ff.
  relation to matter, 150
  sciences related to, 158
  subject of, 128
  by way of learning, 169-81
Matter
  divisibility of, 156 f.
  and form, 110
  and motion: divine science and, 159-68; natural science and, 143-48
  as principle of diversity, 111

# INDEX

Medicine, 138 f.
Metaphysics: mathematics in relation to, 141; natural science in relation to, 141
Mind, human: dependence on divine light, 20-27; natural light of, 22; need of divine operation, 25
Morality, science of, 138
Motion and matter: divine science and, 159-68; natural science and, 143-48
Motion in God, 165
Mutability of creatures, 148

Natural philosophy; see Science, natural
Natural science; see Science, natural
Natural sciences by way of reason, 169-81
Non-intelligibility, 119
Number, diversity according to, 104-13, 123
Numerical difference: variety of accidents and, 72; variety of location and, 121-24

Obscurity, proper use of, 64 ff.
Operation, divine, 25
Opinion, faith and, 76
Origen and doctrine of Trinity, 93 f.
Otherness as cause of plurality, 71, 99-104

Pavia, Boethius, at, 2
Perfection of man, 47
Phantasms, 183 ff., 195
Philosophy: its use in sacred doctrine, 60; the order in, 9; theology and, 9, 163 f.
Philosophy, natural; see Science, natural
Place: relation of bodies to, 116; two bodies in same, 113-21
Planets, motion of, 114
Plato, theory of ideas, 144
Platonists and doctrine of Trinity, 93
Plurality, cause of, 99-124; otherness as, 71, 99-104
Potencies, active and passive, 23

Practical intellect, 134
Preface (Boethius'), 12
Principles, self-evident, 142

Quadrivium, the, 137
Quantity, 110

Reason: and knowledge of the Trinity, 38-44; natural sciences by way of, 169-81
Religion: acts of, 83 ff.; distinction between faith and, 82 f.; and faith compared, 82-86
"Religion," derivation of, 83

Sacred doctrine, use of philosophy in, 60
Science
  divine; see Theology
  of divine truths, 50-55
  essence of, 52
  faith and, 50, 55, 76
  faith as principle of, 55
  first; see Metaphysics
  objects of, 147
  theology the ultimate, 142
Science, natural: metaphysics in relation to, 141; as part of speculative science, 131 ff.; things in motion and matter, 143-48
Science, speculative, 125, 128, 194: division of, 131-68; and knowing the divine essence, 192-97; modes attributed to, 169-97; procedure in, 195
Sciences: differentiated by formal objects, 140; distinguished by objects, 136; methods of the, 178; related to mathematics, 158; subordination of the, 140
Sensible things, knowledge of, 52 f.
Society, faith necessary for, 76
Species, diversity according to, 124
Speculative intellect, 134
Speculative science; see Science, speculative
Stars, substance of, 121
Subordination of the sciences, 140
Substance of heavenly bodies, 121

Theology
  and matter and motion, 159-68
  objects of, 129
  the order in, 9
  as part of speculative science, 131 ff.
  philosophy and, 9, 163 f.
  the ultimate science, 142
  use of imagination in, 181-87
  by way of intellect, 169-81
*Theosebia*, 83
Thomas Aquinas, St.: contents of Commentary, 5 ff.
Trinity, doctrine of, 70: an article of faith, 41, 90-98; Origen and,

Trinity (*continued*)
  93 f.; Platonists and, 93
Trinity, our knowledge of the, 38-44
Trinity, treatises on the, 5 ff.
Trivium, the, 137
Truth, discriminate teaching of, 64 ff.
Truths, some not evident, 76 f.
Two bodies in same place, 113-21

Variety of accidents, 104-13
Variety of location and numerical difference, 121-24

Words, use of obscure, 62-66

# INDEX

## Unicity of the Intellect

Accidents, not beings, 230
Agent, instrument and principal, 257
Albert, St., 202
Alexander of Aphrodisias on the intellect, 239
Algazel: on equality of souls, 273; opinion of, 241
Anaxagoras: on nature of the intellect, 260; on simplicity of the intellect, 221
Aphrodisias, Alexander of: on the intellect, 239
Arabian philosophers on the intellect, 240
Aristotle
on existence of man from eternity, 261
interpretation of, 201
on nature of man, 251
St. Thomas' use of, 208
Scholasticism and, 208
on sensation, 219
on the soul, 211
Averroes: followers of, 201; perverter of Peripatetic philosophy, 275; on the possible intellect, 243; refutation of theory of, 244
Averroism: condemned, 206; consequences of, 202; at Paris University, 205
Averroist doctrine, 202
Avicenna, 202: on the soul, 274; on the intellect, 240

Bernier of Nivelles (Averroist), 201, 203
Body: intellectual soul the act and form of the, 211 ff.; soul substantially united to the, 215; soul

Body (continued)
the act of the, 216, 225; soul the form of the, 254; union of soul and, 245 ff.
Boethius of Dacia (Averroist), 201, 203: De sompniis by, 204 f.; De Summo Bono by, 204

Cause, efficient, 249

De sompniis by Boethius, 204 f.
De Summo Bono by Boethius, 204
Duval, Simon (inquisitor), 203

Empedocles on knower and thing known, 220

Faculties of the soul, 217
Faith, reason versus, 276
Form, matter and, 233 f.
Forms, species of, 228

Gregory of Nyssa, St.: on nature of man, 251; on the soul, 228

Incorruptibility of the soul, 228
Individuation, matter as principle of, 265
Instrument, principal agent and, 257
Intellect
the active, 218
Alexander of Aphrodisias on, 239
Anaxagoras: on nature of, 260; on simplicity of, 221
Arabian philosophers on, 240
Avicenna on, 240
comes from without, 233
dependence on phantasms, 231
as faculty of the soul, 227 ff.

287

# INDEX

Intellect (*continued*)
  locus of the species, 261
  organ of the, 223
  the possible, 218, 242 ff.: Averroes on, 243; not one for all men, 256; in potency and in act, 260
  proper operation of, 248
  separability of, 215
  separate, 229
  as separate substance, 224
  the separated, 232
  something belonging to the soul, 211 ff.
  soul moved by, 250
  Themistius on the, 237 ff.
  Theophrastus on, 239
  and will, 252
Intellects: multiplication of, 267; plurality of possible, 264
Intelligible species, 270: phantasms and, 262 f.

John Philopon, 202

Knower and thing known, 220 f.

Man
  Aristotle on nature of, 251
  Gregory of Nyssa on nature of, 251
  not intellect alone, 251
  not soul alone, 251
  Plato on nature of, 250
  Plotinus on nature of, 250
  principally intellect, 258
Matter: the cause of number, 264; and form, 233 f.; as principle of individuation, 265
Meteorology Commentary on, 204

Number, cause of, 264

Paris, St. Thomas at, 201
Paris University, Averroism at, 205
Peripatetics, opinions of, 237 ff.
*Periphrastica Hermolai Barbari translatio Themistii,* 278 ff.
Person, nature of individual, 246
Phantasms: intelligible species and, 262 f.; soul's dependence on, 231

Philopon, John, 202
Plato: intellect compared to the sun, 256; on nature of man, 250; on objects of science, 268; on souls in man, 213
Plotinus on nature of man, 250
Principal agent and instrument, 253

Reason, faith versus, 276

Scholasticism, Aristotle and, 208
Science, Plato on objects of, 268
Sensation, Aristotle on, 219
Separability of the intellect, 215
Separate substances, individual and singular, 266
Separated substances, 262, 265
Siger of Brabant (Averroist), 201, 203, 205 f.: death of, 206; works of, 206
Simplicius, 202
Soul, the
  act of the body, 216, 225
  Aristotle on the, 211
  Avicenna on the, 274
  definition of, 211
  effects of, 213
  faculties of, 217
  form of the body, 254
  incorruptible, 228
  intellect as faculty of, 227 ff.
  intellect something belonging to, 211 ff.
  the intellectual: act and form of the body, 211 ff.
  moved by the intellect, 250
  in potency and in act, 234
  the sensitive, 234, 236
  separated from the body, 272
  substantially united to the body, 215
  union of body and, 245 ff.
  vegetative, 236
Souls: Algazel on equality of, 273; individually distinct, 257
Species, distinction of, 252
Species, intelligible, 270: phantasms and, 262 f.
Substances, separated, 262, 265; individual and singular, 266

# INDEX

Tempier, Stephen (bishop of Paris), 205 f.
Themistius, 230: on the intellect, 237 ff.; on science and health, 249; on unicity of the intellect, 274
Theophrastus on the intellect, 239
Thomas Aquinas, St.: his use of Aristotle, 208; at Paris, 201

*Tractatus modis significandi,* 204

*Unicity of the Intellect:* purpose of, 209; summary of, 207 f.

Will: intellect and, 252; and moral responsibility, 252 f.

www.ingramcontent.com/pod-product-compliance
Lightning Source LLC
Chambersburg PA
CBHW050338230426
43663CB00010B/1908